Welcome to the Webelos Scout Book!

Contents

33108

ISBN 0-8395-3108-7

©1998 Boy Scouts of America

Revised 2001

10 9 8 7 6 5 4 3 2 1

Welcome to
Webelos Scouting!

This book tells you all about the great new adventures you and your friends in Webelos Scouting can choose.

If you've been a Cub Scout, you probably know Webelos Scouts in your pack, and you've seen their plaid neckerchiefs and the colorful activity badges they've earned. Now you're a Webelos Scout—one of the older boys in the pack—and ready for challenging activities and outdoor fun.

If you already have your Bobcat badge, skip to page 12.

If You Are New to Webelos Scouting and the Pack

Webelos Scouting is part of Cub Scouting. It's for the older boys in the Cub Scout pack, and it will prepare you for being a Boy Scout. Here's what to do if you've just joined:

First, register. Ask your den leader for an application to join the pack. (All dens belong to a Cub Scout pack.) Fill out the application and have your parent sign it. Give it to your Webelos den leader along with your registration fee.

Second, earn your Bobcat badge. Bobcat is the rank everyone in the pack works on first. It won't take long, and you'll learn the Cub Scout Promise, the Law of the Pack, and other things all Cub Scouts know. The requirements are explained on the next few pages. When you complete them, have your parent sign the Bobcat badge scoreboard.

Earning the Bobcat Badge

Welcome to the Webelos den and the Cub Scout pack! It's great to have you with us!

If you weren't a Cub Scout, start earning the Bobcat badge right away. The requirements are listed below. You'll learn what you need to know for the Bobcat badge by reading the following pages.

When you're ready, show your parent what you know about each requirement. Then ask him or her to sign each line in the Bobcat scoreboard below. Take your book to your den leader, and you'll receive your Bobcat badge at a pack meeting.

Bobcat Badge Scoreboard

Requirements   **Approved by:**

1. Learn and say the Cub Scout Promise. _____

2. Say the Law of the Pack. Tell what it means. _____

3. Tell what *Webelos* means. _____

4. Show the Cub Scout sign and handshake. Tell what they mean. _____

5. Say the Cub Scout motto and give the salute. Tell what they mean. _____

6. With your parent or guardian, answer the questions in the "What If . . ." section of "How to Protect Your Children from Child Abuse: A Parent's Guide." _____

Cub Scout Promise

I, [say your name], promise

To do my best

To do my duty to God

And my country

To help other people, and

To obey the Law of the Pack.

What the Promise Means

I Promise

When you promise to do something, you mean you will do it. Even if it is difficult, a Webelos Scout keeps his promise, because it's the right thing to do. He wants people to know he can be trusted.

To Do My Best

When you say, "I will do my best," you mean, "I will try as hard as I can." One boy's best can be different from another boy's best. Webelos leaders don't expect you to be perfect, but they want you to do your best.

To Do My Duty

When you do your duty, you do your share. You do what you ought to do.

Your duty to God is done with God's help. That means you practice your religion at home, in your church or synagogue or other religious group, and in everything you do.

Your duty to your country means being a good American. You obey the laws. You're a good citizen, and you help your community in any way you can.

To Help Other People

This means thinking about other people and their needs. Sometimes this isn't easy, but a Webelos Scout will help others when he can.

Law of the Pack

The Cub Scout follows Akela.

The Cub Scout helps the pack go.

The pack helps the Cub Scout grow.

The Cub Scout gives goodwill.

What Obeying the Law of the Pack Means

"The Cub Scout Follows Akela."

Who is Akela? (Say Ah-KAY-la.)

Akela is the Webelos Scout name for a good leader. Some of the people you may call Akela are your father or mother, your teacher, your den chief, your Webelos den leader, your Cubmaster, or anybody who is a good leader.

Good leaders first learn to follow. That's why the first part of the Law of the Pack asks you to follow. Follow good leaders. Follow Akela.

"The Cub Scout Helps the Pack Go."

When you become a Webelos Scout, you're a member of a Webelos den and a Cub Scout pack. You'll help the pack GO by doing whatever you can to help the pack run smoothly. By doing your part, you'll help everyone in your den and pack get the most out of all their activities.

Help the pack GO by attending all meetings and following the leaders. Your pack will be better in every way because you're in it.

"The Pack Helps the Cub Scout Grow."

You'll "grow" in skills and knowledge while you're a Webelos Scout. That's what all the pack leaders want for you, so they plan den and pack activities to help all the Cub Scouts grow.

In your den meetings, while you're having fun earning activity badges, you'll learn new skills and new ways of doing things. Earning the Arrow of Light Award, the highest award in Cub Scouting, will help you prepare for Boy Scouting. That's how the pack helps you "grow."

"The Cub Scout Gives Goodwill."

Goodwill means cheerfulness and kindness. You give goodwill by having a cheerful attitude, by being kind in what you say and do, and by looking for ways to help other people.

Smile and *help*—those are two Webelos Scout words to remember.

The Meaning of Webelos

The word *Webelos* (say WEE-buh-lows) has a special meaning for Cub Scouts and Webelos Scouts. Webelos is made up of the first letters of these words: "**WE**'ll **BE LO**yal **S**couts." Loyal means you'll keep your Cub Scout Promise.

The Cub Scout Sign

Make the sign with your right hand, holding your arm straight up. The two extended fingers stand for two points of the Promise—*help* and *obey*. Give the sign whenever you repeat the Promise or the Law of the Pack.

The Handshake

When you shake hands with another Webelos Scout or Cub Scout, hold out your right hand as you do for an ordinary handshake. But place your first two fingers along the inside of the other Scout's wrist. This means both of you will *help* others and *obey* the Law of the Pack.

"Do Your Best."

The Motto

"Do Your Best"—That's the Cub Scout and Webelos Scout motto. Do your best when you're helping your family at home, learning in school, or working on a project for a Webelos activity badge. Even when something seems difficult, you'll feel good if you've done your best.

The Salute

Salute with your right hand. Hold your fingers as you do for the sign but with the first two fingers close together. Touch the tips of those fingers to your cap's bill. If you aren't wearing a cap, touch your forehead above your right eyebrow. Salute the U.S. flag during ceremonies.

Sometimes you may also salute your leaders or other Webelos Scouts to show goodwill and courtesy.

Child Abuse

Your parent has a booklet that came with your *Webelos Scout Book*. It's called "How to Protect Your Children from Child Abuse." With your parent, talk about the questions and answers in the section called "What If . . ."

Ready for Webelos Adventures

When you pass all the Bobcat requirements and your parent signs the scoreboard on page 6, you'll be ready for Webelos Scouting fun.

Read on to find out more about being a Webelos Scout.

Fun and Adventure in the Webelos Den

Get set for fun and adventure!

As a Webelos Scout, you'll explore adult careers and learn a lot of new skills. You'll go camping with your den, along with your parent or an adult relative or friend.

Everything in Webelos Scouting is more advanced and challenging than the activities younger Cub Scouts do.

You'll earn special badges that only Webelos Scouts can wear. At the same time, you'll be getting ready to become a Boy Scout.

Read the next section to find out all about Webelos Scouting. Good luck on the Webelos trail!

Your Webelos Den Meeting

Your Webelos den will meet each week. This is where you'll learn new skills. Go to all the meetings so you won't miss any of the fun, excitement, new information, and badge work.

Den meetings often include games, sports, and making things. Sometimes the den will go on special outings, like a nature hike or an overnight campout.

Your Webelos Den Leader

Your Webelos den leader understands boys your age. He or she knows about Boy Scouting and will help you get ready for it.

Your den leader can teach you the right way to build a fire, cook a meal, pitch a tent, and many other skills that are fun.

Den leaders know the importance of the Cub Scout motto, "Do Your Best." They'll help you do your best in improving your skills and learning new ones.

They know the importance of ideals. They believe in God and the greatness of the United States of America. They believe in you and your future. That's why they take the time to lead your Webelos den.

The Webelos Den Chief

Den chiefs are Boy Scouts, Varsity Scouts, or Venturers. They help the den leader by leading games and teaching you many skills you'll need to know when you move into a Boy Scout troop.

The Webelos Denner

Your Webelos den members will elect a denner. The denner helps the den leader and den chief at meetings and outdoor events. If you're elected denner, do your best.

The Pack Meeting

Your Webelos den plays an important part in the monthly pack meetings. You and your den might demonstrate the new skills you've learned in the past month or exhibit projects you've completed for an activity badge. Because your age group is ready for more responsibility, the Cubmaster (the adult leader of the pack) may ask your den to help set up chairs before the meeting or show adults to their seats.

Each pack meeting includes a special ceremony for Webelos Scouts who have earned badges during the month. Your Webelos den leader will present your badge to you.

Your New Uniform

As a Webelos Scout, you may choose between two uniforms. One is the blue uniform you wore as a Cub Scout. The other is the uniform you can take with you into Boy Scouting—the tan Boy Scout shirt and olive green trousers. You and your family choose which uniform you'll wear.

You'll have three special uniform parts to show you're a Webelos Scout: a cap in two shades of blue with the Webelos emblem on the front, a plaid Webelos neckerchief, and a Webelos neckerchief slide.

You'll be proud to wear your uniform at all Webelos den meetings, pack meetings, and special events. It shows you're one of the older boys in the pack, on the trail to Boy Scouting.

How to Put on the Neckerchief

You may wear your neckerchief either over or under the collar, but all members in your pack wear it the same way. If it is worn over the collar, turn the collar under.

Roll the long edge over several times, until the neckerchief is about 6 inches long from the rolled part to the tip. Place the neckerchief around your neck and pull the neckerchief slide up snugly. Tie the loose ends or leave them loose, according to the rule of your pack.

The neckerchief should lie smoothly on the back of your shirt.

Fun and Adventure

Earning Your Uniform

You can help earn the money to buy your uniform. Consider asking about extra chores at home or in your neighborhood: washing windows, weeding gardens, caring for pets while their owners are away, baby-sitting, running errands, shoveling snow.

You may know other ways to earn money for your uniform. Talk over your ideas with your parents and Webelos den leader.

Invite Your Friends

If you have friends who are not Cub Scouts, why not ask them to join your Webelos den? Invite them to a den meeting and introduce them to your Webelos den leader and the Webelos Scouts. Help them join in games and activities.

Follow the Webelos trail!

All About the Webelos Advancement Trail

Advancement in Webelos Scouting means growing in knowledge and skills, and you do this through all the experiences that lead to earning activity badges and other awards. This moves you upward along the trail to Webelos Scouting's highest award, the Arrow of Light Award. By that time you'll be close to joining a Boy Scout troop.

The requirements for each badge and award are in this book, along with detailed information you'll need for each subject.

You'll do much of your badge work with your den and some of it at home. Read on to learn about these experiences and awards.

Activity Badges

In Webelos Scouting, there are 20 possible activity badges! You can earn all 20 or as many as you like. You earn them by completing the requirements with your den or at home (with your den leader's approval). During den meetings one month, you might concentrate on swimming, and the next month you could be conducting scientific experiments.

Activity badges are colorful metal emblems you pin on the front of your Webelos cap. Or you can pin them to the Webelos colors, which are the gold, green, and red ribbons you may decide to wear on your right sleeve.

Webelos Badge

As soon as you start earning activity badges, you can look forward to earning the Webelos badge. The Webelos rank is the fourth rank in Cub Scouting (higher than Bobcat, Wolf, and Bear). As you earn it, you'll learn a lot about Webelos Scouting and Boy Scouting.

As part of your Webelos badge work, you need to earn three activity badges, each one from a *different* activity badge group. One of the badges must be Fitness, from the Physical Skills Group. The other two badges may be from the Mental Skills, Community, Technology, or Outdoor Group. (You'll find all the activity badges listed in their groups on page 22.)

You wear the Webelos badge on your left shirt pocket.

Compass Points Emblem

The compass points emblem is awarded after you have earned the Webelos badge and four additional activity badges, for a total of seven. After you receive the emblem, you'll add a metal "compass point" to it for each additional four activity badges you earn. The emblem hangs from the button on your right shirt pocket.

Arrow of Light Award

The Arrow of Light Award is the highest rank in Cub Scouting. Set your sights on it now.

It's more challenging to earn than the Webelos badge, but you can do it! First you'll need the Webelos badge. You need a total of eight activity badges, including Citizen, Readyman, and Fit-

ness. (You'll already have three badges, including Fitness, from earning your Webelos badge.) The total must include at least one badge from each of the five activity badge groups.

You'll wear your Arrow of Light Award on your left shirt pocket flap.

By the time you've earned the Arrow of Light Award, you'll have gained knowledge and skills in a lot of subjects, and you'll know a lot about Boy Scouting. You'll be ready to graduate into a Boy Scout troop!

What Happens Now?

In the pages that follow, you'll find the details on each activity badge. The requirements for the Webelos badge, compass points emblem, and Arrow of Light Award are near the end of the book, beginning on page 414.

Other awards are explained there, too: Religious emblems, the Cub Scout World Conservation Award, and the Cub Scout Academics and Sports program.

Earning Activity Badges

If you were a Cub Scout before becoming a Webelos Scout, you had a chance to earn three badges—Bobcat, Wolf, and Bear. You also may have earned arrow points and Progress Toward Ranks beads.

But in Webelos Scouting, you can earn many badges and awards! Most of the rest of this book gives you details about the 20 activity badges. Earn as many as you like!

Activity badges are colorful metal emblems that you pin on your Webelos cap or Webelos colors. You can earn them by completing the requirements during den meetings and at home (with your den leader's approval).

All the instructions for earning activity badges are in this book. The 20 badges are divided into five groups.

Physical Skills			
Aquanaut	Athlete	Fitness*	Sportsman

Mental Skills			
Artist	Scholar	Showman	Traveler

Community			
Citizen**	Communicator	Family Member	Readyman**

Technology			
Craftsman	Engineer	Handyman	Scientist

Outdoor			
Forester	Geologist	Naturalist	Outdoorsman

* Fitness—Required for the Webelos badge
** Citizen and Readyman—Required for the Arrow of Light Award

Physical Skills Activity Badge Group

Aquanaut

Athlete

Fitness

Sportsman

Physical Skills Group

Aquanaut

Aquanauts are people who are at home in and around the water. When you're an aquanaut, you enjoy the water, but you also respect it. You master the water skills you need.

Swimming, floating, snorkeling, water rescue, and boating are all skills of aquanauts.

Aquanauts know water can be dangerous. They know how to be safe in and on the water, and they never take foolish chances or break safety rules. They know that rules protect everyone. They help others enjoy the water safely and help them improve their skills.

So splash right in and become an aquanaut! The better you become at water skills, the more fun you'll have.

Are You an Aquanaut?

Doing the tests for this activity badge will tell you whether you're an aquanaut. You'll enjoy trying them. If you can't do all of them right away, keep practicing. You'll improve all the time. The aquanaut tests will help you get ready for more advanced aquatics in Boy Scouting.

Do These:

1. **Jump into water over your head. Level off and swim 100 feet, at least half of this using the elementary backstroke.**

2. **Stay in the water after the swim and float on your back in a resting position with as little motion as possible for one minute.**

And Do Three of These:

3. **Do a surface dive and swim under water for two strokes before coming up.**

4. **Swim on the surface for 50 feet while properly using a mask, fins, and a snorkel.**

5. Demonstrate three basic water rescue methods. Demonstrate reaching and throwing. Describe going with support.

6. Know the rules of small-boat safety. Show that you know how to handle a rowboat.

7. Put on a personal floatation device (PFD) that is the right size for you. Make sure it is properly fastened. Wearing the PFD, jump into water over your head. Show how the PFD keeps your head above water by swimming 25 feet. Get out of the water, remove the PFD, and hang it where it will dry.

8. While you are a Webelos Scout, earn the Cub Scout Sports belt loop for swimming.

When you pass each requirement, ask your den leader or Aquanaut counselor to initial your Aquanaut scoreboard on page 42.

Have Fun—Be Safe

Swimming and boating are lots of fun. The water skills you learn now can lead to even greater adventure as you grow up.

You'll be safe around water if you understand its dangers, always follow safety rules, and improve your swimming and boating skills.

Swimming Safety

Can you swim now? How far can you swim? And how deep is the water where you want to swim? The answers to these questions will help you swim where the water is safest for you.

■ **If you can't swim,** stay in water that is not more than 3½ feet deep.

■ **If you can swim 50 feet,** you may go in water that is 6 feet deep but you may not go more than 25 feet from shore.

■ **If you can swim 100 yards or more,** you may swim in water that is more than 6 feet deep but you may not go more than 50 yards from shore.

Make plans to improve your swimming ability with adult supervision. Swim only when a lifeguard or an adult is along who is a skilled swimmer.

Always Swim With a Buddy

Swimming with a buddy is good common sense for people of all ages. You and your buddy can help each other if either of you gets into trouble in the water. And you'll both improve your swimming skills by making a game of practicing. The buddy system is used for all swimming in Scouting. (See "Safe Swimming" in the Readyman badge section, pages 241–242.)

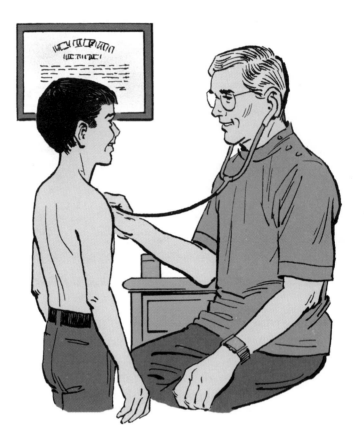

Have a fitness checkup with your family physician. If you don't have any health problems, you can swim with confidence.

Rules on the waterfront protect you. Check a "Do" or "Don't" on each line to make the rules read correctly:

☐ DO ☐ DON'T swim with adult supervision.

☐ DO ☐ DON'T show off in the water.

☐ DO ☐ DON'T dive into unfamiliar or shallow waters.

☐ DO ☐ DON'T go swimming right after strenuous physical activity.

Aquanauts Swim Well

Aquanauts learn several different swim strokes. Each stroke has its purpose. You can learn all of them with the help of a swimming coach or teacher. Follow the pictures and directions for the right way to do the elementary backstroke, sidestroke, and crawl.

Floating on Your Back

Most boys can float on their backs. About one in 20 can't float unless he moves his arms and legs. See if you can float without moving.

Start by arching your back. Take a deep breath and hold it. Put your head back until your ears are in the water. Slowly put your arms out with palms up.

If you're a floater, your body will rise slowly to the surface. When you take a breath, do it fast to keep your lungs full of air. Try to float with as little motion as possible for one minute.

Elementary Backstroke

Start by floating on your back, arms at your sides. Keep your eyes looking down toward your feet, over the surface of the water.

Bring your cupped hands up over your chest to your shoulders. At the same time, drop your heels downward. They should be beneath your knees.

Turn your toes outward and swing your feet outward in a circular motion without stopping. At the same time, reach your arms straight out. Then sweep them down to your sides as your legs come together in a straight-out position, with toes pointed. The arm pull and leg kick happen at the same time.

You should end up the same way you were at the start.

Physical Skills

Sidestroke

Lie on your side with one ear in the water. Stretch your bottom arm out ahead of you. Your top arm is at your side, along your leg.

Start with your feet together, and then bend your knees, pulling your heels toward your hips.

Cup your reaching hand a little. Sweep it down in front of your chest.

Move your feet apart by moving your top leg forward and your bottom leg backward.

Notice the hand and arm movement. As your lower hand pushes down, your upper hand moves toward your chest. They nearly meet.

When your legs are as far apart as possible, snap them together quickly as if closing a pair of scissors.

Your upper hand is pushing down. Your lower hand is reaching out ahead of you, returning to its starting position.

Stop your feet as they come together. Repeat arm and leg movements.

Crawl Stroke

Float face down in the water with your arms and legs extended.

Move your legs up and down. Press down on the water with the top of your foot. (This is called the *flutter kick.*)

Still kicking, pull downward with your right arm. Breathe out through your nose and mouth while your face is in the water.

As your right-arm stroke ends, begin a stroke with your left arm. Raise your face by turning your head to the right so you can breathe in through your mouth.

Reach ahead again with your right arm. At the end of the left-arm stroke, begin a new one with the right arm. Turn your face under water again to breathe out.

Keep strokes and leg kicks even.

The crawl stroke is a fast way to swim, but it's tiring. It's great for racing and for swimming a short distance.

Surface Dive

Float face down with your arms out ahead of you. Sweep your arms back toward your hips.

At the same time, bend forward sharply at the hips. Aim the top part of your body toward the bottom.

Turn your hands palms down. Push them toward the bottom. Raise your legs above the surface as high as you can.

Your head will be pointing downward. The weight of your legs in the air above the water will drive you down.

Swim underwater for two strokes before coming to the top again.

Swimming Underwater

Never overbreathe (hyperventilate) before swimming underwater. Take regular breaths. Whenever you feel you want to breathe while underwater, do so right away by coming to the surface and lifting your face out of the water. Then you won't be taking a chance on underwater blackout.

Snorkeling

There's a way you can move about the surface with your face underwater, see the scene beneath you, and still breathe. How? Use a snorkel. Would you like to become a "snorkeler?"—learn to use a face mask, a snorkel, and swim fins? First, you must be a good swimmer. You must be able to surface dive and swim underwater.

The Mask

Your vision is blurred under-water by the water against your eyes. A face mask puts air in front of your eyes, which helps you see clearly.

A good mask should cover only your eyes and nose. As a test, when you're out of the water, hold the mask to your face without using the head strap. Take a breath through your nose. When you do this, a mask that fits well will cling to your face. The window should be safety glass, with a metal band to hold the glass tightly in place.

When you go underwater with a face mask, it may fog over. To minimize fogging, spit on the glass and rub the spit around. Then rinse the glass before you put on your mask.

Try out your face mask in shallow water. When you need to breathe, raise your head from the water and breathe through

your mouth. This is the only way to breathe when using a face mask by itself. Your view of the underwater scene will be interrupted each time you take a breath.

The Snorkel

The snorkel is a J-shaped tube with a soft rubber end that fits in your mouth. You breathe through your mouth, through the tube that reaches upward above the surface of the water.

When you use a snorkel, put it inside the headband of your mask. It should slope backward. Adding a snorkel should not break the seal between your face and the mask. Hold the mouthpiece in your mouth. Blow out before you breathe through your snorkel. Breathe only at the surface. Feel the back of your head to see whether the tube is out of the water. If it is, you can breathe through it.

Swim Fins

You can swim faster with swim fins. There are several kinds. Some have heel straps, and others have full foot pockets. The fins with heel straps fit any foot because you can adjust the size of the straps. The fins with pockets cost more and must be fitted to your feet. They can't be too tight or too loose. They protect your feet like shoes when you walk on sharp rocks.

With fins, your feet have more surface area in the water, giving you the swimming advantage a fish has with its tail and fins. Use slow, easy flutter kicks, keeping your knees well bent. This will move you through the water at a good speed. Don't work too hard at first. Your legs will tire quickly. Train slowly and build your ability until you can use the fins for a longer time.

Snorkeling = Swimming on the Surface

When you swim, your body is at the surface. Looking through your mask and breathing through your snorkel, you swim with your eyes and thoughts directed below. Unless you're a good swimmer, don't dive under. When you become skilled at swimming and snorkeling on the surface, you may wish to learn the sport of skin diving, which is underwater exploration using a mask and fins but not the snorkel. Then you can see many more wonderful underwater sights.

Safe Snorkeling

While snorkeling, stay near your buddy at all times. Wise aquanauts obey the chief point of all aquatic safety:

Never swim alone! Always use the buddy system!

Aquanauts Know Water Rescue Methods

Webelos Scouts are not expected to do the rescue work of a trained adult. Still, they should know some simple rescues. You might save a person in trouble when no one else is around.

But remember, swimming rescues are for trained older people. Swimmers need to be strong and know exactly what to do to rescue someone. Therefore, never try a water rescue by swimming if you can do it another way.

The safest ways are

Reach!

Throw!

Go! with support

1. **REACH** toward the person in the water with whatever is available. For instance, you can use your hand or foot, a tree branch, a canoe paddle, or a towel.

2. **THROW** a line, buoy, or floating object (like a beach ball) to the person.

3. If you can't help someone by reaching or throwing, **GO WITH SUPPORT.** The best support is a rowboat, canoe, or surfboard.

Aquanauts Are Safe Boaters

Whenever aquanauts use a rowboat, a motorboat, or any other type of water craft, they keep in mind being safe and the safe ways of handling their craft.

Personal Flotation Devices

Webelos Scouts participating in boating activities must use a Type I, Type II, or Type III personal flotation device (PFD). The Type I PFD provides the most buoyancy. It can be used in open, rough, or remote waters. The Type II and Type III PFDs will help keep a person in a vertical or slightly backward position in the water. They are recommended for water sports and close-to-shore operations on lakes and ponds. The BSA recommends using the Type I PFD.

Boating Safety Rules

■ Know your boat—don't overload it. In a rowboat, one person per seat is a good rule.

■ Put on a PFD before getting into the boat. Everyone should wear a PFD when in a boat less than 20 feet long. In some states, it's the law.

■ Balance your load. Divide weight evenly from side to side and from bow (front) to stern (back).

■ Step into the center of the boat when boarding or changing seats, and always keep low.

- If your boat tips over or fills with water, hang on. You can kick the boat to shore or drift in, but don't leave it. Let help come to you.

- Watch the weather. Head for shore if it begins to look bad. If you're caught on the water in bad weather, seat your passengers on the floor of the boat. Have everyone in the craft sit as low as possible. Head your boat into the waves.

- If you use a motor, use one that is appropriate for the boat. Too much power can damage your boat or even swamp it. Look on the boat for the capacity plate. It shows how many people the boat should hold and the recommended horsepower for the motor.

- Sharp turns are dangerous, so take it easy.

- Keep a lookout for other boaters and for swimmers.

Cub Scout Sports Participation

Recognition for Swimming

Did you earn the Swimming belt loop when you were in a Cub Scout den? If you did, great!

But that won't count for Aquanaut requirement 8. For requirement 8, you must earn the Swimming belt loop while you are a Webelos Scout. It should be fun—and easy, too.

Aquanaut Scoreboard

Requirements	Approved by:

Do These:

1. Jump into water over your head. Level off and swim 100 feet, at least half of this using the elementary backstroke. _____

2. Stay in the water after the swim and float on your back in a resting position with as little motion as possible for one minute. _____

And Do Three of These:

3. Do a surface dive and swim under water for two strokes before coming up. _____

4. Swim on the surface for 50 feet while properly using a mask, fins, and a snorkel. _____

5. Demonstrate three basic water rescue methods. Demonstrate reaching and throwing. Describe going with support. _____

6. Know the rules of small-boat safety. Show that you know how to handle a rowboat. _____

7. Put on a personal flotation device (PFD) that is the right size for you. Make sure it is properly fastened. Wearing the PFD, jump into water over your head. Show how the PFD keeps your head above water by swimming 25 feet. Get out of the water, remove the PFD, and hang it where it will dry. _____

8. While you are a Webelos Scout, earn the Cub Scout Sports belt loop for swimming. _____

On to Athlete!

Athlete

Strength and good health are important to you now for sports and games. They'll be important to you all your life.

Athletes know that a good training program includes exercises that build strength and endurance. *Endurance* means the ability to keep going in a race or in playing a sport.

The Boy Scouts of America has standards to test the strength and endurance of boys. The standards for 9-, 10-, and 11-year-old boys are shown on the following pages.

See if you can meet the standards. If you can't meet all of them the first time you try, don't let that stop you. The more you work on each test, the higher your rating should be. This means you're growing stronger.

Keep a record of all your scores.

Do These:

1. **Explain what it means to be physically healthy.**
2. **While you are a Webelos Scout, earn the Cub Scout Sports pin for physical fitness.**

And Do Five of These:

3. **Lie on your back. Have another person hold your feet to the floor and do 30 curl-ups.**
4. **Do two pull-ups on a bar.**
5. **Do eight push-ups from the ground or floor.**
6. **Do a standing long jump of at least 5 feet.**
7. **Do a vertical jump and reach of at least 9 inches.**
8. **Do a 50-yard dash in 8.2 seconds or less.**
9. **Do a 600-yard run (or walk) in 2 minutes 45 seconds or less.**

When you pass each requirement, ask your den leader or counselor to initial your Athlete scoreboard on page 63.

Staying Physically Healthy

When your body feels good and you aren't sick, you are physically healthy.

This means your body is strong and resists diseases. Take care of your body, exercise often, and get lots of rest. Eat balanced meals, with the right amounts of grains (bread, cereal, rice, and pasta), fruits, vegetables, milk products, and foods rich in protein. See the Food Guide Pyramid on page 67.

Cub Scout Sports Pin for Physical Fitness

If you've already earned this Sports pin as a Cub Scout, you must earn another pin as a Webelos Scout for requirement 2.

Ask your den leader to either get you a copy of the book called *Cub Scout Academics and Sports Program Guide* or photocopy the pages about earning the Physical Fitness pin. You'll find that to earn the pin you need to complete five of nine requirements. The requirements include such things as understanding the Food Guide Pyramid and tracking the foods you eat in a week, setting up and following an exercise program for two weeks, and visiting a local gym and talking to a trainer about exercises for young people. You'll find that you can learn a lot about physical fitness while you also have fun!

Exercise the Right Way

Before you begin the following exercises, do stretching exercises to limber up your muscles. You can learn about good stretching exercises by checking out a book from the library, reading about warming up exercises on the Web, or talking to a physical education instructor.

You can keep track of your improvement on the Fitness Progress Chart on page 53.

Curl-Ups

Starting Position: Lie on your back with your legs bent and feet flat on the floor. Cross your arms over your chest. Have a partner hold your ankles, to keep your feet on the floor, and count each curl-up.

Action: Sit up and touch your elbows to your thighs. Return to the starting position.

Count one curl-up each time you go back to the starting position. See how many you can do in one minute.

Pull-Ups

Equipment: Use a bar high enough and easy to grip.

Starting Position: Hold the bar with your thumbs facing one another. Hang with your arms and legs fully out and feet not touching the floor.

Action: Pull your body up with your arms until your chin is over the bar. Then lower your body until your arms are straight.

Rules: The pull must not be a snap movement. Don't raise your knees or kick your legs. Don't let your body swing. If this happens, your partner should stop the motion. Count one pull-up each time you place your chin over the bar.

Push-Ups

Starting Position: Lie face down on the ground or floor. Put your hands on the ground beside your shoulders.

Action: Push up with your arms, keeping your back and legs as straight as possible. Then lower your body and touch your chest to the ground. Repeat as many times as you can.

Rules: For each push-up, your body must be straight and your arms must be extended full length. Count one push-up each time your chest touches the ground.

Standing Long Jump

Equipment: You will need a level surface and a tape measure.

Starting Position: Stand with your feet apart and your toes just behind the starting line. Prepare to jump by bending your knees and swinging your arms back and forth.

Action: Jump, swinging your arms ahead and upward hard. Take off from the balls of your feet.

Rules: Three jumps are allowed. Distance is measured from the starting line to the place nearest the starting line that your body touches. Record the best of the three jumps.

Jump and Reach

Equipment: Chalk and a ruler or tape measure.

Starting Position: Stand next to a wall with your feet flat on the floor. With the chalk in your hand, reach as high as you can and make a mark.

Action: Now jump as high as you can and make a mark above the first one. Your score is the number of inches between the two marks.

50-Yard Dash

Starting Position: Stand behind the starting line. The starter will be at the finish with a stopwatch. He will raise one hand before giving the starting signal.

Action: The starter lowers his hand and hits the side of his leg. This is the signal to start. As you cross the finish line, your time is noted.

Rules: The score is the time between the starter's signal and the instant you cross the finish line.

Athlete

600-Yard Run (or Walk)

Starting Position: Stand behind the starting line.

Action: On the signal "Ready-Go!" begin running.

Rules: You can run or walk. However, you want to cover the distance in the shortest possible time. Record your time in minutes and seconds. Don't try to set a record the first time out. Practice each day and slowly build up your pace. Remember, you can walk.

   A regular football field can be used for both running tests. The 50-yard dash would cover half the field between the goal lines. The 600-yard run (or walk) would be six lengths of the field.

FITNESS PROGRESS CHART

Name_____

Pack _____ Medical Checkup _____
Date

TEST	1	2	3	4	5
DATE					
Curl-ups					
Pull-ups					
Push-ups					
Standing Long Jump					
Jump and Reach					
50-Yard Dash					
600-Yard Run (or walk)					

Athlete

Exercises to Make You Strong

Exercising can be fun, whether you're by yourself or with a friend. Webelos Scouts should exercise at least 20 minutes a day, at least two or three times a week.

The exercises shown on these pages need little or no equipment. You can do them at home. Active games, sports, swimming, hobbies calling for action, and home chores will strengthen you, too.

Paper Crunch: This will build strong hands and fingers. Squeezing sticks, rocks, or sponge balls; hand wrestling; and rowing boats will also develop your hands.

Biceps Builder: Push up with the right hand and arm. Push down with the left hand at the same time. Hold as you count to 10. Repeat five times for each arm.

Physical Skills

Trunk Stretch: Strengthens the back and stretches the chest muscles. Lie face down with your hands at the back of the neck and elbows out. Raise your head and chest and hold.

Walking: Considered a perfect aerobic exercise. *Aerobic* means it helps your body use oxygen and it improves your heart and lungs. Aerobic exercise, such as walking, running, and swimming, increases your endurance and fitness. It helps prevent heart disease.

Stretcher: Done best in slow motion. Curl up your body slowly from a flat-on-your-back position until your knees touch your chin. Count to five. Return to the starting position.

All the Way: Strengthens stomach muscles for tough jobs. Lie back on the floor, with your hands above your head. With your arms and legs straight, raise your body and touch your toes.

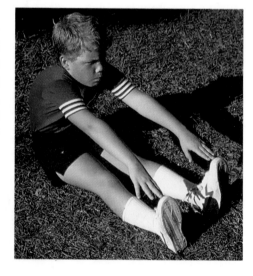

Physical Skills

Neck Builder: You need a bath towel. Pull it hard across the back of your neck. Hold 10 seconds and release. Repeat 10 times.

Butterfly: Strengthens the back. Lie on your stomach. Raise your arms, chest, and legs. Spread your arms and legs 10 times. Return to the starting position and repeat.

Trunk Bend: Strengthens trunk muscles. Bend sideways and down. Touch your toes—first left, then right. Spread your legs. Keep the elbows and knees straight.

Leg Stretch: Builds stomach muscles. Raise and spread your legs slowly three times without touching the floor. Hold for 10 seconds, lower your legs, and rest. Repeat.

Squat Thrust: Take a squatting position, with your hands in front of you on the floor. Thrust your legs back until your body is straight from the shoulders to the feet. Return to a squat. Stand up. Then repeat.

Toe Exercise: Conditions the feet. Practice walking pigeon-toed with your toes curled. Try picking up and carrying small rocks, marbles, or pencils with your toes.

Athlete

Dual Contests

These two-boy contests will test your strength, balance, and ability to react quickly. **Note:** Do *not* do these contests with someone who is bigger or older than you. You and your partner should be about the same size.

Arm Wrestle: Try to force your opponent's hand to the ground or raise his elbow. You must do this without moving your own elbow. Try changing hands.

Stick Fight: Grip the stick firmly—left hand up, right hand down. Try to force the right end of the stick to the ground. Repeat several times.

Physical Skills

Stick Pull: Sit on the ground facing each other. Put the soles of your shoes together. Grasping a broomstick, try to pull your opponent forward to his feet.

Pull Apart: Sit foot to foot, with your hands locked and legs spread wide apart. Try to pull your opponent forward. The winner is on his back at the end of the contest.

Duck Fight: Grasp your ankles in a low squat position. Push your opponent with your shoulders only. The winner forces his opponent to let go of his ankles or fall.

Chest Push: Start the contest between two lines, 10 feet apart. Push chest against chest, arms out, hands touching. The winner must force his opponent back over the line.

Leg Wrestle: Lie side by side on your backs, head to feet, and link inside elbows. Raise inside legs three times. On the third count, try to catch your opponent's heel and flip him.

Physical Skills

Athlete Scoreboard

Requirements	Approved by:

Do These:

1. Explain what it means to be physically healthy.

   _____

2. While you are a Webelos Scout, earn the Cub Scout Sports pin for physical fitness.

   _____

And Do Five of These:

3. Lie on your back. Have another person hold your feet to the floor and do 30 curl-ups.

   _____

4. Do two pull-ups on a bar.

   _____

5. Do eight push-ups from the ground or floor.

   _____

6. Do a standing long jump of at least 5 feet.

   _____

7. Do a vertical jump and reach of at least 9 inches.

   _____

8. Do a 50-yard dash in 8.2 seconds or less.

   _____

9. Do a 600-yard run (or walk) in 2 minutes 45 seconds or less.

   _____

Physical Skills Group

Fitness

What does *fitness* mean? It means being healthy and in good physical shape.

One of your jobs in life is taking care of your wonderful and complex body. You need to become an expert at keeping it working at its best.

That means you must have a healthy diet and plenty of exercise and rest. You must avoid harmful substances.

You can earn the Fitness activity badge at home, on your own and with a family member. You'll learn about taking care of yourself, so you'll be your best when you work, play, and learn.

Do Six of These:

1. With a parent or other adult family member, complete a safety notebook, which is discussed in the booklet "How to Protect Your Children from Child Abuse" that comes with this book.

2. Read the meal planning information in this chapter. With a parent or other family member, plan a week of meals. Explain what kinds of meals are best for you and why.

3. Keep a record of your daily meals and snacks for a week. Decide whether you have been eating foods that are good for you.

4. Tell an adult member of your family about the bad effects smoking or chewing tobacco would have on your body.

5. Tell an adult member of your family four reasons why you should not use alcohol and how it could affect you.

6. Tell an adult member of your family what drugs could do to your body and how they would affect your ability to think clearly.

7. Read the booklet *Take a Stand Against Drugs!* Discuss it with an adult and show that you understand the material.

When you have passed each requirement, ask an adult member of your family to initial the Fitness scoreboard on page 77.

Your Safety Notebook

Part of taking care of yourself is knowing how to be safe and how to react in an emergency. In requirement 1, when you make a safety notebook with your parent or other adult family member, you'll have a place to keep emergency telephone numbers, your parent's work number, and other important numbers to have on hand. You'll write down the safety rules that you and your family follow. For more details on requirement 1, check the booklet "How to Protect Your Children from Child Abuse" that comes with this book.

How to Plan Meals

There's a great advantage to requirement 2: You help choose the menus for meals you might eat for a whole week! But choose wisely and include foods that are best for you.

How to start? You'll find what you need for planning right here:

■ The Food Guide Pyramid shows you types of foods to include and tells how many servings you need each day.

■ The serving size list gives you examples of foods and tells how much makes one serving.

■ The sample menu for a day gives you an idea how it's done.

Plan your menus with a parent or family member. If you or any family member has any dietary restrictions, keep those in mind.

In this chapter, you'll also find out how to read labels on food packages so you can compare foods.

The Food Guide Pyramid Helps You Plan

By using the pyramid as a guide, you'll plan a balanced diet that includes protein, vitamins, minerals, carbohydrates, and fiber.

You need the most servings each day from the widest area at the bottom of the pyramid. These are in the bread, cereal, rice, and pasta group. You need good amounts of fruits and vegetables, too.

A Guide to Daily Food Choices

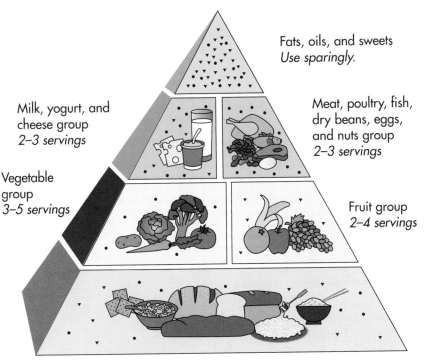

Fats, oils, and sweets
Use sparingly.

Milk, yogurt, and cheese group
2–3 servings

Meat, poultry, fish, dry beans, eggs, and nuts group
2–3 servings

Vegetable group
3–5 servings

Fruit group
2–4 servings

Bread, cereal, rice, and pasta group
6–11 servings

Source: U.S. Department of Agriculture and the U.S. Department of Health and Human Services

Much of your protein, which is necessary for your body's growth and maintenance, comes from the next two groups up the pyramid—milk products and the group that includes meat, beans, and eggs. Milk products also provide most of your calcium. In the smallest section at the top of pyramid are the fats, oils, and sweets. You don't need a lot of them. They are high in calories and low in nutrients.

The pyramid doesn't tell you exactly how many servings of each food to eat. It gives you a range, such as two to four servings of fruit. For a boy your age (around 9 to 11 years old), if you are average in size and activity, you can *aim* for the middle number of servings in each group. Sometimes the number of servings you actually eat may be toward the low or high end of the range.

Be sure you drink water, too, especially if you've been playing hard, hiking, or exercising.

What Counts as a Serving?

The serving size can vary for different foods. As you plan your meals, check the following list of examples from each food group. The list may give you ideas for meals, too.

If eight or nine servings from the bread, cereal, rice, and pasta group seems like a lot, look at the list carefully. You already may be eating that much, because you get two servings in a sandwich or in one cup of pasta.

Some dishes are combinations. Pizza combines a bread crust, cheese, tomato sauce, and possibly vegetables and meat. You'll have to guess at the serving sizes in a piece of pizza.

Serving Sizes

Each of the following portions counts as one serving, except where otherwise noted.

Bread, Cereal, Rice, and Pasta Group
1 slice of bread (a sandwich has two servings)
1 tortilla
½ cup cooked rice, pasta, or cereal
1 ounce ready-to-eat cereal
½ hamburger bun, bagel, or English muffin (one whole bun has two
   servings)
3 to 4 plain crackers (small)
1 pancake (a stack of three pancakes has three servings)
½ doughnut or Danish (medium)
1/16 cake (average)
2 cookies (medium)
1/12 pie (two-crust)

Vegetable Group
½ cup chopped raw or cooked vegetables
1 cup raw, leafy vegetables
¾ cup vegetable juice
½ baked potato

Fruit Group
1 apple, banana, orange, pear, nectarine, peach, or melon wedge
¾ cup fruit juice
½ cup chopped, cooked, or canned fruit
¼ cup dried fruit

Milk, Yogurt, and Cheese Group
1 cup low-fat or skim milk
1 cup yogurt
1½ ounces natural cheese
2 ounces processed cheese
½ cups cottage cheese
1 cup frozen yogurt

Meat, Poultry, Fish, Dry Beans, Eggs, and Nuts Group
2½ to 3 ounces cooked lean beef, pork, lamb, veal, poultry or fish. Also
   equal to 1 ounce of meat: ½ cup cooked beans, one egg, 2 tablespoons peanut butter, or 1/3 cup nuts.

69

Fats, Oils, and Sweets

Use sparingly. Examples of fats and oils are butter (one pat), margarine
(1 tablespoon), oils used in cooking, and shortening used in pastry.
Many salad dressings contain varying amounts of fat (usual serving
size, 2 tablespoons), but fat-free dressings are available.

Sweets include most desserts, cookies, candy, cakes, pies, puddings, and
syrups. Some reduced-fat products are available.

What About Snacks?

Everyone likes snacks! You'll want to include a couple of
healthful snacks in each day's plan. A snack can provide nutrients and give you energy between meals. Each low-fat snack
listed below can count as one serving in your day's plan.

Fruits

1 apple, banana, orange, pear, nectarine, or peach
¾ cup orange or grape juice
½ cup pineapple or grapes
¼ cup prunes or raisins

Vegetables

1 carrot
¾ cup mixed vegetable juice
1 stalk celery (1 cup chopped)

Grains (bread group)

1 graham cracker, wheat cracker, ½ English muffin, or rice cake
½ bagel
1 low-fat granola bar
1 cup popcorn, light (not much fat added)
1 ounce pretzels

Dairy (milk group)

1 ounce skim mozzarella cheese
1 cup of 1 percent chocolate milk
1 cup powdered breakfast drink made with skim milk
1 cup skim milk
8 ounces yogurt with fruit

Low-sodium (low-salt) soups
1 cup chicken noodle or vegetable
1 cup chicken broth

Sweets (for snacks or desserts)
1 slice angel food cake (bread group)
3 gingersnaps or vanilla wafers (bread group)
½ cup ice milk (milk group)
1 juice bar (fruit group)

A Sample Menu

Make different daily plans with a variety of foods. Check to see if you have enough servings from each food group.

Meal	Number of servings in each group				
	Bread/cereal/ rice/pasta	Vegetables	Fruits	Milk/yogurt/ cheese	Meat/poultry/fish/ beans/eggs/nuts
Breakfast					
Orange juice			1		
Milk				1	
Cereal with raisins	1		1		
Toast	1				
Lunch					
Ham sandwich	2				1
Carrot sticks		1			
Apple			1		
Milk				1	
Cookies (2)	1				
Afternoon snack					
Carrot		1			
Bagel	2				
Dinner					
Chicken					1
Peas		1			
Rice	1				
Tossed salad		1			
Ice milk				1	
Evening snack					
Popcorn	1				
Daily totals	9	4	3	3	2

What About Fat?

You hear and read a lot about people avoiding fat in foods. But our bodies actually need some fat in our diets, and we can't avoid fat altogether, anyway.

But a diet high in fat can be harmful in terms of weight gain and health. A good rule is to eat a balanced diet, be aware of high-fat foods, and make low-fat choices when you can.

Experts say we should get no more than 30 percent of our daily calories from fat. A *calorie* is a unit of energy stored in food.

A 10-year-old boy who needs 2,000 calories per day should have *no more than* 600 calories from fat:

$$2{,}000 \times 0.30 \text{ (or 30\%)} = 600 \text{ calories from fat}$$

Some health experts say less than 30 percent of calories from fat is better.

Most people don't keep an accurate count of calories they consume each day and the percentage that comes from fat. That would take a lot of time. What you can do is be aware of some choices you can make every day between high-fat and low-fat foods.

An apple and other fruits and fruit juices are obvious low-fat choices for snacks. Skim milk has very little fat compared with whole milk. Although children younger than 2 years need whole milk, a better choice for older children, teens, and adults is low-fat or skim milk.

If you make good choices every day, an *occasional* higher-fat choice, like fast food or real ice cream, shouldn't be a problem.

One way to identify high-fat foods—and learn more about foods you eat—is to read food labels.

Read Those Labels

You can learn a lot from a food label. Compare these labels from two snack food products.

Fat-free pretzels

Nutrition Facts

Serving Size 1 oz. (28g/About 12 pretzels)
Servings Per Container 15

Amount Per Serving

Calories 110	Calories from Fat 0

	% Daily Value*
Total Fat 0g	0%
Saturated Fat 0g	0%
Cholesterol 0mg	0%
Sodium 520mg	22%
Total Carbohydrate 23g	8%
Dietary Fiber 1g	5%
Sugars less than 1g	
Protein 2g	

Vitamin A 0%	•	Vitamin C 0%
Calcium 0%	•	Iron 10%

*Percent Daily Values are based on a 2,000 calories diet. Your daily values may be higher or lower depending on your calories needs.

Calories:		2,000	2,500
Total Fat	Less than	65g	80g
Sat Fat	Less than	20g	25g
Cholesterol	Less than	300mg	300mg
Sodium	Less than	2,400mg	2,400mg
Total Carbohydrate		300g	375g
Dietary Fiber		25g	30g

Calories per gram:
Fat 9 • Carbohydrate 4 • Protein 4

Cheese-flavored snack food

Nutrition Facts

Serving Size 1 oz. (28g/About 12 pieces)
Servings Per Container 10

Amount Per Serving

Calories 150	Calories from Fat 90

	% Daily Value*
Total Fat 10g	15%
Saturated Fat 2.5g	12%
Cholesterol less than 5mg	1%
Sodium 350mg	14%
Total Carbohydrate 15g	5%
Dietary Fiber less than 1g	1%
Sugars 1g	
Protein 2g	

Vitamin A 0%	•	Vitamin C 0%
Calcium 2%	•	Iron 2%

*Percent Daily Values are based on a 2,000 calories diet. Your daily values may be higher or lower depending on your calories needs.

Calories:		2,000	2,500
Total Fat	Less than	65g	80g
Sat Fat	Less than	20g	25g
Cholesterol	Less than	300mg	300mg
Sodium	Less than	2,400mg	2,400mg
Total Carbohydrate		300g	375g
Dietary Fiber		25g	30g

Calories per gram:
Fat 9 • Carbohydrate 4 • Protein 4

Look at each label. What makes one serving for each? Is that about the amount you might eat for a snack, or would you eat more?

Notice the calories in one serving and the number of calories from fat. You can figure the percentage of calories from fat in one serving of the cheese-flavored snack this way:

90 (calories from fat) ÷ 150 (calories per serving) = 0.60
(60% of calories from fat)

(Note: If the label lists only grams of fat, you can figure calories yourself: 1 gram fat = 9 calories.)

If you ate this for a snack, the rest of your food for the day might have enough low-fat items in it to keep your daily calories from fat less than 30 percent. But you can also see how a person who eats many high-fat items in a day may end up with more than 30 percent.

If you read labels, you begin to get an idea of the nutritional content of different types of foods. Some have higher sodium (salt) content than others. Some products have protein, and some have none. Some have fiber, and some don't.

Eating right is a kind of balancing act. What you don't get from one food you may get from another. The more you learn about what your body needs, the better prepared you'll be to make wise choices about food.

Dangers of Smoking and Chewing Tobacco

Why do some kids smoke or chew tobacco? They do it because they think it makes them more grown up.

In fact, smoking and using chewing tobacco are bad choices for anyone—child, teen, and adult. Many adults have given up smoking and chewing tobacco because scientists have shown that these habits are very harmful to health.

Cigarette smoking has these bad effects:

- It causes lung cancer, heart disease, and other ailments.
- It reduces a person's ability to breathe deeply. Athletes who smoke cannot play as hard or as long as those who don't.
- Smoke may irritate the eyes, making them red and sore.
- Smoke stains teeth and fingers.

Chewing tobacco is as dangerous as smoking.

- The tobacco may damage the delicate tissues of your mouth.
- It causes diseases.
- It certainly will stain your teeth.

Using tobacco is like putting sand in the gas tank of a new car. The beautiful car won't run, and the engine will be ruined.

Dangers of Alcohol and Other Drugs and Inhalants

Drinking alcoholic beverages and doing drugs are even more dangerous than smoking because these actions can have terrible consequences the very first time a person tries them.

The effects of alcohol: Perhaps you have seen someone unsteady on their feet because he or she has drunk too much beer, wine, or liquor. Alcohol slows down the brain and body. It destroys balance. It may make a person see double.

Alcohol makes some people do bad things they would never consider doing when they are sober. Drunk drivers are responsible for thousands of deaths on our nation's streets and highways every year.

A person who drinks too much for several years may suffer from serious illnesses of the liver and other organs.

The effects of drugs: Some drugs are prescribed by doctors to ease pain or relieve symptoms of disease, but prescription drugs are dangerous if they are misused. You should never take a prescription drug unless it is prescribed for you by a doctor. All other drugs are dangerous for you—whether they have been legally prescribed for someone else or sold illegally on the street.

Sniffing glue and inhaling the fumes of paint thinner or gasoline can be dangerous and even fatal. These substances contain toxins that can affect the liver, kidneys, and muscular system. Inhaling these poisonous substances can also cause psychological problems.

Stay away from inhalants and drugs and people who sell them. Marijuana, cocaine and "crack," heroin, "speed," "pep pills," LSD, and other illegal drugs bring nothing but trouble.

Some drugs make people drowsy. Some make it hard to know what is real and what is a dream. Others make people feel so awake and active that they cannot relax and rest. Overdoses are often fatal.

All illegal drugs are bad news.

Drugs: A Deadly Game

Requirement 7 asks you to read a booklet called *Take a Stand Against Drugs!* It's meant to be another reminder about the dangers of drugs—*all drugs*—including cigarettes and beer. Maybe you'll learn something you didn't know about drugs. You can discuss what you learn with adults or members of your den. You can never know too much about the bad news of drugs.

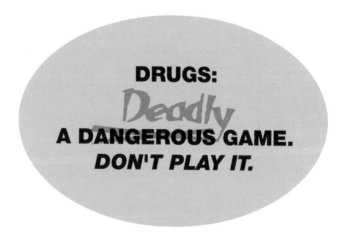

Fitness Scoreboard

Requirements	Approved by:

Do Six of These:

1. With a parent or other adult family member, complete a safety notebook, which is discussed in the booklet "How to Protect Your Children from Child Abuse" that comes with this book. _____

2. Read the meal planning information in this chapter. With a parent or other family member, plan a week of meals. Explain what kinds of meals are best for you and why. _____

3. Keep a record of your daily meals and snacks for a week. Decide whether you have been eating foods that are good for you. _____

4. Tell an adult member of your family about the bad effects smoking or chewing tobacco would have on your body. _____

5. Tell an adult member of your family four reasons why you should not use alcohol and how it could affect you. _____

6. Tell an adult member of your family what drugs could do to your body and how they would affect your ability to think clearly. _____

7. Read the booklet *Take a Stand Against Drugs!* Discuss it with an adult and show that you understand the material. _____

Physical Skills Group

Sportsman

America is a sports-loving country. We cheer our school teams. College and professional games draw crowds, and we watch all kinds of sports on television.

These games are great fun to watch, but too many Americans are spectators. Be a player!

In the Sportsman activity badge, you'll play team sports like basketball, baseball, and soccer. You'll go out for individual sports like bicycling, swimming, and tennis. You may try a sport you'll play all your life.

Sports build your body and improve your skills. Some sports sharpen your eye and your accuracy. Some require you to move carefully and deliberately, while others demand quick thinking, speed, and endurance. Choose your sports and play!

Do These:

1. **Show the signals used by officials in one of these sports: football, basketball, baseball, soccer, or hockey.**

2. **Explain what good sportsmanship means.**

3. **While you are a Webelos Scout, earn Cub Scout Sports belt loops for two individual sports (badminton, bicycling, bowling, fishing, golf, gymnastics, marbles, physical fitness, skating, skiing, swimming, table tennis, or tennis).**

4. **While you are a Webelos Scout, earn Cub Scout Sports belt loops for two team sports (baseball, basketball, soccer, softball, volleyball, or ultimate).**

When you pass a requirement, ask your den leader or counselor to initial your Sportsman scoreboard on page 81.

Learning Officials' Signals

You'll find pictures of officials' signals starting on page 82. You may already know many of them from watching sports events. For requirement 1, you'll learn the signals for one sport, but look at the others. You'll enjoy watching games even more when you know instantly the decisions officials make on exciting plays.

Good Sportsmanship

What is good sportsmanship?

You may say, "It's being a good loser."

That's part of it. If you lose, try to take the loss bravely. Don't gripe about bad luck or blame the officials or your teammates. Practice, do your best, and see what happens the next time you compete.

Good sportsmanship also means being a good winner. You'll be happy, but don't put the other team down. Take time to tell your opponent he played a good game.

A good sport plays by the rules and never cheats. Playing fairly is a matter of honor and self-respect, as well as respect for opponents. Play hard and play to win—but to win *fairly*.

Playing Sports

For requirements 3 and 4, you'll earn the belt loops for two individual sports and two team sports in the Cub Scout Academics and Sports program.

If you earned some of those awards when you were in a Cub Scout den, they won't count toward these requirements. You could choose different sports this time, or you could earn a second belt loop in any sport you want to repeat for this badge.

The book called *Cub Scout Academics and Sports Program Guide* tells you what you need to do to earn a belt loop for each of the sports listed in requirements 3 and 4. Generally, you need to understand the rules of the sport, practice some of the skills, and then play a game of the sport itself.

Sportsman Scoreboard

Requirements   **Approved by:**

Do These:

1. Show the signals used by officials in one of these sports: football, basketball, baseball, soccer, or hockey.   _____

2. Explain what good sportsmanship means.   _____

3. While you are a Webelos Scout, earn Cub Scout Sports belt loops for two individual sports (badminton, bicycling, bowling, fishing, golf, gymnastics, marbles, physical fitness, skating, skiing, swimming, table tennis, or tennis).   _____

4. While you are a Webelos Scout, earn Cub Scout Sports belt loops for two team sports (baseball, basketball, soccer, softball, volleyball, or ultimate).   _____

OFFICIALS' SIGNALS

FOOTBALL

OFFSIDE

ILLEGAL PROCEDURE

ILLEGAL MOTION

ILLEGAL SHIFT

ILLEGAL RETURN

DELAY OF GAME

CLIPPING

ILLEGAL USE OF HANDS (HOLDING)

ILLEGALLY PASSING OR HANDING BALL FORWARD

PASS INTERFERENCE

INELIGIBLE RECEIVER DOWNFIELD

ROUGHING THE KICKER

INCOMPLETE PASS— PENALTY DECLINED— NO PLAY— NO SCORE

TOUCHDOWN OR FIELD GOAL

TIME OUT

FIRST DOWN

START THE CLOCK

BASKETBALL

TIME OUT— FOUL

TECHNICAL FOUL

ILLEGAL USE OF HANDS

TRAVELING

HOLDING

PUSHING— CHARGING

ILLEGAL DRIBBLE

CANCEL SCORE

BASEBALL

STRIKE

SAFE

OUT

FAIR BALL— POINTS TOWARD OUTFIELD

FOUL BALL— POINTS AWAY FROM OUTFIELD

TIME OUT

TIME IN

HOCKEY

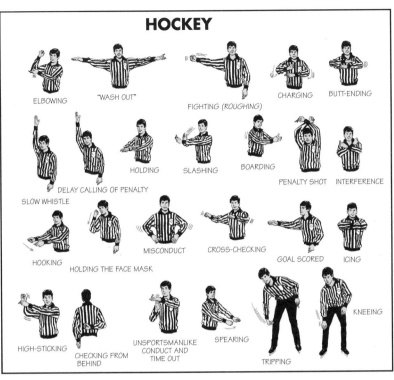

ELBOWING

"WASH OUT"

FIGHTING (ROUGHING)

CHARGING

BUTT-ENDING

DELAY CALLING OF PENALTY
SLOW WHISTLE

HOLDING

SLASHING

BOARDING

PENALTY SHOT

INTERFERENCE

HOOKING

HOLDING THE FACE MASK

MISCONDUCT

CROSS-CHECKING

GOAL SCORED

ICING

HIGH-STICKING

CHECKING FROM
BEHIND

UNSPORTSMANLIKE
CONDUCT AND
TIME OUT

SPEARING

TRIPPING

KNEEING

SOCCER

CAUTION OR EXPULSION

PLAY ON—ADVANTAGE

INDIRECT FREE-KICK

GOAL-KICK

OFF-SIDE

SUBSTITUTION

PENALTY.KICK

DIRECT FREE-KICK

CORNER KICK

OFF-SIDE

THROW-IN

OFF-SIDE

OFF-SIDE

SUBSTITUTION

CORNER KICK

GOAL-KICK

Mental Skills Activity Badge Group

Artist

Scholar

Showman

Traveler

Mental Skills Group

Artist

Paints, brushes, crayons, clay. Soft colors, bright and dark ones. Shapes you haven't tried before. When you create a work of art, you stir up a fascinating mixture of materials and ideas.

Making art is a constant experiment. You try many ways of working. Your art is like no one else's because you are unique. So are your ideas and your vision of the world around you.

Art is about making your ideas visible and even changing them as you work. It's also about playing with materials until an idea takes hold. You'll go your own individual way on this badge.

Do Five of These:

1. Draw or paint an original picture, using the art materials you prefer. Frame the picture for your room or home.

2. List the primary and secondary colors. Explain what happens when you combine colors.

3. Using a computer, make six original designs using straight lines, curved lines, or both.

4. Draw a profile of a member of your family.

5. Use clay to sculpt a simple subject.

6. Make a mobile, using your choice of materials.

7. Make an art construction, using your choice of materials.

8. Create a collage that expresses something about yourself.

When you pass each requirement, ask your den leader or counselor to initial your Artist scoreboard on page 107.

Choosing a Medium

An artist chooses a *medium* to use in creating a work of art. Watercolor paint is a medium. Pencil is a medium. So is clay. The medium is whatever you use to make art.

When you combine two or more materials, you are using *mixed media*. (*Media* means more than one *medium*.) An example of mixed media would be using crayon for the lines of a drawing and then brushing watercolor paint into some areas.

As you work on the Artist badge, you'll experiment with several media.

Drawing and Painting Media

Some ideas for drawing media:

■ Pencil

■ Ink (black and other colors)

■ Crayon

■ Marker (fine or broad-tipped)

■ Oil pastels

With pencil and ink, a fairly smooth paper gives you clean lines. With crayons and markers, use either smooth or rougher-textured paper for different effects.

Some choices for painting (these paints clean up with soap and water):

Watercolor paint. Watercolor comes as a set in a box. Perhaps you use a set like this at school or have one at home. You can use this kind of paint for your painting. Watercolor in separate tubes or in kits is more expensive. Paint on drawing paper or watercolor paper. Watercolor paper is more expensive but also more absorbent.

Tempera paint or poster color is liquid and dries quickly. It comes in small bottles or large squeeze bottles. Paint on manila paper or heavy white drawing paper.

Acrylic paint. "School acrylic" comes in large squeeze bottles. Acrylic paint in tubes is thicker and more expensive. Paint on canvas board or heavy paper.

Because of the cost of tempera and acrylic paints, it's probably more thrifty to do this kind of painting as a den project. The cost of the pint squeeze bottles can be split.

Comparing paint: With tempera and acrylic, you can paint over areas you want to change. Watercolor won't hide a color you've already painted, but it lets the white of the paper shine through, adding light to the color.

Compare paint prices. To start, you need only red, yellow, blue, black, and white. You can mix other colors from these. (See

the color wheel on page 94.) If you buy a paint kit, it may include more than the basic colors.

Brushes: Inexpensive brushes with synthetic bristles will work for tempera or acrylic. (For acrylic, you must have synthetic bristles because the paint will ruin natural hair bristles.) Watercolor brushes are softer, and camel hair is the least expensive. It's helpful to have at least two sizes of brushes—one for larger areas and one for detail.

Maybe you have other art materials on hand. You decide what to use. Remember, you can combine drawing and painting materials in one picture.

You also need:

■ A mixing palette or tray. You can use a large plastic lid from a food container for tube acrylics. For tempera, school acrylics, and watercolor, which are more runny, use several jar lids or buy an inexpensive plastic paint tray with wells for colors.

Mental Skills

- For tube acrylics: a palette knife (a flexible mixing tool). For the other paints, mix colors with your brush.

- A sturdy water container for rinsing paint from brushes before using another color. (Change water often.)

- A sponge for pressing excess water from brush before dipping in paint.

- Rags for spills.

Cleanup: Make cleanup easy. If possible, work at a table with a washable surface. Before you start, cover it with layers of newspaper to protect it.

When you stop, wash brushes promptly with soap and warm water. Store them with bristles up, in a jar, can, or mug. Wash and dry all tools.

What Will It Be?

You decide what to draw or paint. The choices are endless. Ideas could come from thinking about your family, celebrations, vacations, a pet, playing basketball with friends, or anything else. Just standing outside and looking at your house or apartment building or neighborhood could give you ideas. The view from a window could give you a starting point. Something you remember or wish for could go into your drawing or painting.

A work of art doesn't have to look exactly like your actual house or your friends or your dog. It's your own personal expression, not an exact likeness. You could even decide to create a mystery of shapes, lines, and colors that makes everyone guess what it is, and each person will have a different guess.

Drawing

You could draw something from your imagination, like a dinosaur, or you could draw while you look at your subject: a person, a house, or a collection of items on a table top—that's called a *still life*.

A simple still life setup might include a mug, an apple, and a cereal box, to give you different shapes to draw. Or gather a few of your favorite things together.

Whether your subject is a cup or a person, notice the form— how the subject is shaped. Imagine the whole form, even the part around the back that you can't see. If you want to, you can use light pencil lines to sketch the general shapes first, as a guide.

Look for shadowed areas and see if you can shade them in. Light, medium, and dark areas help show the form, so the subject won't look flat. If you're using color, you can apply the color more heavily in the shadows and make it thinner in the light places.

Color Wheel and Mixing Paint

The *primary colors* are red, yellow, and blue. The *secondary colors* are orange, green, and violet.

Look at the color wheel on the next page. You mix yellow and blue (primary colors) to make green (a secondary color). Green is on the wheel halfway between yellow and blue. If you add more yellow, you get a yellow-green. If you add more blue instead, you get a blue-green.

If you want a red-orange, you can use the wheel to find out which primary colors it lies between—red and yellow.

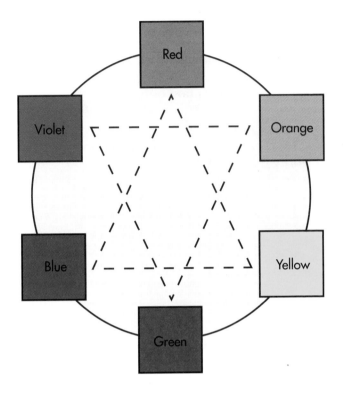

Using the wheel, you can find out which primary colors to use to mix the other colors.

You can use a small amount of white to lighten a color you've mixed, or black to darken it. Or try adding only water to get a pale color. For brown, experiment with combinations of red, yellow, and blue. Try adding a little black.

If you're not sure about a color you've mixed, try it first on a piece of scrap paper. The more you paint, the more you'll remember about mixing colors.

Art supply stores sell paints in many colors. After working with the primary colors, you may decide to buy a few other colors to see what they're like.

Experiment!

You can use a brush in different ways. You know you can use it for lines, details, and larger areas of color. A wet brush makes a different pattern than a mostly dry brush. Discover other marks and textures you can make by holding the brush differently. Lay it flat, so it makes a mark the shape of its bristles. Touch the tip of it to the paper and see if it leaves a dot or a texture.

You can use tools other than brushes. A sponge dipped in paint adds texture. A string dragged through paint and pressed down on the paper or canvas leaves a line. Crumpled paper dipped in paint makes unpredictable patterns.

Making a Frame

You don't have to buy a frame for your drawing or painting. Make one instead. Here are three simple kinds of frames to make.

Tape or glue your picture to a piece of cardboard that is about 1 inch bigger all around than the picture. (Use glue only on the edges so the paper won't buckle.) From a second piece of cardboard, cut out the frame. Glue that to the back cardboard.

If you have a woodworking shop, you can make a wood frame.

An old weathered board makes a good frame. You have to sand the board very smooth in the area where the picture will be glued.

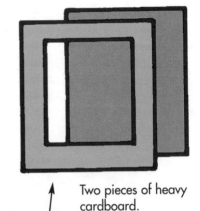

Two pieces of heavy cardboard.

Cut frame to fit picture.

Simple wood frame with mitered corners.

Glue picture on weathered board.

Mental Skills

Computer Designs

When artists create designs, they think about shape, line, color, placement, the feeling they want to convey, and more.

If you do requirement 3, you'll create original designs using a computer drawing program. You'll use straight lines or curved lines or a combination of both. You could try arrangements of thin lines or marks, or use lines to make shapes that you leave empty or fill with color.

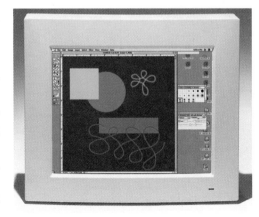

The result probably won't look like any object in the real world, although you might have been thinking about an ocean wave, a storm, a birthday party, or traveling through outer space. Sometimes a design expresses a feeling. We don't know what was on the artist's mind, but the design might make us think of a happy time, or a peaceful night, or an adventure.

Your designs can be as simple or as complicated as you want. Have fun and experiment with the drawing and painting "tools" and colors you can use. Learn how to move pieces of the design until the arrangement on the screen pleases you and feels right to you. Save and print your designs.

Drawing a Profile

A profile is a side view of a person. Try drawing one of a member of your family.

Note the shape of the subject's head and sketch that in first. Then start adding features.

If you have trouble drawing a profile, try this. Tape your drawing paper to a wall. Ask your subject to stand in front of the paper. Then shine a bright light on him or her. The shadow will outline the profile and you can trace it.

Sculpture

When you have a piece of clay in your hands, what happens? You squeeze it, twist it, pull it, roll it, and shape it. You are sculpting. Some sculptors say this is like "thinking with your hands."

What will you make? It could be the figure of a person, or just the head and neck. It could be an animal or a fantastic creature no one has ever seen before. You could even sculpt your own design of a futuristic car. You decide.

What to Work With

Plasteline, a commercial modeling clay, is oily and plastic, meaning you can shape it. It never dries out. It works easily when kept at room temperature.

If you stop working, put the sculpture away until you can return to it. You'll find it is still soft and ready to be worked. Plasteline costs more than natural clay in the beginning. But you'll save money in the long run because you can use it again and again.

Moist clay comes from the earth. It can be worked easily when damp. As it dries, it becomes stiffer and is good for detail work. Because natural clay does dry out, it must be kept covered when not being worked. Use wet cloths and a plastic bag. If it dries out, you can soak it and knead it until it becomes soft again.

Self-hardening clay is a prepared clay. It costs more than the moist kind. It is as easily worked, as long as it is kept wet and soft. It is self-drying and becomes very hard. When it has dried, it cannot be softened for reuse.

Tools

Your best tools for working clay are your fingers, but sometimes another tool comes in handy. Try these:

■ Dull kitchen knife for cutting clay

■ Tongue depressor or craft stick for detail work and smoothing

■ Homemade modeling tool (see instructions)

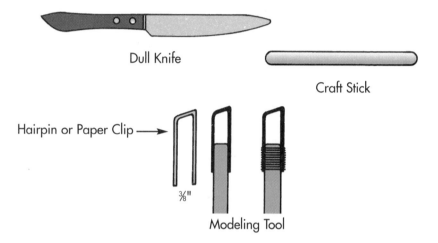

Dull Knife

Craft Stick

Hairpin or Paper Clip ⟶

⅜"

Modeling Tool

Make a modeling tool with a wooden dowel for a handle. Shape a hairpin or paper clip and attach it to the dowel by wrapping with thread. Coat the thread with model cement.

Sculpting a Head

When you start sculpting, make the head small, about 3 or 4 inches wide. This size takes less clay, but it's large enough for you to be able to work on detail.

Work in a well-lighted room. Your workbench or table should be solid. The clay should be at eye level. Do this by sitting on a low chair or stool. Or put your clay on a box on top of your workbench.

Work in a place that is easy to clean. Clay dropped on a good floor or rug leaves stains.

How to Get Started

1. Make a support. Use a 1-inch dowel 12 inches long. Have an adult drill a 1-inch hole in the center of a 6-by-6-inch block of wood.

2. Start putting clay on and around the dowel stick. Build up an egg shape about 3 to 4 inches wide.

3. Push in the eye spaces with your thumbs.

4. Note the shape of a normal head. Most beginners forget the forehead and back of the head.

5. Add bits of clay to build up the chin, nose, neck, brows, hair, and ears.

6. Refine lips, eyes, and shape of the head.

   You can change clay while it is soft—take a pinch off here, add a little more there. Turn your work around and look at it from the top, sides, back, and front.

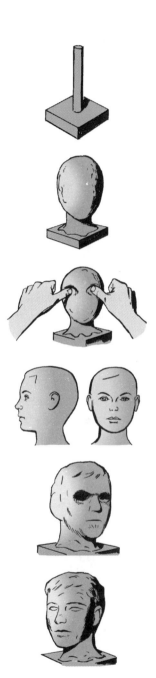

Artist

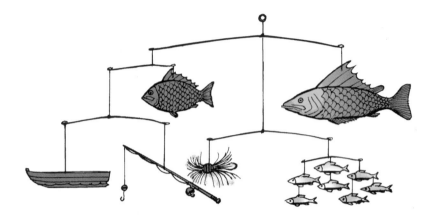

Mobiles: Sculpture in Motion

A *mobile* (MO-beel) is a hanging sculpture. It has many light-weight parts hanging from arms that move in the slightest breeze.

Making a mobile is a matter of thinking of a design, creating the parts, and balancing them as you put the mobile together.

What will your mobile be? It could be about your favorite sport—or someone else's favorite sport if the mobile is to be a gift. It could have butterflies or imaginary insects flying from it. It could simply have curious shapes of things that no one can identify. Draw a simple plan so you know how many hanging items to make. They can be different sizes.

You'll need: Several metal wire clothes hangers, heavy thread or lightweight string, flexible wire (the kind that comes on spools in craft shops), materials for making the hanging items (see below). Tools: wire cutters, pliers, a hammer or a vise.

To make the designs you'll suspend from the arms: Use cardboard, foil, thin wood, metal, or any lightweight material. You can add color to the designs if you wish.

Finding the balance point:

■ You're going to make a hole at the top of the design so you can hang it. If you want the design to hang level like the designs in the fishing mobile pictured, you need to find the balance point—the right place to make the hole. Push a pin through the top of the design and hold onto the pin. The design should be loose on the pin so it can move. If your design takes a nose-dive, this isn't the balance point. Move the pin until you find the balance point.

- Punch or drill a hole at the balance point. This is where the thread or string goes that will fasten your design to an arm of the mobile.

Making the wire arms:

- Use coat hanger wire for the arms. With wire cutters, cut one length each of 12 inches, 19 inches, 24 inches, and 25 inches.

- Straighten each wire arm by hammering or pressing in a vise. Then bend it into a smooth arc.

- With pliers, bend up about ½ inch from each end, making a right angle.

Putting the mobile together:

- Make a mobile from the bottom up.

- Hang a design on each end of one wire arm.

- Tie a thread or string to the center of the wire arm and slide it until the two designs balance. Make a loop in the top end of this thread. With the flexible spool wire, make a small ring through this loop.

- Slip the ring over the end of a second wire arm. Fasten another design to the other end of this second wire.

- Find the balance point of the second arm as you did for the first one by attaching a thread and sliding it. Again, make a thread loop at the top of the thread and add a ring made of spool wire.

- Add the other wire arms and designs to the mobile. You may decide to move items and rebalance arms. When it's right, bend the ends of the wire arms to keep the designs in place.

- Hang the top of the mobile from fishing line, kite string, or other strong string.

Constructions

Constructions are fun. You "build" a sculpture, using all sorts of objects. For the base, start with a handful of clay or a piece of wood.

Collect odds and ends you'd like to combine. These might be scrap items, things you've saved, things no one wants. Ideas: Tongue depressors, ice cream sticks, toothpicks, bits of wood; buttons, cloth, yarn, spools, string; plastic spoons, forks, and knives; wire, chicken wire, screen wire, pipe cleaners, corks; straws, keys, bottle caps, egg cartons (you can cut shapes from them); seed pods, pinecones, nuts, sticks, seashells.

Mental Skills

Clay Base

Start with your base. Experiment. You might begin by pushing a stick or a wire into the clay. Then add items to the construction; change them around; figure out how to attach things and link them together.

Wood Base

■ Drill holes in the base the right size to hold any sticks or wires you want to use for main supports. Insert ends. For wire, a slight bend just above the base will help hold it in place.

■ Add items; try connecting parts of the construction by criss-crossing with yarn, wire, or string. With flexible materials, try bending and twisting them. Experiment until the design pleases you.

Collages

Collage (co-LAZH) is a French word. A collage is a work of art made by gluing materials to a surface.

How do you make a collage that expresses something about yourself? It could include a small photo of yourself and pictures out of magazines that show a sport you like, your favorite food, or a place you dream of visiting. Maybe you've saved the ticket stubs after going to a movie. Maybe you have something with your name on it, like the envelope from a letter addressed to you. A photo of your family, a photo of a pet, anything you decide on.

Start with a blank poster board or a big piece of cardboard. Collect the items you want to use. Anything made of paper works well, although you can use other materials.

Arrange things on the poster board and move them around. A collage is a very casual thing—you can do whatever looks good to you. You can tilt and overlap items. You can cut your paper items in shapes you want or use them as they are. For added color, cut or tear pieces of colored paper or scraps of gift wrap and slip them in. Try to cover all or most of the surface of the poster board.

When you're ready to glue everything in place, use a glue stick that won't make ripples in the paper items when you glue them on. If you feel like your collage needs some finishing touches, consider cutting words from magazines or writing or drawing in a few places.

If you want to frame your collage, look for a simple poster frame made of a backing, a sheet of clear acrylic, and clips that hold everything together. This will work if your collage is flat, but not if you've glued anything bulky to it.

Mental Skills

Artist Scoreboard

Requirements	Approved by:

Do Five of These:

1. Draw or paint an original picture, using the art materials you prefer. Frame the picture for your room or home. _____

2. List the primary and secondary colors. Explain what happens when you combine colors. _____

3. Using a computer, make six original designs using straight lines, curved lines, or both. _____

4. Draw a profile of a member of your family. _____

5. Use clay to sculpt a simple subject. _____

6. Make a mobile, using your choice of materials. _____

7. Make an art construction, using your choice of materials. _____

8. Create a collage that expresses something about yourself. _____

Mental Skills Group

Scholar

School is a big part of your life. You study math, science, language, and other subjects, but you also learn about yourself—what subjects you like best, what areas you want to explore further.

You learn how to concentrate and how to find out what you want to know. To be a good scholar, you have to be curious and determined to gain everything you possibly can from your education.

You're probably already doing some things that will help you earn this badge: going to school, earning the best grades you can, and behaving well in school.

Do Three of These:

1. Have a good record in attendance, behavior, and grades at school.
2. Take an active part in a school activity or service.
3. Discuss with your teacher or principal the value of having an education.
4. List in writing some important things you can do now because of what you've learned in school.

And Do Three of These:

5. Trace through history the different kinds of schools. Tell how our present public school system grew out of these early schools.
6. Make a chart showing how your school system is run.
7. Ask a parent and five other grown-ups these questions:
   - What do you think are the best things about my school?
   - What are its main problems?

   What do you think were the best answers? Why?
8. List and explain some of the full-time positions in the education field.

9. Help another student with schoolwork. Tell what you did to help.

When you complete each requirement, ask your teacher, principal, den leader, or counselor to initial your Scholar scoreboard on page 116.

Do Your Best in School

As a Webelos Scout you have promised to "do your best." That is the Cub Scout motto, and you should follow it in everything—work, play, and school.

Are you doing your best in school? Do you always go to school, except when you are sick? Do you behave well in school? Do you try hard to get good grades? These are things you need to do for requirement 1.

Do you take part in school activities, like clubs and sports? Do you do a Good Turn for the school now and then? If you do, you may be earning requirement 2 right now. If you need ideas for ways you can become involved in activities and in helping your school, ask your teacher or principal.

When you do requirement 1 or 2, or both, ask your teacher or principal to initial your Scholar scoreboard.

The Value of an Education

Why go to school? There are lots of reasons. Requirement 3 asks you to think about them.

From kindergarten on, your studies help you make your way in the world. You're gaining knowledge that helps you right now, and it will help you later as you continue your education and when you begin your adult career.

In school, you can explore many subjects on your own, too. If you want to find out about dinosaurs or volcanoes or tropical fish, your school library or media center may have just what you're seeking.

What are your ideas about the value of an education? If you're doing requirement 3, discuss this with your teacher or principal. Then ask him or her to initial your Scholar scoreboard.

What You've Learned So Far

This list will help you start thinking about requirement 4 and the things you can do now because you are going to school:

- Reading
- Writing
- Math
- History of your state and country
- Geography
- Science
- New games and songs
- Arts and crafts

Can you think of other knowledge and skills you have acquired in school? If you're doing requirement 4, write these down in a list. Show it to your teacher or principal and ask him or her to initial the scoreboard.

History of Schools

Your school is the latest step on a long trail going back to people who lived long ago, before written history began.

Everyone needed to learn about food, shelter, clothing, and safety. When they were old enough, children learned skills like hunting and fishing from their parents and other adults. Their school was life itself and the daily activities that helped them survive.

The earliest written records of ancient civilizations have stories of schools. These schools were in the temples where people worshiped their gods, and the schools taught mostly about religion. In Egypt, the temple schools taught more subjects as the years went on.

The ancient Greek and the Roman civilizations believed schools and teachers were important. Their schools were not like ours. Sometimes teachers just walked around the streets with their pupils and talked with them.

A great Greek teacher named Plato met his students in a garden in Athens called the Academy. That's where the word *academy*, meaning school, came from.

Mental Skills

Early schools in America. America's early colonists soon set up schools. The Pilgrims landed in 1620, and by 1647 Massachusetts Colony had a law providing for free public schools. Few were started, though. Most schools were still private.

The New England Colonies had schools in homes, where children learned Bible verses and the alphabet. Academies trained students for college. The Middle Colonies had both public and church-run private schools. In the Southern Colonies, each plantation had its own teacher.

But by the early 1800s, schools still were not free. There were charity schools, but many parents didn't like them. If they could afford it, parents sent their children to private academies. The main subjects were "The Three Rs"—**R**eading, w**R**iting, and a**R**ithmetic.

Usually there was just one room for school. Boys sat on one side and girls on the other. Sometimes, children—especially those from farms—came only when there was no work at home. Often, everyone studied aloud at one time in the classroom! This was called a "Blab School."

The common school movement in America. People were demanding free schools, paid for by taxes. The first "common schools" (public schools) were opened in New York and Pennsylvania.

Horace Mann and the state of Massachusetts led in changing the system of education. Mann campaigned successfully for better teachers and buildings. In his state, children between the ages of 8 and 14 had to attend school. Schools were divided into grades.

These ideas spread, and by 1855, America had 81,000 common schools.

Since then, schools have continued to change. You learn about many more subjects than "The Three Rs." New ideas about the best ways to learn are constantly being brought into schools. Families have choices of public schools, private schools, schools run by churches and other religious groups, and home schooling, where a parent teaches his or her child.

Who Runs Your School?

You may answer this question by saying "the principal."

But there is more to it than that. In a public school, the principal works with teachers. He or she also works with the school superintendent, who is in charge of all the schools in the district. See if you can make a chart showing how your school system is run. Ask your principal about it.

This is how a chart of a school system might look:

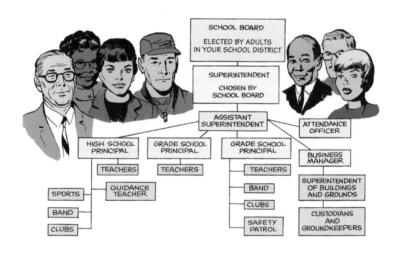

Your School's Strengths and Weaknesses

You may think there are good things and bad things about your school. If you have attended more than one school, you may have an idea how your present school compares with another school. But to get a good idea of what people in your community think about your school, you need to ask them. This will help you earn requirement 7.

Ask your Webelos den leader to invite the den's parents to a den meeting. Ask them: What are the best things about the schools? What are the problems?

What are your own answers to these questions? What can be done to improve your school?

Careers in Education

If you're interested in a career in education, you should know about teaching jobs plus all the other jobs connected with schools.

You can think of jobs right in your school. Who works there besides teachers and a principal? Start a list of careers in your school. This will get you started on requirement 8.

Also, ask your teacher about the types of careers in your school system. You may be surprised at the different kinds of skills that are needed to run it. Add these careers to your list and be ready to explain what these people do in their jobs.

Scholar Scoreboard

Requirements   **Approved by:**

Do Three of These:

1. Have a good record in attendance, behavior, and grades at school.   _____

2. Take an active part in a school activity or service.   _____

3. Discuss with your teacher or principal the value of having an education.   _____

4. List in writing some important things you can do now because of what you've learned in school.   _____

And Do Three of These:

5. Trace through history the different kinds of schools. Tell how our present public school system grew out of these early schools.   _____

6. Make a chart showing how your school system is run.   _____

7. Ask a parent and five other grown-ups these questions:

   • What do you think are the best things about my school?

   • What are its main problems?

   What do you think were the best answers? Why?   _____

8. List and explain some of the full-time positions in the education field.   _____

9. Help another student with schoolwork. Tell what you did to help.   _____

On to Showman!

Mental Skills Group

Showman

Everybody loves to see a show. And it's fun to be on stage. Behind the scenes are people who enjoyed creating the script, songs, and scenery.

For the Showman activity badge, you'll choose puppetry, music, or drama.

For puppetry, you might decide to write a play for puppets, make the puppets, and put on the play.

For music, you can learn a folk song, play a musical instrument, or tell about music you like.

For drama, you can be an actor in a play for your den. Or you can attend a play or read one.

You have a lot of choices! On with the show!

Choose one set of requirements for this badge: Puppetry (below), Music (page 127), or Drama (page 132).

Puppetry

Do Four of These:

1. Write a puppet play about one of your Webelos den activities or a subject of your choice.

2. Make a set of puppets or marionettes for the play you have written or for another play.

3. Build a simple stage for marionettes or puppets.

4. Alone or with the help of others, put on a puppet show for your den or pack.

5. Make a set of four paper bag puppets for a singing group. With the help of three other den members, sing a song with the puppets as the performers.

6. There are sock, stick, and finger puppets. There are paper bag puppets and marionettes. Explain their differences and show any puppets you have made for this badge.

When you pass each requirement, ask your den leader or counselor to initial your Showman scoreboard for Puppetry on page 141.

Writing a Play

A puppet play is just like a play with live actors. It can be funny or sad.

Your play could have a plot like a television show. The hero overcomes obstacles and defeats the bad guys, or he or she finds a way to get out of a comical situation.

Or your play might be a joke with a surprise ending. You would act out the joke with puppets instead of just telling the joke.

As you write your puppet play, think about how you'll perform it. Remember, you only have two hands. You can have several characters, but you can only have two puppets on stage at once, unless you ask someone to be a puppeteer with you.

A Play With a Plot

What do you need? A story that will hold the audience's attention. One event in it leads to another, and puppet characters have to make decisions and take action. It doesn't have to be something that has actually happened. You can make it up. In most plays, the action builds up through the play.

Mental Skills

This is an example of an idea for a play about a den activity. Notice how the plot starts out with an easy task for two Webelos Scouts, but then they deal with one challenge after another.

Title: "The Adventures of the Pebble Pups"

Characters: Two Webelos Scouts, Jason and Brian; their Webelos den leader, Mr. Mason; a bull

Props (things you need): Poison ivy plants (made of paper), a huge outcropping of granite (made of something lightweight), a small piece of granite a puppet can hold

Plot idea: Jason and Brian are looking for samples of granite to complete their rock collections for the Geologist activity badge. Mr. Mason tells them he is sure there is a granite outcrop on a hill not far away.

Jason and Brian start out. They climb a steep hill. They cross a pasture and are chased by a bull. They walk through poison ivy and start itching.

Finally they get to the granite outcrop on a hill. Suddenly they realize they forgot to bring a hammer and chisel. As they start back, Jason stumbles over a rock. It's a piece of granite!

They hike back to Mr. Mason. He says, "Well boys, how did it go?"

Jason shows him the rock and says, "It was easy. Here's the stone, Mr. Mason."

How to put your play on paper: Put down what each character says and does. Here's an example of the way the middle part of the above play could be written:

Brian: Let's cut through this pasture. *(They walk along.)*
Jason: Hey, Brian, what's really big and runs fast?
Brian: I don't know. What?
Jason: That! *(He points offstage right.)*
Brian: A bull! Come on, run! *(They run offstage left and the bull follows them across.)*

The characters have to talk about where they're going and what they're seeing so the audience understands what is happening. They have to show how they feel—happy, excited, scared.

Make your play a different idea from the example. If you work with another puppeteer, give him a copy of your play script to study so he is familiar with his lines and the action. Have a rehearsal before you present your play to the den.

A Joke You Act Out

Just as in writing a play, you need to write out your actors' lines for the joke.

Title: "Matching Pairs"

Characters: Webelos Scout Jonathan, Webelos den chief, two other Webelos Scouts (who don't have lines to say)

The joke: The den chief is inspecting the den's uniforms. He comes to Jonathan and looks him over carefully. Then he notices that Jonathan is wearing one red sock and one blue sock and calls his attention to them. The end of the script for the joke would go like this:

Jonathan: That's funny.
Den chief: What's funny?
Jonathan: I have another pair just like them at home!

Making Puppets

Simple Puppets

Paper Bag Puppet. Use a small paper bag. Use crepe paper for hair and mustaches. Mark features with felt-tip pens. Look at the picture: Draw the upper lip on the edge of the sack's bot-

Mental Skills

tom and the lower lip on the side of the sack so you can make the mouth open and close.

Finger Puppet. Draw a puppet without legs on heavy paper. Make it 2 or 3 inches high. Cut holes for your first two fingers where the legs should go. You may want to wear a glove as a "costume" for your fingers.

Stick Puppet. This is the simplest kind of puppet. Draw the figure on cardboard and cut it out. Glue on a handle of heavy cardboard or use a craft stick.

Puppets in Motion

Moving stick puppet. May be cut from cardboard or light wood. Join with paper fasteners so parts can be moved. Use a dowel or balsa wood stick for the body stick and thinner balsa wood sticks for the moving parts. Hold the body stick in one hand while moving the other sticks to make the legs walk, tail thrash, or jaws bite (depending on your puppet). You can make a stick puppet of a person with only one moving arm or leg, which is easier to work.

Sock Puppet. Cut the foot off the sock as shown. Take the ankle part and stuff it into the toe to make the puppet's head. Fasten it in with a strong rubber band or ribbon.

Use felt-tip marking pens to draw features. Cut holes on each side of the body for the arms (your thumb and middle finger). You can put on a glove first, if you want to cover your fingers. Your forefinger moves the head.

Marionettes. Traditional marionettes are jointed, which means their necks, wrists, knees, and ankles can bend. Their strings are attached to a crosspiece made of two wooden sticks. The puppeteer holds the crosspiece and tilts it to make the marionette move in different ways.

You can make marionettes from simpler materials, as shown here. The football player is cut from cardboard. The parts are connected by paper fasteners. Attach threads or string to the head and hands. Tie the threads to a wooden dowel or a balsa wood stick. Hold the stick in one hand and use your other hand to pull strings and make the arms move.

Puppet Stages

Carefully turn table on its side. Kneel behind it and hold puppets over edge of table.

Hang a cloth across a doorway. Keep the room behind the stage dark. Light the front.

Take the top off a heavy cardboard carton that is not too deep. Cut the stage opening out of the bottom and decorate it. Put it on a table with cloth draped around the legs.

Marionette Stage

Drape a cloth or old sheet behind a doorway. The performer is hidden behind the backdrop, which is a folding table on its side or a large carton. Tape paper scenery to the backdrop.

Mental Skills

Music

Do Four of These:

1. Play four tunes on any band or orchestra instrument. Read these from music.

2. Sing two songs alone or with a group.

3. Make a collection of three or more records, tapes, or compact discs. Tell what you like about each one.

4. Tell what folk music is. Hum, sing, or play a folk tune on a musical instrument.

5. Name three American composers. Name a famous work by each.

6. Draw a staff. Draw on it a clef, with a sharp, flat, natural, note, and rest. Tell what each is used for.

7. Show the difference between 2/4, 3/4, and 4/4 time by beating time or playing an instrument.

When you pass each requirement, ask your den leader or counselor to initial your Showman scoreboard for Music on page 142.

The Joy of Music

If you are taking music lessons, the music requirements will be easy for you.

Why not form a den band or singing group and perform at a pack meeting? You will have fun, and so will the other boys and their parents.

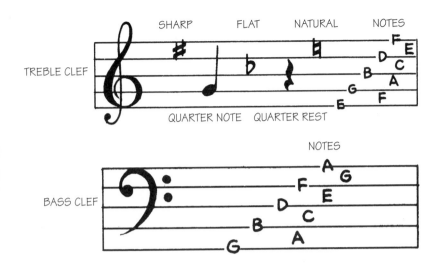

Folk Music

A folk tune is one that has been handed down from generation to generation. There is no known composer. People heard it, learned to play it, and sang it, often in different versions. Many years later, someone wrote down the music and words.

Many folk tunes we hear today came from other countries. Other tunes and songs were made up by people in America. The songs tell of the joys and sorrows of the people living then. Some songs are humorous, and some music is for dancing. The fiddle, guitar, banjo, and dulcimer are often used to play folk music or accompany folk singers.

You might know a few folk songs, like "Down in the Valley," "Hush Little Baby," and "Polly Wolly Doodle." Songwriters have continued to compose in the folk style, so you may know newer songs that fit in with the folk tradition. An example is "This Land Is Your Land," written by Woody Guthrie.

If you don't know much folk music, you have fun ahead of you. Look for a folk song book at your library and learn a few folk songs. Some libraries might have tape recordings of folk music and videos of performers, so you can hear the music.

American Composers

Ragtime, blues, jazz, classical and popular music—American composers have created wonderful music in many styles. Here are just a few titles from six composers:

Stevie Wonder (1950–)

Singer and writer of popular songs. Some of his songs:

"You Are the Sunshine of My Life"
"Superstition"
"Isn't She Lovely"

Aaron Copland (1900–1990)

Composer of symphonies, concertos, and music for ballets. Some of his works:

Symphony for Organ and
  Orchestra
Appalachian Spring
Billy the Kid
El Salón México
Lincoln Portrait

W.C. Handy (1873–1958)

Composer of the blues; wrote a book called, and came to be known as, "Father of the Blues." Some of his songs:

"Memphis Blues"
"Beale Street Blues"
"St. Louis Blues"

George Gershwin (1898–1937)

Composer of popular songs, folk opera, and jazz compositions. Some of his works and songs:

Porgy and Bess
Rhapsody in Blue
Piano Concerto in F
An American in Paris
"Swanee"
"I Got Rhythm"

Woody Guthrie (1912–1967)

Folk singer and composer. Some of his songs:
"This Land Is Your Land"
"So Long, It's Been Good to Know You"
"This Train Is Bound for Glory"

Leonard Bernstein (1918–1990)

Composer of musicals and symphonies. Some of his works:

West Side Story
Wonderful Town
Fancy Free
Jeremiah
Mass

Drama

Do Four of These:

1. Give a monologue (a talk) on a patriotic, humorous, or holiday subject or another subject of your choice.
2. Attend a play. Describe the story. Tell what you liked about it.
3. Read a play. Make a model stage setting for one of the acts.
4. Write, put on, and take part in a one-act play.
5. Make a list of stage directions. Tell what they mean.
6. Describe a theater-in-the-round. What are its good and bad points?
7. Explain the difference between a grand opera and a light opera. Explain the difference between a musical and a play.
8. Read about William Shakespeare. Draw a picture of his Globe Theater.

When you pass each requirement, ask your den leader or counselor to initial your Showman scoreboard for Drama on page 143.

Mental Skills

Performing a Monologue

A single actor recites or acts out a *monologue*. It can be a poem, a story, or an essay. It may be on a serious subject, such as patriotism. Or it may be a funny story.

Choose a short story or long poem that you like. Try to memorize it. Practice often and show all the humor, sadness, or excitement that is in it. Then perform your monologue for the den.

Attending Plays

Have you ever been to a play in a theater? It's different from watching a comedy or drama on television. It's almost as if the actors are living their roles right before your eyes.

Stage actors have demanding jobs. They must become the character, remember the lines and actions exactly, and portray every emotion so it is believable. The cast does this again and again, for every performance.

Actors in television and movies also have demanding roles, but they often have many chances to get it right. A scene can be filmed many times until no one makes a mistake and the director is satisfied. You see the best of their work on the screen.

Ask an adult to take you to a play staged by a local high school drama club, college drama department, or theater group. Some groups put on plays just for children.

Reading and Writing Plays

You can find books of plays in your school or public library.

As you read, picture the characters on stage. What would the actors be doing as they speak the lines? How would they show humor or fear or anger? Say the lines out loud, as if you are acting in the play.

The plays you read may be divided into three acts, or they may be shorter, one-act plays. If you decide to do requirement 4 and write your own one-act play, you can get some tips from the section above on writing a play for puppets (pages 120–122).

Stage Setting

A play director often makes a model of the stage setting for a play to help him or her plan the action. Set designers also make models. You can make one, too. Read a play and then make a model stage setting for it.

■ First, sketch your idea on paper. Draw it as the audience would see it. Then draw it as a floor plan of the stage, as if you were looking down at the stage. Show where furniture or other large objects will go. Use these sketches as a guide. (You can change your mind about your design at any time.)

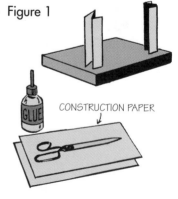

Figure 1

CONSTRUCTION PAPER

GLUE

■ Cut two strips of light cardboard about 10 inches long and 3 inches wide. Make two lengthwise folds, so the ends look like a "Z" shape. Glue them to a box as shown in figure 1. These represent the curtains at the side of the stage.

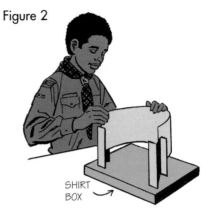
Figure 2

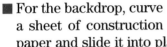

■ For the backdrop, curve a sheet of construction paper and slide it into place (figure 2). Or fold it to make two corners of a room. This is the backdrop.

■ If it is an indoor scene, mark lightly in pencil the places where you want doors and windows on the backdrop. Then remove the backdrop and use crayons or paints to add line and color. If it's outdoors, paint trees and other features. Glue or tape the backdrop in place when it's ready.

■ Keep it simple. The audience comes to the theater ready to use imagination, so you don't have to fill in every detail.

■ Make simple furniture from cardboard or use dollhouse miniatures. Don't clutter the scene with things that won't be used. The action in the play will tell you what must be there.

Stage Directions

As the director of the play you write, you will have to give stage directions to the actors. Read your play and think about what each character does. Make notes in your script where you want each actor to stand, sit, and move on the stage. Here's a way to note the locations:

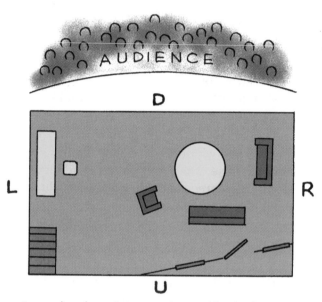

D—Down (toward audience); **U**—Up (toward back of stage); **L**—Left (your left as you face audience); **R**—Right (your right as you face audience); **C**—Center; **DC**—Down center; **UC**—Up center; **LC**—Left center; **RC**—Right center

For the play you write, your stage may be an area of your den meeting place. Keep the setting simple. Use the furniture that is available and movable. Let the audience imagine a sofa when you line up three folding chairs.

Mental Skills

Theater-in-the-Round

Two main kinds of stages are used today. One is the kind of stage you usually think of when you hear the word "stage." It's a raised platform at one end of the room, with a curtain between it and the audience that can be opened and closed.

The other kind of stage is called *theater-in-the-round*. The stage is in the center of the room. The audience sits around all sides of it. There is no curtain. Instead of a curtain closing, the theater is darkened between scenes or acts.

Theater-in-the-round works well for plays with small casts and action that needs to be seen close up. The actors enter and leave the stage along aisles through the audience.

There's no backdrop or solid scenery that would block anyone's view of the actors. A window frame hanging from the ceiling might be the only suggestion of a wall of a house.

If the theater is small, everyone in the audience is fairly close to the stage—much closer than most people would be in a traditional theater. Watching a play this way can make the audience feel very involved in it.

Showman

For a director, staging the play can be challenging. Actors' moves must be planned so they don't have their backs to one part of the audience for too long a time.

For plays with a large cast or a lot of action, theater-in-the-round is not a good choice. The audience is too close to the stage to see everything clearly when many actors are moving about. A great deal of fast action can be confusing.

Opera and Musicals

Opera and musicals are alike in this way: Both are plays with music and singing.

Opera

There are different kinds of opera:

- **Grand opera** has a serious theme. Every word in it is sung by the actor-singers. An example of a grand opera written in English is *Amahl and the Night Visitors*, by Gian-Carlo Menotti.

- **Light opera** has a humorous, romantic plot. It can have a combination of musical numbers and spoken lines. Other names for light opera are *comic opera* and *operetta*. An example of an operetta is *The Pirates of Penzance*, by Sir William Gilbert and Sir Arthur Sullivan.

Grand operas are sometimes shown on television. Watch one if you can. It might be sung in Italian, German, or French. Usually English subtitles are shown so you can follow the story.

Musicals

A musical can be serious or funny. Much of the plot unfolds in the spoken lines. There may be a great deal of variety, with solo singers and choruses, a lot of action, and exciting dance numbers. Actors in musicals are talented in acting, singing, and dancing.

Some examples of musicals:

- *Oklahoma!*, with music by Richard Rodgers and lyrics (words) by Oscar Hammerstein II.

- *My Fair Lady*, with music by Frederick Loewe and lyrics by Alan Jay Lerner.

- *West Side Story*, with music by Leonard Bernstein and lyrics by Stephen Sondheim.

- *Cats* and *Phantom of the Opera*, with music by Andrew Lloyd Webber.

You may have a chance to see an opera or a musical on stage. That will be quite an experience. If you can view videos at home, find out if your public library loans out videos of musicals and operas.

Shakespeare and His Theater

William Shakespeare (1564–1616), who lived in England, has been called the greatest playwright in history. Indeed, he is considered to be one of the greatest writers of any kind.

His plays are still popular today, centuries after his death. He wrote both comedies and tragedies. Examples of his many plays are *Hamlet*, *A Midsummer Night's Dream*, *Romeo and Juliet*, and *Much Ado About Nothing*.

Not very much is known about his life, and there is even an argument among scholars as to whether he really wrote all the plays that bear his name.

During much of his career, he was an actor as well as a playwright. He performed at the Globe Theater in London.

Watch for announcements of productions of Shakespeare's plays by local colleges or theater groups. Many of the plays may be available on video, as well as movie versions of them.

Look for books about Shakespeare and his plays in the library. If you can't find books, read about him in an encyclopedia or on the Internet.

Showman Scoreboards

Do the requirements for only **one** of the following: Puppetry, Music, or Drama.

Puppetry

Requirements   **Approved by:**

Do Four of These:

1. Write a puppet play about one of your Webelos den activities or a subject of your choice.   _____

2. Make a set of puppets or marionettes for the play you have written or for another play.   _____

3. Build a simple stage for marionettes or puppets.   _____

4. Alone or with the help of others, put on a puppet show for your den or pack.   _____

5. Make a set of four paper bag puppets for a singing group. With the help of three other den members, sing a song with the puppets as the performers.   _____

6. There are sock, stick, and finger puppets. There are paper bag puppets and marionettes. Explain their differences and show any puppets you have made for this badge.   _____

Music

Requirements

Approved by:

Do Four of These:

1. Play four tunes on any band or orchestra instrument. Read these from music. _____

2. Sing two songs alone or with a group. _____

3. Make a collection of three or more records, tapes, or compact discs. Tell what you like about each one. _____

4. Tell what folk music is. Hum, sing, or play a folk tune on a musical instrument. _____

5. Name three American composers. Name a famous work by each. _____

6. Draw a staff. Draw on it a clef, with a sharp, flat, natural, note, and rest. Tell what each is used for. _____

7. Show the difference between 2/4, 3/4, and 4/4 time by beating time or playing an instrument. _____

Drama

Requirements

Approved by:

Do Four of These:

1. Give a monologue (a talk) on a patriotic, humorous, or holiday subject or another subject of your choice.
   _____

2. Attend a play. Describe the story. Tell what you liked about it.
   _____

3. Read a play. Make a model stage setting for one of the acts.
   _____

4. Write, put on, and take part in a one-act play.
   _____

5. Make a list of stage directions. Tell what they mean.
   _____

6. Describe a theater-in-the-round. What are its good and bad points?
   _____

7. Explain the difference between a grand opera and a light opera. Explain the difference between a musical and a play.
   _____

8. Read about William Shakespeare. Draw a picture of his Globe Theater.
   _____

Showman

143

Mental Skills Group

Traveler

Traveling is one of humankind's greatest adventures. Early explorers sailed across vast oceans, floated down mighty rivers, and journeyed through high mountain country to see what they could find.

You can be an explorer, too. You won't be traveling in unknown territory, but it will be new to you. You'll enjoy the thrill of discovery wherever you travel.

Be curious, ask questions, read signs about points of interest, notice the sights and sounds.

In earning the Traveler activity badge, you'll learn how to help plan family trips. You'll also learn how to use public transportation—buses, planes, and trains. Let's go!

Do Five of These:

1. **Get a map or timetable from a railroad, bus line, airline, subway, or light rail. The line should serve the place where you live or near where you live. Look up some places it goes.**

2. **Use a timetable to plan a trip from your home to a city in another state by railroad, bus, airline, or ferry.**

3. **With your parent or guardian, take a trip to a place that interests you. Go by car, bus, boat, train, or plane.**

4. **Figure out what it costs per mile for the trip you have taken in requirement 3.**

5. **List four nearby trips you would like to take with your parents or guardian. Lay out the trips on a highway map. Using the map, act as navigator on one of these trips. It should start at your home, be at least 25 miles long, and have six or more turns.**

6. **Pack a suitcase for a trip.**

7. **Check the first aid kit in the family car to see if it contains what is needed.**

When you pass each requirement, ask your den leader or counselor to initial your Traveler scoreboard on page 153.

All Aboard!

Has most of your traveling been by car? It's fun to find out about other kinds of travel—by bus, ship, train, or plane. Then when you do take a trip, you'll know how to read schedules and plan.

Each kind of travel has advantages and disadvantages. Buses go to more places, like small towns, than planes and passenger trains do. Usually the bus is the least expensive of these three, but not always. Airlines sometimes have special low fares.

Many people choose a long train trip mainly to enjoy seeing the country. Long-distance trains have more room for moving about than other forms of transportation, and everything a passenger needs is on the train.

These trains usually have lounge cars and dining cars. Some even have observation cars, where you sit up high for an even better view of the countryside. You may have your own room, called a compartment. It is a tiny living room, bedroom, and washroom, all in one.

A plane is the fastest way of traveling on long trips. The view of the earth from high in the sky is breathtaking. You have a bird's-eye view of mountains, rivers, and cities far below. Flying through and above clouds gives you a feeling of being in another world.

Mental Skills

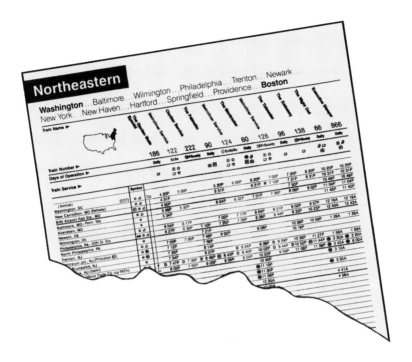

Your Schedule

Railroads, buses, airlines, and ship lines have schedules called *timetables*. These list the places they go and show the times they leave and arrive at each place.

Timetables look hard to read. But they're not, when you learn how. For instance, some timetables use arrows to show the direction of travel. Noon to midnight hours (P.M.) are usually shown in heavy type. Look at the beginning of the timetable for instructions on how to use it.

Read your timetable with care when you are planning a trip. Be sure the train, bus, airplane, or ferry goes on the day you want. Check with a ticket agent for any recent changes in the departure and arrival times.

You can get a timetable at a railroad or bus station, ferry line, airline terminal, or travel agency.

How Much Does It Cost?

Requirement 4 asks you to figure out how much it costs to go on a trip. If you travel by bus, rail, or plane, you can find out the cost per mile if you know two things: the fare and the distance.

> Here is the formula to use:
> Fare ÷ Distance = Cost Per Mile

Suppose you are going to take a bus trip to a city 180 miles from your town. The fare is $37.50. Then:

> $37.50 ÷ 180 Miles = $0.208 Cost Per Mile

It would cost a little more than 20 cents per mile to travel by bus.

But because you are younger than 12 years old, you might be able to go at half-fare. That means your cost would be about 10 cents a mile.

Many airlines, bus lines, and railroads have special fares. Fares may be lower on weekends or at certain times of the year. It's a good idea to check for special fares before you plan a trip.

How much it costs to take a trip by car may be harder to figure. There are many "hidden" costs when traveling by car, such as the cost of the car insurance, the cost of wear and tear on the car and tires, and the cost of engine oil. But you can easily figure out the cost of the gasoline used per mile of your trip by dividing the total fuel cost by the total miles you travel.

Packing Your Suitcase

■ Make a list of things you'll need. Check it with an adult member of your family.

■ Fold your clothes and press down on them as you pack so you will have as many as you need.

■ If you're using a suitcase, put extra shoes at the back. When the suitcase is standing up, the shoes will be on the bottom.

■ Tuck socks into shoes to save room.

Mental Skills

- Put things that might break and spread throughout your clothes, such as toothbrush, toothpaste, and shampoo, in a plastic jar or bag. (A jar won't crush easily.)

- If you're using public transportation, you should have name tags on all your luggage. Some tag holders have a cover that opens so the name and address aren't visible to everyone who passes by. The tag helps if your luggage is lost or if several passengers have similar bags. Some people also tie a piece of brightly colored yarn to the handle so they can find their luggage quickly when they arrive at their destination.

A Family Trip by Car

When traveling by train, bus, or airplane, you really don't have much to do. You just pack your bag and get to the train station, bus station, or airport ahead of time. But when you go by car, you have to do more planning.

Your parent or parents have to get the car ready. That means making sure the brakes, lights, and steering are okay. The oil level in the engine and the air pressure in the tires must be checked. The gas tank should be full. Before a long trip, a mechanic should take care of any regular maintenance that is due.

Planning a Car Trip

You can help plan the trip. How do you find the best way to get where you want to go? How do you know the best roads? By using road maps.

Look for maps of your own state and neighboring ones at state tourism offices, the highway department, or a gas station. Some families use a road atlas, which is a book of state maps.

If your parent is a member of an automobile club, it provides maps of states and street maps of large cities. A club may also plan your route for you.

Study the maps. For a long trip, decide how far you'll travel each day. Where will you stop? At a hotel, a motel, or a camping ground? Your parent may need to phone and make reservations. Find out whether your library has recent travel guides that list places to stay. Automobile clubs may have these, too.

Family Camping Trips

Many American families take vacation trips by camping along the way at public or private campgrounds. They may stay a day or two and then move on again. If they especially like a campground and the recreation the area offers, they may spend most of their trip there. This can be an inexpensive and enjoyable vacation.

There are four main kinds of public campgrounds.

National Forests

The United States has more than 150 national forests. National forests cover one-tenth of the whole area of our country. The U.S. Department of Agriculture controls them.

The national forests have more than 2,000 campgrounds. Most have tables, benches, rock fireplaces, a water supply, and toilets. Many are free. They don't accept reservations.

National Parks

The National Park Service controls our national parks. A park may be the site of a great natural wonder, like the Grand Canyon in Arizona and Mammoth Cave in Kentucky.

Most of the national parks have campgrounds. (Look for a campground symbol on the map.) These have a water supply, tables, fireplaces, and restrooms. Some have laundry rooms, showers, and stores. Besides the cost to go into the park, some campgrounds charge an extra fee.

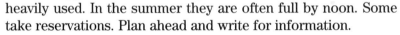

With the increase in camping interest, most campgrounds in national parks are heavily used. In the summer they are often full by noon. Some take reservations. Plan ahead and write for information.

National Monuments

National monuments are places that preserve

- Prehistoric sites, such as Petroglyph National Monument in New Mexico.

- Historic sites, such as Fort McHenry National Monument in Maryland.

- Places of scientific interest, such as Agate Fossil Beds National Monument in Nebraska.

A national monument could be almost anywhere—in the heart of a city or in the wilderness. Some have camping places, or there might be a campground nearby.

Check the map for national monuments along your route. They are worth a visit.

State Parks

Each state has state parks. Some of them are for day use only, for picnics and other recreation. Others may have campgrounds ranging from basic campsites to those with showers and laundry facilities. Most have a small daily charge.

Finding Places to Camp

Perhaps your family would like to know more about campsites. Check some current guidebooks on camping. Find out where to write for more information about camps in each state you plan to visit.

Before you go on a camping vacation, try to earn your Outdoorsman badge. Everything you learn about outdoor living will be helpful on your trip.

Car First Aid Kit

Be sure to have a first aid kit in the car. Naturally, you hope you will not need it, but a Scout should be prepared. Check the first aid kit in the car before you go. The things that should be in the kit are listed on pages 245–246.

Traveler Scoreboard

Requirements	Approved by:

Do Five of These:

1. Get a map or timetable from a railroad, bus line, airline, subway, or light rail. The line should serve the place where you live or near where you live. Look up some places it goes. _____

2. Use a timetable to plan a trip from your home to a city in another state by railroad, bus, airline, or ferry. _____

3. With your parent or guardian, take a trip to a place that interests you. Go by car, bus, boat, train, or plane. _____

4. Figure out what it costs per mile for the trip you have taken in requirement 3. _____

5. List four nearby trips you would like to take with your parents or guardian. Lay out the trips on a highway map. Using the map, act as navigator on one of these trips. It should start at your home, be at least 25 miles long, and have six or more turns. _____

6. Pack a suitcase for a trip. _____

7. Check the first aid kit in the family car to see if it contains what is needed. _____

Community Activity Badge Group

Citizen

Communicator   **Family Member**

Readyman

Community Group

Citizen

I n the Cub Scout Promise, you say you will do your duty to your country. This means being a good citizen.

There are many ways to be a good citizen, not only of your country but in your community and your state, and even closer to home, in your neighborhood and school. And think about this: What does it mean to be a good citizen of the planet Earth?

As you earn the Citizen activity badge, you'll find out what it takes to be a good citizen.

Do All of These:

1. **Know the names of the president and vice president of the United States. Know the names of the governor of your state and the head of your local government.**

2. **Describe the flag of the United States and give a short history of it. With another Webelos Scout helping you, show how to hoist and lower the flag, how to hang it horizontally and vertically on a wall, and how to fold it.**

3. **Explain why you should respect your country's flag. Tell some of the special days you should fly it. Tell when to salute the flag and show how to do it.**

4. **Repeat the Pledge of Allegiance from memory. Explain its meaning in your own words. Lead your Webelos den in reciting the pledge.**

5. **Tell how our national anthem was written.**

6. **Explain the rights and duties of a citizen of the United States. Explain what a citizen should do to save our natural resources.**

7. **Alone or with your Webelos den, do a special Good Turn. Help your church or other religious organization, school, neighborhood, or town. Tell what you did.**

And Do Two of These:

8. Tell about two things you can do that will help law enforcement agencies.

9. Visit a community leader. Learn about the duties of the job or office. Tell the members of your Webelos den what you have learned.

10. Write a short story of not less than 50 words about a former U.S. president or some other great American man or woman. Give a report on this to your Webelos den.

11. Tell about another boy you think is a good citizen. Tell what he does that makes you think he is a good citizen.

12. List the names of three people you think are good citizens. They can be from any country. Tell why you chose each of them.

13. Tell why we have laws. Tell why you think it is important to obey the law. Tell about three laws you obeyed this week.

14. Tell why we have government. Explain some ways your family helps pay for government.

15. List four ways in which your country helps or works with other nations.

16. Name three organizations, not churches or other religious organizations, in your area that help people. Tell something about what one of these organizations does.

When you pass each requirement, ask your den leader or counselor to initial your Citizen scoreboard on pages 176–177.

Statue of Liberty's 100th birthday, 1986.

Government and You

Good citizens know what their government is doing—that means national, state, and local government. They try to find out what is happening. They read newspapers. They watch and listen to the news on television and radio.

You may not understand everything you read or hear about government in the news. Talk it over with your parent or other adult. What happens in government affects everyone's life.

Know These Names

For requirement 1, learn the names of the president and vice president of our country. Find out who the governor of your state is. Learn the name of the head of the government of your city, town, or county. Ask your parent what the duties of each one are.

The U.S. Flag

You'll learn about our flag for requirement 2: its history, how to raise and lower it, how to hang it on a wall, and how to fold it.

History of Our Flag

Red Ensign Flag. An English flag that flew over the American colonies before the American Revolution.

Grand Union Flag. George Washington flew this flag over his army headquarters near Boston in 1776. The Revolutionary War had started the year before.

Old Glory. The first official flag of the United States. It was created by the Continental Congress on June 14, 1777. This is why June 14 is celebrated as Flag Day.

Star-Spangled Banner. This flag flew over Fort McHenry near Baltimore, Maryland, during the War of 1812 against Great Britain. Francis Scott Key watched it waving as the British bombarded the fort. Then he wrote our national anthem, "The Star-Spangled Banner."

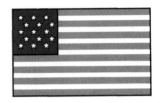

Today's Flag. The 13 stripes represent the original 13 states. Each of the stars in the blue field represents one state. The 50th star—for Hawaii—was added on July 4, 1960.

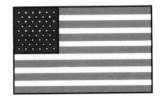

Hoisting and Lowering the Flag

The flag can be attached to the halyard (the rope on the flagpole) with two half hitches or with two snap hooks, which fasten the flag more securely.

It takes two people to hoist and lower the flag correctly. One person holds the flag. The other attaches it to the halyard and hoists the flag, keeping it close to the pole by holding the line taut (see hand positions in the illustration above). He finally fastens the halyard to the cleat on the pole.

Displaying the Flag

Flag at speaker's right

Flag horizontal

Flag vertical

Flag vertical

Folding the Flag

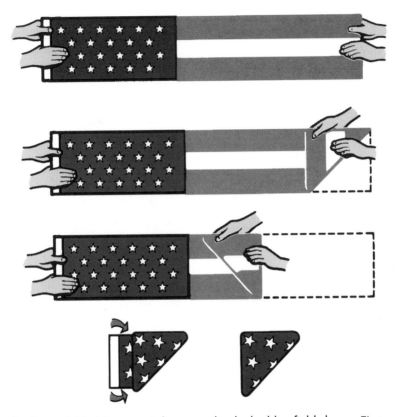

The flag is folded in a special way until only the blue field shows. First, fold the flag lengthwise, in half, then lengthwise again with the blue starred area on the outside. Then make triangular folds, starting from the striped end, until only the blue field is showing. Tuck in the loose end. Never let the flag touch the ground, the floor, or water.

Showing Respect to the Flag

We show respect to the flag in many ways. For requirement 3, think about some ways you show your respect. Read on for some clues.

Flying the Flag

The flag is flown on public buildings every day when weather permits. Some citizens fly it at home every day, too.

It should be flown especially on the following days:

New Year's Day, January 1

Inauguration Day, January 20 after a presidential election

Martin Luther King Jr. Day, third Monday in January

Lincoln's Birthday, February 12

Washington's Birthday or Presidents' Day, third Monday in February

Mother's Day, second Sunday in May

Armed Forces Day, May 20

Memorial Day (half-staff until noon, full-staff to sunset), last Monday in May

Flag Day, June 14

Father's Day, third Sunday in June

Independence Day, July 4

Labor Day, first Monday in September

Constitution Day, September 17

Columbus Day, second Monday in October

Veterans Day, November 11

Thanksgiving Day, fourth Thursday in November

It is also flown on other days proclaimed by the president of the United States, on the birthdays of states (dates of admission to the Union), and on state holidays.

Saluting the Flag

If you are in uniform, give the Cub Scout salute:

■ When the flag is being hoisted or lowered.

■ When the flag passes by or you pass the flag. In a parade, salute just before the flag passes and hold the salute until the flag has gone by.

■ When you recite the Pledge of Allegiance.

If you are not in uniform, greet the flag by placing your right hand over your heart. Take off your hat, if you are wearing one.

The Meaning of
the Pledge of Allegiance

When you pledge allegiance to your flag, you promise loyalty and devotion to your nation. Each part of the pledge has a deep meaning:

I pledge allegiance . . . I promise to be true

. . . **to the flag** . . . to the sign of our country

. . . **of the United States of America** . . . a country made up of 50 states, each with certain rights of its own

. . . **and to the Republic** . . . a country where the people elect their fellow citizens to make laws for them

. . . **for which it stands,** . . . the flag means the country

. . . **one nation under God,** . . . a single country whose people believe in religious freedom

. . . **indivisible,** . . . the country cannot be split into parts

. . . **with liberty and justice** . . . with freedom and fairness

. . . **for all.** For every person in the country.

Our National Anthem

Every good citizen knows "The Star-Spangled Banner," our national anthem. If you have forgotten it, see the *Wolf Cub Scout Book.*

How the anthem was written: From 1812 to 1815, the United States fought England in the War of 1812. In September 1814, English ships fired on Fort McHenry, near Baltimore, Maryland. The fort returned fire.

Francis Scott Key, an American lawyer and poet, was on an English ship. He had come earlier, under a truce flag, to rescue Dr. Beans of Baltimore. The battle lasted into the night.

Key anxiously awaited sunrise. The Stars and Stripes still waved proudly. The fort held out! Meanwhile, Key had begun the poem in the light of the rocket's red glare. He finished it the next night, and it was later set to music.

Your Rights and Duties

As a citizen of the United States, you have both rights and duties. Some are your rights and duties now. For others—like voting and serving on a jury—you must wait until you are an adult. Meanwhile, you can encourage your parent to vote and to use other rights.

Examples of rights. As citizens, you and your family can

- Worship where you like
- Say what you think (freedom of speech)
- Join other people at "peaceful" meetings (the right to assemble)
- Own property and choose where to live
- Go to a good school
- Vote (age 18 or older)
- Have a trial by jury
- Keep people from searching your home—unless they have a special paper, called a *warrant*, issued by a judge

These are a few examples of the freedoms Americans have. Along with your many freedoms comes the responsibility to use them in ways that don't harm other people.

Examples of duties. As citizens, you and your family should

- Obey laws
- Respect the rights and property of others
- Help the police
- Keep informed on what is going on around you
- Help change things that are not good

When you are an adult, you also should

- Vote
- Pay taxes
- Serve on a jury when asked to do so

Saving Our Resources

A good citizen helps save America's natural resources. You and your den can do many conservation projects to improve our nation's air, water, and soil and to keep America beautiful. For example:

- Clear trash out of a stream or lake.
- Take part in a block cleanup campaign.
- Plant trees. Trees provide shelter and food for birds and animals. Trees also take in carbon dioxide and give off oxygen, making the air purer. (See "Photosynthesis," page 339.)
- Save water and energy at home. Fix leaks and don't use more water than necessary when you shower and brush your teeth.

Citizenship and You

Citizenship starts close to home. In fact, it begins with YOU. You know that a good citizen obeys the law, respects the rights of others, and always tries to be fair. But he does even more than that. He does a Good Turn to help other people whenever possible. A Good Turn is an extra act of kindness that you go out of your way to accomplish. (The Scout slogan is "Do a Good Turn Daily.")

What can you and your den do to help your church, synagogue, school, or community? Talk about this with your Webelos den leader. You'll do a Good Turn, either by yourself or with your den, for requirement 7.

Helping the Police

The police and other law enforcement agencies need your help in fighting crime. Here's what you might do:

- Burglar-proof your home with good locks and windows that cannot be easily pried open.
- Protect the family car by always making sure the key is removed and the doors are locked.
- Safeguard your bicycle by locking it in the daytime and bringing it indoors at night.

■ Report to the police any suspicious-looking people you see around the neighborhood.

Learning About Your Community

Your community is where you live. It may be just a few square blocks in a big city, or perhaps your community is a small town. If you live in the country, you're part of a rural community of neighbors, even though you live some distance apart.

Wherever your community is, learn how it works. You can find out by asking a community leader.

Depending on where you live, some community leaders might be

■ Mayors or city managers
■ Municipal department heads
■ City council members
■ County commissioners
■ School board members
■ Service club presidents
■ Municipal judges

■ Ethnic group leaders
■ City attorneys
■ Directors of youth-serving agencies or the Red Cross
■ School superintendents
■ Church leaders
■ Block leaders
■ United Way officials

What Makes a Good Citizen?

Three of the optional requirements ask you to think about this question. For one of them, you learn about a former president of the United States or other great American. For another, you tell why a boy you know is a good citizen. For the third, you tell about three other good citizens.

How can you tell whether a person is a good citizen? Here are some signs:

- Good citizens obey the law. If they think a law is wrong, they try to have it changed. They do this by telling what they think to the people who are elected to make laws.

- Good citizens respect the rights of others. They don't try to get special privileges for themselves.

- Good citizens try to be fair and honest with everyone.

- Good citizens try to make their community, state, or nation better.

- School-aged good citizens "do their best" to learn all they can about their country.

- Adult good citizens learn all they can about their government. Then they vote on election day.

Why We Need Laws and Government

We've said a good citizen obeys the law. But why have laws or a government?

Laws

If there were no laws, people could do anything they wanted. Does that sound wonderful? Think about it. If someone stole your bike, could you get it back? Probably not, especially if the thief were bigger than you.

Laws help us have an orderly society. Many laws are designed to protect people, property, and natural resources. There are laws against littering, driving while under the influence of alcohol, and selling certain drugs, to name a few.

Our nation has *federal laws* that are for everyone in the country. Each state has *state laws*. Cities, towns, villages, and counties have *ordinances*. If your city requires dogs to be penned up or on a leash at all times, that's a city ordinance.

Laws You Obey

You obey laws every day of your life. Perhaps you don't even know you are doing it. Here are some times when you obey laws:

- When you're riding your bike and stop for a red traffic light.
- When you go to school. Your state has a law saying you must attend school unless you are sick.
- When you follow the school crossing guard's orders.
- When you cross streets only at corners when it is safe.
- When you take good care of your pet. There is a law stating that you must not mistreat or harm animals.
- When you're fishing and stop when you've caught the number of fish allowed. A law sets that limit.

These are just a few examples. Talk with your parent or other adult about other laws you obey.

Why We Have Government

What if there were no government? There would be no police officers to see that the laws were obeyed. There would be no firefighters to save your house if it caught fire. There would be no military to fight for our country if it were attacked. Government takes care of all these things and much more.

Paying for Government

The United States has four levels of government—federal, state, county, and city. They give us a lot of services, and they cost a lot of money. Soldiers, police officers, firefighters, teachers, and other government workers have to be paid. Roads, highways, bridges, dams, and parks are expensive to build and maintain.

All citizens help pay for these services. Most of the money comes from taxes like income tax, sales tax, real estate tax, and property tax. Some money comes from license fees or charges for using public parks.

Citizenship in the World

Our country is full of good citizens. And it is a good citizen, too, because it helps other countries. The United States is one of the richest countries in the world. Some nations are so poor, many children go hungry and have no schools. Our country tries to help other nations in several ways. Here are some:

- By giving them food and services

- By lending money at little cost

- By buying the products other countries make and by selling them our products (this trade helps us, too)

- By sending teachers, farming advisers, doctors, scientists, and engineers to work in other countries

- By bringing students from other countries to the United States to study

Americans help in other ways, too. For example, there is the Cooperative for American Relief to Everywhere, commonly known as CARE. Our citizens give money to CARE. CARE sends food and clothing to poor people in other countries. The Boy Scouts of America helps other countries through its own World Friendship Fund. Cub Scouts, Boy Scouts, Varsity Scouts, and Venturers give money to help Scouting groups around the world.

Citizenship in Your Town

Many people in your community show good citizenship by working without pay. They are volunteers. They care about other people, and they find their work enjoyable and worthwhile. These are some volunteer groups that may make your community a better place:

- Volunteer fire department
- Rescue squad
- Red Cross
- Hospital volunteers
- Recreation associations
- United Way
- Humane Society
- The Salvation Army
- Boy Scouts of America
- Girl Scouts of the United States of America

Many people help these volunteer organizations by donating money to them.

Rescue team at work

Citizen Scoreboard

Requirements   **Approved by:**

Do All of These:

1. Know the names of the president and vice president of the United States. Know the names of the governor of your state and the head of your local government. _____

2. Describe the flag of the United States and give a short history of it. With another Webelos Scout helping you, show how to hoist and lower the flag, how to hang it horizontally and vertically on a wall, and how to fold it. _____

3. Explain why you should respect your country's flag. Tell some of the special days you should fly it. Tell when to salute the flag and show how to do it. _____

4. Repeat the Pledge of Allegiance from memory. Explain its meaning in your own words. Lead your Webelos den in reciting the pledge. _____

5. Tell how our national anthem was written. _____

6. Explain the rights and duties of a citizen of the United States. Explain what a citizen should do to save our natural resources. _____

7. Alone or with your Webelos den, do a special Good Turn. Help your church or synagogue, school, neighborhood, or town. Tell what you did. _____

8. Tell about two things you can do that will help law enforcement agencies.

   _____

9. Visit a community leader. Learn about the duties of the job or office. Tell the members of your Webelos den what you have learned.

   _____

10. Write a short story of not less than 50 words about a former U.S. president or some other great American man or woman. Give a report on this to your Webelos den.

   _____

11. Tell about another boy you think is a good citizen. Tell what he does that makes you think he is a good citizen.

   _____

12. List the names of three people you think are good citizens. They can be from any country. Tell why you chose each of them.

   _____

13. Tell why we have laws. Tell why you think it is important to obey the law. Tell about three laws you obeyed this week.

   _____

14. Tell why we have government. Explain some ways your family helps pay for government.

   _____

15. List four ways in which your country helps or works with other nations.

   _____

16. Name three organizations, not churches or other religious organizations, in your area that help people. Tell something about what one of these organizations does.

   _____

Community Group

Communicator

A communicator is a person who shares information. We all do that constantly. We tell or show what we know, how we feel, and what we think.

When you speak or write, you communicate. And when you yawn, smile, or frown, you're showing other people that you're sleepy, happy, or unhappy. You can communicate by drawing pictures and by using sign language and codes.

We communicate over long distances by telephone and computer. Communications keep our personal, business, and government worlds going. As you earn this activity badge, you'll learn about the many careers in communications.

Do Seven of These:

1. Play the Body Language Game with your den.

2. Prepare and give a three-minute talk to your den on a subject of your choice.

3. Invent a sign language or a picture writing language and use it to tell someone a story.

4. Identify and discuss with your den as many different methods of communication as you can (at least six different methods).

5. Invent your own den secret code and send one of your den members a secret message.

6. With your den, visit a library and talk to a librarian. Learn how books are cataloged to make them easy to find.

7. Visit the newsroom of a newspaper or a radio or television station and find out how they receive information.

8. Write an article about a den activity for your pack newsletter or local newspaper.

9. Invite a person with a visual, speaking, or hearing impairment to visit your den. Ask about the special ways he or she communicates. Discover how well you can communicate with him or her.

10. Use a personal computer to write a letter to a friend or relative. Create your letter, check it for grammar and spelling, and save it to either a hard drive or a diskette. Print it.

11. Under the supervision of a parent or adult, search the Internet and connect to five Web sites that interest you. Exchange e-mail with a friend or relative.

12. Earn the Academics belt loop for Computers.

13. Earn the Academics belt loop for Communicating.

14. Find out about jobs in communications. Tell your den what you learn.

When you pass each requirement, ask your den leader or counselor to initial your Communicator scoreboard on pages 205–206.

Body Language

We often send messages without meaning to do it. People can see how we feel by our frown or smile or by a shrug of our shoulders. Such facial expressions and gestures are called *body language.*

Animals use body language, too. When a dog wags its tail, you know the dog is happy. When a cat arches its back or bares its claws, you know the cat is prepared to fight.

Body Language Game

To play this game, give your den members paper and pencils. Ask them to think about feelings they can show by body language only—without making a sound. Have them make a list of at least five feelings they can show.

Den members take turns showing one of their feelings. The others try to guess what the feelings are. The den leader or den chief can be referee and decide whether the body language really does show the feeling.

If a den member guesses correctly, he gets one point. If nobody guesses correctly, the boy who performed the body language gets one point. The final winner is the boy with the most points.

Here are examples of feelings that you can show by body language. Probably you can think of other body language that shows feelings.

Happiness or pleasure—big smile

Fear—protecting head with arms

Indifference—shrugging shoulders

Anger—shaking fist

Communicator

Unhappiness—big frown

Sleepiness—yawning

Puzzlement—scratching
head and looking doubtful

Anxiety—tensing body
and looking worried

Boredom—slouching and
looking blank

Giving a Talk

Most of our communication is done through speaking and listening. It's important to learn to speak so that everyone understands what you're saying, and you need to listen carefully when others are speaking. It's also important to ask questions when you don't understand or want more information.

For requirement 2, you'll give a three-minute talk in front of your den. This can be like telling a story about something you have done. You can answer questions after the talk.

Suppose you plan to tell the den about an exciting soccer game you played recently. Would the story sound like this?

"Boy, did we have a great game Saturday, you know? In the last seconds, I passed off to Jason, and he kicked the winning goal. It was great!"

Your listeners will know it was a soccer game and your team won by one goal, but they're going to ask questions. What teams were playing? What was the final score? Who is Jason? How far was he from the goal when he scored? Where were the defenders and goalkeeper? This story could have had a few more details in it.

Think through your story before you tell it. You might even make a list of the important points to fix them in your mind. You don't have to tell *everything* that happened, but include the basic information, the highlights, and why the game was exciting.

Try to avoid using words and phrases that don't move your story along. Expressions like "you know?" just slow it down.

What will *your* story be? Will it be about an exciting game, or a holiday with your family, or an outdoor adventure? When you decide, practice your talk and time it.

Sign Language and Picture Writing

If you met a French boy, how could you communicate with him? You couldn't talk with him unless he knew English or you knew French.

You would try signs or gestures. Maybe you would draw pictures, too. That's what American Indians did when they wanted to communicate with people from a tribe that spoke a different language.

If you have a *Wolf Cub Scout Book*, look in it for the sign language used by deaf people. You'll also find signs used by American Indians and samples of picture writing. On pages 193 to 196 in this book, you'll find the Cub Scout Promise in sign language.

Now see if you can invent your own sign language or picture writing and use it to communicate with your den. First explain the meaning of each sign or picture. Then tell a simple story using them.

Here is a sample story in an invented sign language.

I

Am Hungry

Give

Me

Ice Cream Cone

Thank

You

Tastes Good

Methods of Communication

Each day, you share your thoughts and ideas with other people. You ask questions and answer them. You receive information from all sorts of sources. It's all communication. How many methods of communication touch your life?

Spoken words: Talking directly or by telephone, cellular telephone, CB radio, ham radio, announcements on the school public address system; translating spoken words from one language to another.

Signed words: Communicating with sign language to someone who is deaf.

Written words: Notes, letters, newspapers, magazines, school books, fiction books, nonfiction books, computer e-mail, posters, notices on bulletin boards, braille books; translating written words from one language to another.

Recorded words: Compact disks, tape recordings of books or instructions.

Audiovisual: Motion pictures, videos, television.

What important messages do signs on the street give you? Do they all use words? Do you get information from radio programs? Can art and music communicate? Can a look from a person communicate? What else do you know that is a form of communication?

Secret Codes

Secret codes are fun. Perhaps you learned how to make and figure out secret codes for elective 1 in the *Wolf Cub Scout Book*.

For requirement 5, invent a secret code that only your den members know. Send them a short message and see if they can decode it.

Here's a simple code that is tough to break, unless you know the secret. The secret: Pick out every third letter.

ATWRQESNBZTELULCAOPVSCLSBTCRVONMUZOT
GXIRUNMFGHIIWNSYFFDRUTMN

WEBELOSSCOUTINGISFUN
Webelos Scouting is fun.

For a tougher code to crack, try this grid code device. On a square piece of paper, draw lines to make a grid. Put a second piece of paper under the first. Now use a paper punch to make a hole through both sheets in each of the squares. Make curved marks above and below some of the holes on both sheets as shown.

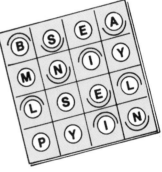

Give one sheet of the code device to another den member. Place the other code sheet over a blank piece of paper. Now you are ready to scramble a message. Let's say you want to code the message, "BILL IS AN ENEMY SPY."

Starting at the top left box with the ⌒ over it, fill in the first five letters of the message in the holes marked ⌒. Fill in the next five letters in the holes marked ‿. Then fill in the six remaining letters in the unmarked holes.

If an "enemy agent" found the coded message, this is what he would see:

All your den members have to do is put their code device over the sheet. Presto! They are in on the secret.

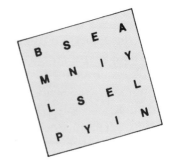

Using a Library

You've probably visited a library. Do you know how to use the library's computer catalog or card catalog to find a book you want? If you don't, learn now. It's a skill you'll need all through school.

Libraries have separate sections for fiction, biographies, and nonfiction. Usually, fiction books are arranged alphabetically by the last name of the author, and biographies are shelved alphabetically by the last name of the subject.

Nonfiction books are grouped by subject. Many libraries use the Dewey decimal system to group nonfiction books. All sports books, for example, have numbers beginning with 796 on the spines of the books. After you find a book's number in the catalog, you can go to the right shelf. Another way of numbering and shelving books is with the Library of Congress classification system.

When you visit the library with your den, find out which system it uses. Then see if you can find books with the computer or

card catalog. Find out whether the computer catalog can be accessed from a home computer.

Libraries loan out magazines, videos, and books on tape, too.

The library is a great place to go for almost any kind of information. In most city libraries, you can use telephone books from other cities, encyclopedias, and newspapers from many places. Some libraries have computers you can use for writing or to get on the Internet.

You need a library card to check out books and other materials. If your family doesn't have a card, ask your parent about getting one.

Visiting a Newsroom

Where does the news come from? Ask your den leader to help you find out by arranging a den visit to the newsroom of a newspaper, television station, or radio station.

All newspapers and broadcast stations have reporters who cover the news in their areas. For news from farther away, they rely on wire services and satellite communication. The largest wire service is the Associated Press (AP). You may see the words Associated Press at the top of newspaper stories.

Machines in the newsroom receive hundreds of wire service stories and pictures every day. Editors decide which stories and pictures to use in the paper or which to broadcast. Talk to an editor to find out how these decisions are made.

Writing a News Story

If you've ever been a reporter for your school newspaper, you know something about writing news stories. If you haven't, you can learn how.

You can write a news article about a den activity for your pack newsletter or a local newspaper. It will be great to see your article in print!

Decide what you'll write about. A special hike? Or a regular den meeting where you worked on a project, like making hand puppets for the Showman activity badge?

First, write the *lead*. The lead is the first sentence or paragraph of the article. It tells the "five Ws": *Who? What? Where? When?* and *Why?* Here's a sample lead:

> Webelos Den 1 visited Boy Scout Troop 10 at Green Tree Park Saturday to find out about Boy Scouting.

Look for the five Ws in this lead. *Who?* Webelos Den 1. *What?* Visited Boy Scout Troop 10. *Where?* At Green Tree Park. *When?* Saturday. *Why?* To find out about Boy Scouting.

Next, write about the most important parts of the activity.

> The Boy Scouts showed the Webelos Scouts how to set up a tent and build a cooking fire.
>
> Everyone helped cook. Lunch included meat and vegetables wrapped in foil, and cherry cobbler baked in a Dutch oven.
>
> After lunch, the troop and den went on a nature hike together. They saw two red-tailed hawks and raccoon tracks by a creek.

Newspapers use short paragraphs, so instead of putting everything in one big paragraph, write your story in short ones. Many times, a newspaper paragraph is only one sentence long.

Double-space your article. This is easy if you're using a computer. If you're writing with pencil or pen on lined paper, leave every other line blank. This gives you space to make corrections.

Be sure to turn your article in on time. If you miss the deadline, your article may not be published. Include your name, address, and phone number. The person who receives it may have questions only you can answer.

Maybe you'll get a *byline*—your name at the top of the article when it's published!

Other Avenues of Communication

People who are unable to see, hear, or speak learn ways of sharing information that work for them. Many consider themselves *differently abled*, so they don't use the term *disability*.

A blind person may listen to recordings of books or read braille books. Braille is a system of raised dots on a page. A small pattern of dots stands for one letter in a word. Some patterns stand for combinations of letters, like *sh*, or whole words, like *the*. The reader reads by feeling the dots with his or her fingers.

A hearing-impaired person may not be able to hear people speak but may be able to read lips. Some people who have been deaf since birth learn to speak, although their speech may not be clear. Others may write messages instead. People who lost their hearing after learning to speak will communicate by speaking.

Many deaf people know sign language and can communicate quickly and expressively with others who know the language. And hearing people also learn sign language so they can communicate with deaf people.

Mute people are unable to speak. If they can hear, they can listen to you and reply by writing.

If you or someone in your den knows a person who is blind, deaf, or mute, invite him or her to a den meeting. Learn about the ways he or she communicates and deals with a world that offers many challenges.

The Cub Scout Promise in Sign Language

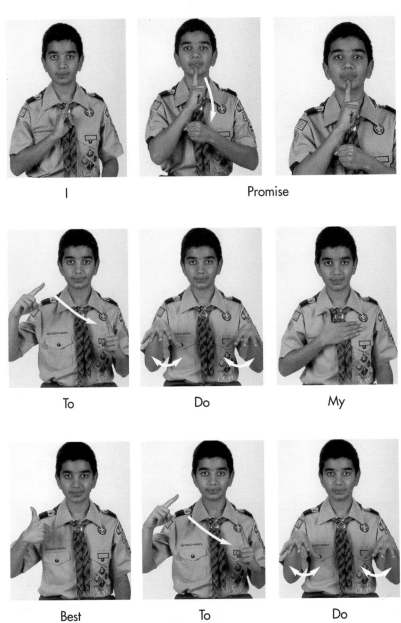

I   Promise

To   Do   My

Best   To   Do

My

Duty

To

God

And

My

Country

To

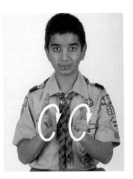

Help

Other

People

And

To

Obey

The

Law

Of

The

Pack

Hello, Computers!

Do you use a computer at school or home? If you haven't been introduced to computers, you'll probably meet one fairly soon, because they're in our lives to stay.

School computers have programs (called *software*) that can help you learn math, English, and other subjects. A home computer could have programs for the family's budget, recipes, games, and much more.

You can use word-processing software to write a school report or a letter. You can even check the spelling and grammar before printing it. It's still a good idea to read your work carefully, though, because the spelling checker will accept the word *here* even though you meant *hear.*

CD-ROMs

CD-ROM drives are standard equipment on most new home computers. *CD* stands for **Com**pact **D**isk (a disk containing a huge amount of information), and *ROM* means **R**ead-**O**nly **Mem**ory. The CD-ROM drive uses a laser to "read" patterns of tiny pits on the disk's surface. It's called "read-only" because you can't add to the information on the disk.

CDs offer games, interactive picture books, cookbooks, encyclopedias, and information on all sorts of subjects. Many CDs are multimedia. That means they present information you can read, pictures (still and moving), recorded voices, music, and other sounds. Some CDs help you work and create on the computer. You could use a CD to make your own greeting cards.

With CDs, you can keep a lot of programs and information on hand that you couldn't keep in your computer for lack of space on the computer's hard disk.

Computer Talk

Computers connected to other computers by telephone lines speed communications in our personal, business, and government worlds every day. Computer talk goes on between computers in one office, across the country, and around the world—almost instantly!

Telephone companies are connected by high-speed networks that communicate by satellite links, underground and undersea cables of various types, and microwave links.

A worldwide network links bank computers, allowing customers to use automatic teller machines (ATMs) to withdraw cash from their accounts, even when they're far from home.

Some people "telecommute." Instead of traveling to a job, they work at home and use a computer to communicate with their employer. They can get company information, exchange messages with the staff, and send their work in—without leaving the house.

A Modem Is the Key

To communicate over telephone lines, a computer must be equipped with a *modem*. A computer sends data in the form of electronic pulses, but a telephone system sends data in the form of waves. The modem changes the computer's pulses into waves that the phone system can use.

At the other end of the line, the receiving computer has a modem that translates the waves back into pulses. Many computers have built-in modems, but a separate modem can be purchased for a computer that doesn't have one.

Communicator

You and the Internet: Get Set to Surf

Have you visited cyberspace? It isn't really one place. *Cyberspace* is the word someone dreamed up for where you "are" when you use your computer to communicate with another—whether those computers are close together or oceans apart.

When you surf (explore) the Internet (the Net), you're in cyberspace. You can "visit" places, watch videos, play games, listen to spoken words and music, and even talk "live" to other people anywhere in the world—all from your computer.

What do you need for surfing the Net? Computer technology changes so fast, new ways to get on the Net can become available at any time. When your *Webelos Scout Book* was published, this is what was needed to get on the Internet using a computer:

■ **A computer.** The best situation is to have a fast computer with a lot of memory capacity and a color monitor, so you can surf efficiently and enjoy the color images the Net offers. But you can still surf the Net without having the latest and greatest computer. Your Internet service provider (see below) can tell you how much speed and memory your computer needs.

■ **A modem.** Having one of the faster modems is an advantage. It will save you time in receiving information on your screen and getting information and new programs from other computers to yours (called *downloading*).

■ **A connection.** This means signing up with a provider of your choice and paying a monthly or annual fee. You have choices. An Internet service provider (or ISP) gives you a connection to the Internet and may provide e-mail and a few other services. An online service offers a wider range of services to its members. For your fee, some providers give you a certain number of hours online each month. After that, you pay an hourly charge.

■ **A Web browser.** This software guides your exploration of the Internet's World Wide Web. Online services have built-in browsers. If you use an Internet service provider, you'll need to get a Web browser. Ask your provider which browser they recommend. Once you're connected, you may be able to download a free or trial copy of a browser, so ask your provider how to do this.

You can learn about choices for hardware, software, and service providers by visiting local computer stores and reading current computer magazines and computer company catalogs.

Safety on the Internet

Just as you have safety rules at home, you and your family should have safety rules for using the Net. That's why requirement 11 says that when you use the Internet to work on the requirement, you must do so with a parent or other adult present.

You should have your parent's approval any time you use the Net because not all sites are suitable for kids. Your family may have rules about whether you can look at certain types of sites. Here are some safety tips:

- Never give out your name, address, telephone number, or school location or send your picture without your parent's OK.
- Never plan to meet in person anyone you meet online, unless your parent approves and goes with you and the meeting is in a public place.
- Always tell your parent if anything you find makes you uncomfortable.

It's important that both you and your parent think about safety on the Internet. Have your parent read the section "Your Child's Safety on the Net" and then discuss it with him or her.

Your Child's Safety on the Net

You need to know that

- The content of some Web sites is not suitable for young people.

- Newsgroups (where anyone can type in a message) and chat rooms (where people talk live) are public; anyone can use them, say what they like, and leave addresses for Web sites you might not want your child to visit.

- If you subscribe to an online service, it may offer monitored chat rooms for kids. If you allow your child to participate, he or she should use a *screen name*, not his or her actual name.

- Online services have methods you can use to block access to selected areas. Ask how this works.

Exploring the Net

What can you do on the Internet? It's impossible to describe it all here, but here are two of the main activities:

- **World Wide Web (WWW).** The Web is made up of Web sites (*home pages*) you can look at (or *access*) by using browser software. You can find home pages for homework help, neat science experiments, space shuttle topics, live tropical fish swimming around, pets, robots, games, video game tips—to name only the very tip of the Web iceberg. Scouting has a home page at http://www.bsa.scouting.org.

Home pages are more than single pages. They're like magazines full of pictures and information, and they may direct you to additional places within the site or to other Web sites. You move around by clicking on highlighted areas on the screen called *links*.

Each Web site has its own computer address called a URL (**U**niform **R**esource **L**ocator). You type the URL to get to the Web site. URLs are long, but you can use the browser to create a "bookmark" for a site. Then you can revisit the site quickly by using its bookmark instead of typing the address.

You can look for a subject you want to explore by using a *search engine,* which is like an index. Choose a subject or some key words, and you'll get a list of sites to visit.

■ **Electronic mail (e-mail)** is a way of exchanging messages with other people. All Internet e-mail participants have a unique e-mail address with their Internet service provider or online service.

If you know a person's address, you can send e-mail no matter which service he or she uses. The messages can contain Web links, files, pictures, sounds, and other features. You write it and send it, and then it waits at the other person's e-mail address until he or she reads the mail.

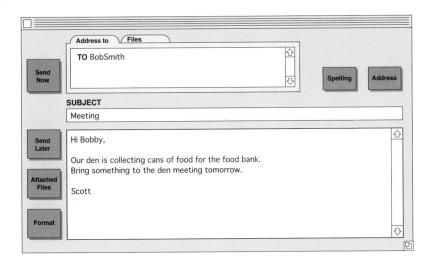

Cub Scout Academics Belt Loops for Computers and Communicating

Even if you earned the Communication or Computers Academics belt loop when you were a Wolf or Bear Cub Scout, you may earn either one again for requirement 12 or 13 of this Communicator activity badge.

communicating

computers

Careers in Communication

Next time you're at the library, choose a book about a career field in communications. Read the book you choose and tell your den what you learned about the field. You could also visit a person who works in communications—a newspaper reporter, an editor, a writer, a print buyer—and share with your den what you learn from talking to him or her.

Communicator Scoreboard

Requirements	Approved by:

Do Seven of These:

1. Play the Body Language Game with your den. _____

2. Prepare and give a three-minute talk to your den on a subject of your choice. _____

3. Invent a sign language or a picture writing language and use it to tell someone a story. _____

4. Identify and discuss with your den as many different methods of communication as you can (at least six different methods). _____

5. Invent your own den secret code and send one of your den members a secret message. _____

6. With your den, visit a library and talk to a librarian. Learn how books are cataloged to make them easy to find. _____

7. Visit the newsroom of a newspaper or a radio or television station and find out how they receive information. _____

8. Write an article about a den activity for your pack newsletter or local newspaper. _____

9. Invite a person with a visual, speaking, or hearing impairment to visit your den. Ask about the special ways he or she communicates. Discover how well you can communicate with him or her. _____

10. Use a personal computer to write a letter to a friend or relative. Create your letter, check it for grammar and spelling, and save it to either a hard drive or a diskette. Print it. _____

11. Under the supervision of a parent or adult, search the Internet and connect to five Web sites that interest you. Exchange e-mail with a friend or relative. _____

12. Earn the Academics belt loop for Computers. _____

13. Earn the Academics belt loop for Communicating. _____

14. Find out about jobs in communications. Tell your den what you learn. _____

On to Family Member!

Community Group

Family
Member

A family is a group of people who care for one another and share their lives and their love.

There are many different kinds of families. Some families have a father, a mother, and children. In other families, children live with one parent. A grandparent or a guardian with a child—that's a family too. And children belong to families in foster homes or boarding schools.

As you earn the Family Member badge, you'll discover new ways to take part in family life and show your family you care about them.

Do All of These:

1. Tell what is meant by family, duty to family, and family meetings.
2. Make a chart showing the jobs you and other family members have at home. Talk with your family about other jobs you can do for the next two months.
3. Inspect your home and surroundings. Make a list of hazards or lack of security that you find. Correct one problem that you found and tell what you did.
4. Explain why garbage and trash must be disposed of properly.
5. Make a list of some things for which your family spends money. Tell how you can help your family save money.
6. Plan your own budget for 30 days. Keep track of your daily expenses for seven days.

And Do Two of These:

7. Prepare a family energy-saving plan. Tell the things you did to carry it out.
8. Tell what your family does for fun. Make a list of fun things your family might do for little cost. Do one of them with a member of your family.

9. **Learn how to clean your home properly. Help do it for one month with adult supervision.**

10. **Show that you know how to look after your clothes. With adult supervision, help at least twice with the family laundry.**

11. **With adult supervision, help plan the meals for your family for at least one week. Help buy the food and help prepare at least three meals for your family.**

12. **Take part in at least four family meetings and help make decisions. The meetings might involve plans for family activities, or they might be about serious topics that your parent wants you to know about.**

When you pass each requirement, ask an adult member of your family to initial your Family Member scoreboard on pages 225–226.

You and Your Family

What Is a Family?

Did you read the first page of this Family Member chapter? It tells what really makes a family, so be sure to read it.

Your Duty to Family

Living in a family means you have support and love. You give support and love, too. When you care about others' feelings and when you listen to their problems and try to help, you're being a good family member.

Being in a family also means doing everyday things like clearing the table after a meal or picking up your belongings. When you hang up your coat and put school books away in your room, that helps everyone else and makes life more pleasant.

Doing your share and helping others is an important part of living together in a family.

What Are Family Meetings?

A family meeting happens when the whole family takes time to talk about what is happening in their lives and about plans and decisions they need to make together. Maybe your family makes plans around the dinner table, and it doesn't seem like a meeting at all.

Sometimes a family may set a special time to plan the coming weekend or talk about family rules. You can read more about family meetings on pages 223–224.

Family Jobs

What are some of the jobs a family does?

Someone cooks the meals, or maybe several people pitch in to help. Family members may take turns setting the table and taking the garbage out. Does one person clean the house, or does each person clean part of it? Then there's lawn mowing and other outdoor chores. All these jobs are important, and they may be shared by family members who are old enough to do them.

For requirement 2, list all your family's jobs around the house. Who does each job? Write in those names beside the jobs. Now you can discuss with your family some other ways you can help out.

Family Member

Neat and Clean

As a family member, your first job is to take care of yourself and your room. If you don't do that, you could add to the work of other family members.

Keep yourself clean. Of course you will get dirty when you play outside or work around the house. Nobody minds that, IF you take a bath or shower afterward.

Brush your teeth regularly. Clean your nails. Don't forget to comb your hair. These simple things show other family members that you care about yourself and want them to be proud of you.

Is your room a mess? Do you just drop your clothes on the floor and expect other family members to pick them up? If you do, what does that tell them about you?

It isn't hard to keep your room neat. Pick up after yourself. Put your books, games, and sports equipment where they belong. Learn to make your bed—and do it every morning.

Doing these things shows you care about others in your family.

Be Safe at Home

A lot of people are hurt or even killed in accidents in their own homes each year. Most of these accidents could be prevented.

Make your home safe by checking it for dangers. Then do something about the dangers.

HOME SAFETY CHECKLIST

PLACE	DANGER	WHAT YOU CAN DO
Living room	Toys on floor	Put toys away.
	Furniture blocking easy passage	Rearrange furniture.
	Electric cords under rugs; worn cords can cause shock, fire	Move cords so people don't walk over them.
	Curtain cords dangling	Keep cords out of children's reach.
Kitchen	Matches in reach of children	Move matches to safe place.
	Knives in reach of young children	Put knives in holder or special drawer.
	Cleaning fluids and other poisons exposed	Put all poisons out of children's reach, in locked area if necessary.
	Spilled grease or water	Wipe up immediately.
Bathroom	Medicines in reach of young children	Put medicines in locked cabinet (in child-resistant containers).
	Radio, hair dryer, or other electrical device near water source	Move away from sink, bathtub, and toilet.
	Toilet lid open	Keep closed when not in use.
	Water too hot	Ask adult to lower water temperature.
Stairways	Boxes, toys, and other items left on stairs	Remove anything people might trip over.
	Handrail loose	Tighten handrail screws.
	Stair covering loose	Tack down covering.
	Light bulb out	Replace bulb.

(Continued)

Family Member

Work area	Tools left out	Put away, out of children's reach.
Furnace area	Waste paper, rubbish near furnace	Move flammable items far away from furnace and throw away.
Outside	Trash, garbage	Keep in tightly covered containers.
	Sandbox, wading pool	Cover when not in use

Other safety tips: If there are young children in the house, add special safety latches to kitchen and bathroom cabinets. They're easy for you and adults to open.

When cooking, use the back burners when you can. Turn pot handles toward the back of the stove so young children can't reach them.

Make sure all purses and briefcases, including those belonging to visitors, are placed out of children's reach.

Garbage and Trash

Garbage can be a health problem unless you dispose of it properly. It can attract flies, roaches, mice, or other pests that carry diseases. It should be taken out of your home and put in garbage cans with tight lids or in sealed plastic bags. The cans or bags should be carried out for each garbage collection day. You can help with this chore.

If your community has a recycling program, recycle glass, metal, plastic, and paper.

Trash and litter outside a home make it look like no one cares. It's also a fire hazard and can cause falls and injuries. Clean it up and get rid of it!

Helping Your Family Save Money

It takes a lot of money to run a household and buy food for a family. Here are a few ways you can help your family hold down the costs.

■ If you are given a weekly allowance, make it last for a week and try to save some of it. Don't spend it quickly and then ask for more. If you need more money, perhaps you could do jobs for neighbors: rake lawns, shovel snow, walk dogs.

■ Take good care of your clothes and shoes. They will last much longer, and that saves money.

■ The monthly bills for utilities—gas, electricity, and water—are a big part of a family's expenses. Turn off lights when you leave a room, and don't waste hot water when you wash or shower. Run the cold water only as long as you need it, too.

Talk with the adults in your family about other ways you can save money for the family.

Your Budget for a Month

A family needs to plan ahead to pay for food, clothing, shelter, activities, and all its other expenses. You can plan ahead for some of your own expenses.

For requirement 6, you'll map out a budget for the month ahead, week by week. First, think about these things:

■ How much money will you have for each week? Do you receive an allowance, payment for a paper route or neighborhood jobs, or money from a parent for certain expenses like school lunches?

■ What are your usual expenses? Think about lunches, school supplies, den dues, snacks, a weekly offering for your church or other religious group.

■ What special expenses are coming up? A gift for a family birthday, a donation to a charity, Webelos Scouting items, a movie with friends?

The money you have to spend depends on the way your family handles children's expenses. In some families, a parent gives a child money as each expense comes up. The child also might have a small allowance to spend as he or she wishes.

In other families, a parent gives a child an allowance to cover lunches and other expenses, and the child has to budget carefully to make the money last.

Because of these differences between families, your budget probably won't look like anyone else's. Plan your month's budget to show the amount of money you expect to have each week and the expenses you will pay out.

How to Plan Your Budget

In planning any budget, it's good to think about *priorities*. A priority is something that comes first. It has to be paid, like your lunch money, so you put it first.

Try planning a budget for the first week. Here's a sample you can fill in, or make a chart of your own:

Where my money will come from:

Allowance .... $_____

Jobs .... $_____

Savings .... $_____

Total money .... **$_____**

Where my money will go:

School lunches (1 week) .... $_____

Den dues .... $_____

Other expenses

_____ .... $_____

_____ .... $_____

Total expenses .... **$_____**

Add up the total money available to you, and then add up the total expenses. If you're not going to have enough money for the first week, decide where you can cut down on expenses. If you expect to have more than enough money, you can increase your savings for another category. Plan the second, third, and fourth weeks. Be sure to include any special expenses you expect and make plans to save for them ahead of time if you can.

Requirement 6 also asks you to keep a record of the money you spend for one week. Each time you spend money, write down what you spent it for and the amount.

When you add up your actual expenses for a week, you'll know whether your budget is working out. You may have to adjust your budget if you didn't include all your expenses, or you may have to cut down your spending so you don't run out of money.

Saving Energy

Saving energy helps your family save money. It also helps conserve our natural resources. Requirement 7 asks you to prepare an energy-saving plan for your family. Check the list below to see what ideas need to go in your plan. Maybe you know other ways to save energy around your home.

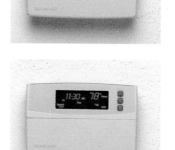

■ Close heating or air-conditioning vents in unused rooms.

■ In winter, close the fireplace damper when the fireplace is not in use, because warm air in the house can be drawn up the chimney.

■ Set the thermostat at the lowest comfortable level in winter and highest comfortable level in summer.

■ In winter, lower the heat at night.

■ Keep windows and outside doors closed when heating or air conditioning is on.

- Don't keep the refrigerator open more than needed.
- Cook several foods at one time. For example, if you cook two things in the oven at one time, the oven doesn't have to be on as long.
- Don't let water run when it isn't needed.
- Use lower wattage bulbs where less light is needed.

Family Fun

A family can have fun together in many ways. Some ways may cost no money, others cost a lot. Try to think of some inexpensive activities your family can do for fun. Here are some ideas:

- Play a new game together
- Make crafts with your family
- Go on a picnic
- Visit a museum, zoo, or park
- Do some community activities together
- Go swimming
- Go on a fishing trip

What are some other things you can do with your family?

Helping With Cleaning

Nobody likes living in a dirty home. It looks bad, and it can even be dangerous to your health because germs breed in dirt, trash, and garbage.

There is no magic way to keep your home clean. Everyone must do his or her part to vacuum or sweep floors, dust and polish furniture, and clean sinks, bathtubs, and toilets.

Cleaning may not be anyone's favorite activity, but when you're done, it's satisfying to have a clean home to live in and enjoy. You are old enough to help, so pitch in willingly. This is another way of showing you care about your family and your home.

Helping With Laundry

Do you take care of your own clothes? When they're dirty, do you put them in the laundry hamper? Once they're clean, do you fold them and put them in drawers or hang them on hangers in the closet?

There is no trick to doing these things. You can learn to fold clothes in about two minutes.

Why not help with the laundry? You'll learn how to operate the family's washing machine or the large machines at the self-service laundry. It will be one more step in showing that you can share in your family's jobs.

Feeding the Family

Everyone likes to eat. But a lot has to happen before the food gets to the table. Planning what to buy, shopping, preparing each dish—that's all part of creating a meal. And cleaning up, too! When you share in this, you learn a lot, and being with your family in the kitchen can be fun.

For requirement 11, you'll help plan at least one week's meals, help shop for the food, and help prepare at least three meals.

Planning Meals

Do you think it would be great to have a hamburger, French fries, and soda for every meal? You'd soon get bored with it, and a diet like that wouldn't do your body any good.

To stay healthy, you need a balanced diet and a variety of foods. When you help an adult in your family plan meals for requirement 11, look at the Food Guide Pyramid on page 67 and the section on meal planning, pages 66–71 (Fitness activity badge). That will tell you about a balanced diet and give you ideas for a variety of foods to choose for your plan.

Shopping for Food

Before you go to the store for food, make a list of the items you'll need for the meals you've planned. This is very important. If you just grab off the shelves the things that look good, you may not have what you need for complete meals. You also need to look for ways to save money on your purchases.

It's a good idea to check the store ads in the newspaper before you shop. Often they will have "specials" that can save you money. An adult member of your family can help you decide whether they are good buys.

In the store, remember to use your list. Ask the adult family member who is with you to help you compare prices. If an 8-ounce can of tomato sauce is 59 cents and a 15-ounce can is 89 cents, which is the better buy? See if you can figure it out. Smart shoppers compare prices.

Price isn't everything, though. Your adult partner may like one brand best, even if it costs more.

Preparing Meals

Have an adult member of your family with you when you pre-pare meals. He or she can help if you don't understand the cook-book recipe or the directions on a box.

For requirement 11, you'll help with at least three meals. Will they be three different breakfasts? Or a breakfast, a lunch, and a dinner?

Getting a meal ready to eat shouldn't be difficult. Maybe you already prepare your own breakfast cereal. But this requirement asks you to help prepare three meals for the whole family. So you might be cooking hot cereal and adding chopped apple to it, or mixing up pancakes to serve with blueberries. Don't forget the other items on your menu plan, like milk and fruit juice.

Lunch can be easy, especially when you know exactly what to get ready. Washing fruit and putting it in a bowl on the table can take just a few minutes. If you get out all the ingredients for the family's favorite sandwiches before you start, you can put them together quickly.

Dinner may take more planning. Since some foods take longer to cook than others, ask an adult to help you decide when to start cooking each dish so everything is ready at about the same time. Or maybe you'll plan a dish you can make earlier in the day, and you can prepare the remaining items just before dinner.

If you use a recipe, read it carefully. Then read it again. Follow it exactly. If the recipe calls for 1 teaspoon of salt and you put in a tablespoon, your dinner will be a disaster!

After dinner, when everyone compliments your good food, you'll feel great. But there's still one thing to do. Clean up! Wouldn't this be a good time for everyone to help?

Family Meetings

Requirement 12 asks you to take part in at least four family meetings. Most families don't have formal meetings, but when your family is at the dinner table, you probably talk about school and events coming up. You make plans for a weekend or a trip. That's one type of meeting that is more like a conversation.

Sometimes families need to sit down and talk at a special time about plans and ideas they need to work out together. These are family meetings, too. The meeting might involve plans for fun, or it might be about serious topics that a parent wants children to know about. Here are some of the subjects that might come up at a meeting like this:

- A schedule to get everyone to music lessons, religious instruction, sports practices, Webelos den meetings, and home again
- Plans for a weekend camping trip or a vacation during the summer
- Family volunteering, like a bike ride for charity or a litter cleanup in your community
- Deciding what to make or buy as a gift for a relative or family friend

- Current events, what is in the news
- Family rules
- Ideas for helping each other
- What everyone needs to know about child abuse, alcoholism, drug abuse, and crime prevention

In the meeting, it's important to listen as well as to talk about your ideas and opinions.

If other family members disagree with you, don't get angry about it. Remember, they have their own interests and ideas, just as you do. Afterward, do your best to do your part in whatever is decided.

Family meetings are important. Talking about things brings all family members closer together.

Family Member Scoreboard

Requirements	Approved by:

Do All of These:

1. Tell what is meant by family, duty to family, and family meetings. _____

2. Make a chart showing the jobs you and other family members have at home. Talk with your family about other jobs you can do for the next two months. _____

3. Inspect your home and surroundings. Make a list of hazards or lack of security that you find. Correct one problem that you found and tell what you did. _____

4. Explain why garbage and trash must be disposed of properly. _____

5. Make a list of some things for which your family spends money. Tell how you can help your family save money. _____

6. Plan your own budget for 30 days. Keep track of your daily expenses for seven days. _____

And Do Two of These:

7. Prepare a family energy-saving plan. Tell the things you did to carry it out. _____

8. Tell what your family does for fun. Make a list of fun things your family might do for little cost. Do one of them with a member of your family. _____

9. Learn how to clean your home properly. Help do it for one month with adult supervision. _____

10. Show that you know how to look after your clothes. With adult supervision, help at least twice with the family laundry.

             _____

11. With adult supervision, help plan the meals for your family for at least one week. Help buy the food and help prepare at least three meals for your family.

             _____

12. Take part in at least four family meetings and help make decisions. The meetings might involve plans for family activities, or they might be about serious topics that your parent wants you to know about.

             _____

On to Readyman!

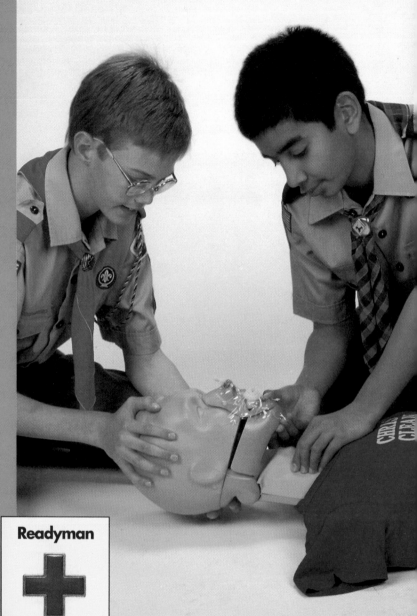

Community Group

Readyman

In emergencies, someone has to be ready to help. After you learn the Readyman badge, you'll know how to react quickly when someone is ill or injured.

You'll be ready to call for emergency help. When you learn first aid, you can care for a sick or injured person until help arrives.

You'll also find out how to prevent accidents and how to be safe when swimming and biking. You'll help your family be safe at home and when traveling by car.

All these skills will make you a Readyman.

Do All of These:

1. **Explain what first aid is. Tell what you should do after an accident.**

2. **Explain how you can get help quickly if there is an emergency in your home. Make a "help list" of people or agencies that can help you if you need it. Post it near a phone or other place with easy access.**

3. **Show what to do for these "hurry cases":**
   - **Serious bleeding**
   - **Stopped breathing**
   - **Internal poisoning**
   - **Heart attack**

4. **Show how to treat shock.**

5. **Show first aid for the following:**
   - **Cuts and scratches**
   - **Burns and scalds**
   - **Choking**

6. **Tell what steps must be taken for a safe swim with your Webelos den, pack, family, or other group. Explain the reasons for the buddy system.**

And Do Two of These:

7. **Explain six safety rules you should follow when driving a bicycle.**

8. **Make a home fire escape plan for your family.**

9. **Explain how to use each item in a first aid kit.**

10. **Tell where accidents are most likely to happen inside and around your home.**

11. **Explain six safety rules you should remember when riding in a car.**

12. **Attend a first aid demonstration at a Boy Scout troop meeting, a Red Cross center, or other place.**

When you pass each requirement, ask your den leader or counselor to initial your Readyman scoreboard on pages 248–249.

What Is First Aid?

You've probably had at least a few scratches and scrapes in your lifetime, and an adult in your family or the nurse at school knew just what to do. Maybe you've taken care of a few small injuries by yourself. All of this is first aid.

First aid is also knowing exactly what to do *first* to help a person with a more serious injury or illness. **First aid is what you must do immediately.** Someone has to help right away, and you might be the only person there who can do this job. It's important to know the right ways to help.

In earning the Readyman badge, you'll find out how to call for emergency help and what to do for different types of illnesses and injuries until help arrives.

What to Do After an Accident

- First, stay calm and think! This may be hard to do—but try. The victim will feel better, knowing you are in control.

- If the victim seems badly hurt, send someone to call for medical help. If no one is there to do that, call for help and give what assistance you can to the victim.

- Do not move a badly hurt person unless the victim is in further danger. It may be necessary to move the person if there is a nearby fire or if the person is lying in the road. But never move an injured person unless it is absolutely necessary.

- Check the victim for "hurry cases" (see pages 232–237).

- Treat the victim for shock (see pages 237–238).

How to Get Help

The way to get help in an emergency is not always the same in every town. Some communities may have different phone numbers for the police, fire department, ambulance, and rescue squad. In many places, the 911 number will put you in touch with all of these services.

Find out how to get help where you live and make a list of the phone numbers. Post your list near the telephone in your home so everyone can find the numbers quickly. It's also a good idea to put your list on a card and carry it with you. You should also carry coins for a pay phone.

Your "help list" should include numbers for

- Police or sheriff's department
- Fire department
- Ambulance
- Utility companies (electricity, gas, water)
- Rescue squad
- Your family doctor
- Poison control center
- A friendly neighbor who can help you

When you call for help, remember the "three Ws": *Who? What?* and *Where?*

Who?   Give your name.
What?   Explain the situation: fire, accident, injury, etc.
Where?   Give the exact location. Give the names of both
              streets or roads at the nearest corner.

Stay on the phone until your message is understood and you have answered all questions.

Sometimes you need to know how to get help, but it may not be an emergency. For problems with your sewer line or other housing problems, call a department of your city or county government. Your church or other religious group, a counseling agency, or friends and relatives might be able to help with a family problem. Find out who to contact in your community.

Hurry Cases

If a person cuts a leg and blood is oozing out, he or she needs first aid but is not going to die. A broken arm is a serious injury, but it won't kill.

Hurry cases are different. Unless you act fast and give the right first aid, the victim may die within a few minutes. The four hurry cases are

■ **Breathing has stopped.** It must be started quickly.

■ **Blood is spurting from a wound.** The bleeding must be stopped quickly.

■ **Poison has been swallowed.** The poison must be made harmless. Get help quickly.

■ **Heart attack.** Get help quickly.

Protective Measures to Take When Handling Wounds and Giving CPR

Treat all blood as if it contains blood-borne viruses. Do not use bare hands to stop bleeding; always use a protective barrier (see the list below). Cover any cuts or scrapes you may have. Always wash exposed skin with hot water and soap immediately after treating the victim, and don't use a sink in a food preparation area.

The following equipment should to be included in all first aid kits and used when giving first aid to someone in need:

■ Latex gloves, to be used when stopping bleeding or dressing wounds

■ A mouth-barrier device, to be used when rendering rescue breathing or CPR (cardiopulmonary resuscitation)

■ Plastic goggles or other eye protection, to prevent a victim's blood from getting into the rescuer's eyes in the event of serious arterial bleeding

■ Antiseptic, for use in sterilization or cleaning exposed skin areas, particularly if soap and water are not available.

Stopped Breathing

In drowning cases and some other accidents, the victim's breathing may stop. It must be started again *quickly*, or the person will die.

Look at the chest. Is it moving up and down? Put your ear to the victim's mouth. Do you feel the victim's breath?

If the answer is no, start rescue breathing. This is a way of blowing air from your own lungs into the victim's lungs.

Rescue Breathing

Don't give up. Continue rescue breathing until medical help arrives and takes over.

Step 1

Note: If available, a mouth-barrier device should be used when rendering rescue breathing or CPR.

Place the victim faceup. Lift the chin with your right hand, and push the forehead down with your left hand.

This shows why it is important to tilt the head back. If the head is not tilted back, the tongue blocks the airway.

Step 2

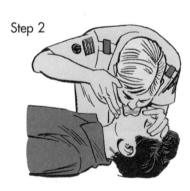

Pinch the victim's nostrils together. Seal your mouth over the victim's mouth. (If the victim is a small child, don't pinch the nostrils. Blow into both the mouth and nose at the same time.) Blow into the victim's mouth to fill the lungs with air. Look to make sure the chest rises.

Step 3

Remove your mouth. Take a deep breath and count slowly to five—about five seconds. (Count to three if the victim is a child.) Watch to make sure the victim's chest falls as air escapes from the lungs. Then give another breath.

If the victim's chest does not rise when you blow in, the airway must be blocked. Turn the head to one side. With your fingers, feel whether something is in the mouth. If there is, pull it out.

If the airway still seems to be blocked, turn the victim's head faceup. Straddle him. Place the heel of your hand midway between the victim's rib cage and belly button. Push upward quickly several times.

Stopping Severe Bleeding

In a bad accident you might see blood spurting out of a wound. It doesn't ooze or flow slowly—it gushes out like a fountain. It must be stopped! **Now!**

Avoid direct contact with the blood. Use latex gloves.

Grab the wound with your gloved hand and **press hard!**

Raise a cut arm or leg above the level of the victim's heart. That will help slow the bleeding.

With your free hand, grab your neckerchief, handkerchief, or other cloth. Fold it into a pad and quickly press it on the wound. Then **press hard** again. If you can, tie the pad in place with a bandage. Don't remove the pad even if it gets soaked with blood. Put another pad and bandage over the first. Send for medical help.

Direct pressure on the wound usually stops bleeding. If it doesn't, **press hard** on one of the pressure points shown to stop bleeding in an arm or leg. The arteries that carry blood from the heart are squeezed against the bone. It's like stepping on a garden hose to stop the water.

 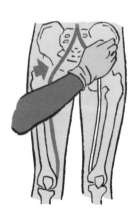

Poisoning by Mouth

Young children will try anything! They will even drink poisons because they don't know any better.

Keep all household cleaners, medicines, weed killers, and insect poisons out of their reach. Locked cabinets are best because children are curious and learn to climb.

If a child does swallow some poison, call a hospital or poison control center immediately. Tell them what the poison is. Follow their directions. Don't give anything to drink unless they tell you to.

Save the poison container so the poison can be identified.

Heart Attack

Heart attack is the number one cause of death in the United States. Most heart attacks happen to adults, especially older people. Here are the signs of a heart attack:

- A feeling of pain or pressure in the center of the chest lasting more than a few minutes. It may come and go. Sharp, stabbing twinges of pain are rarely signals of a heart attack. If in doubt, seek medical help.

- Sweating when the room is not hot.

- Feeling like throwing up.

- Shortness of breath.

- A feeling of weakness.

If you think a person is having a heart attack, call for medical help at once.

First Aid for Shock

Whenever a person is badly hurt, he may also suffer from shock. He will feel weak. His face may get pale. His skin will feel cold and clammy. He may shiver or vomit.

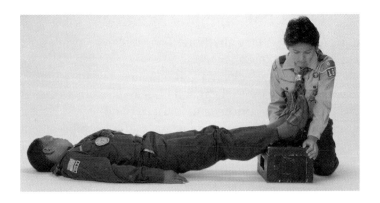

Don't wait for these signals to appear. Give any badly injured person first aid for shock.

■ Have him lie down.

■ Raise his feet slightly, unless you think he has injuries to his head, neck, back, hips, or legs. If you don't know, have him lie flat.

■ If he is not awake, turn him on his side, *not* on his back.

■ If the weather is cool, cover him. If it's hot, don't.

■ Call for emergency help immediately. He needs expert medical care as soon as possible.

Other First Aid You Should Know

Cuts and Scratches

Most scratches, scrapes, and slight cuts are not serious. The main thing is to clean them out with soap and water and then cover them with a sterile dressing. (*Sterile* means free of germs.)

Small wounds: Wash with soap and water. Cover with sterile adhesive bandage from a first aid kit.

Large wounds: Wash with soap and water. Cover with a sterile compress from a first aid kit. Hold the compress on the wound by tying your neckerchief or other cloth around it. If you are unable to stop the bleeding, or you are unsure how bad the wound is, take the victim for medical care.

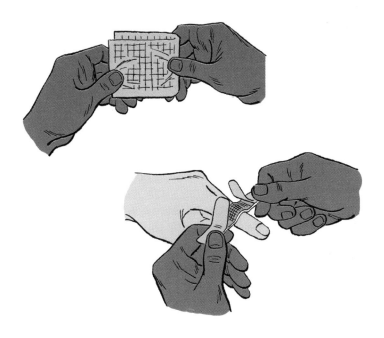

Burns and Scalds

First aid for burns and scalds depends on how serious the injury is. A burn from light contact with a hot object probably is a first-degree burn. Very serious burns are called third-degree burns.

First-degree burn: The skin gets red and sore. Put the burned area in cold water until the pain stops. If you don't have any water, cover the burn with a clean, dry dressing.

Second-degree burn: Blisters form on the skin. Try to protect them from breaking open, as this could cause infection. Cover the burned area with a sterile gauze pad from a first aid kit. Hold the pad loosely in place with a bandage. **Don't** apply creams, ointments, or sprays. All second-degree burns need medical attention.

Third-degree burn: The skin may be burned away. Flesh may be charred. The victim may feel no pain. Don't try to remove clothing from around the burn. Wrap the victim in a clean sheet.

Cover him with blankets if the weather is cool. Rush him to a hospital.

Treat for shock, too: People with second- or third-degree burns will be suffering from shock. So give first aid for shock as well as for the burn.

Sunburn: Most sunburns are first-degree burns. A severe sunburn is a second-degree burn and should receive prompt medical attention. Prevent sunburn by liberally applying sunscreen lotion with a high sun protection factor (SPF) about 20 minutes before you're in the sun. Reapply if you sweat heavily or swim. It's also important to wear protective clothing and a broad-brimmed hat and sunglasses as well as limit your exposure to the sun. The sun's rays are most harmful between 10:00 A.M. and 2:00 P.M. Sunburns should be treated with cool compresses or baths.

Choking

If a bit of food sticks in a person's throat, he will start choking. He may not be able to cough it up by himself. Unless the person is a baby, use the Heimlich maneuver to help him.

Heimlich Maneuver

Stand behind the victim and put your arms around him. Make a fist with one hand just above his belly button. Cover the fist with your other hand. Now make four quick thrusts inward and upward to force air from his lungs.

Heimlich Maneuver

Close-up of hand position for Heimlich maneuver

This should dislodge the food. If it doesn't, repeat until the food is dislodged.

If the person is too big for you to do the Heimlich maneuver standing up, have him lie down faceup. Put one open hand just above his belly button and put the other hand over the first. Make four quick, upward thrusts.

Note: Because of the possibility of injury, **do not practice the thrust part of the Heimlich maneuver on a person.** Thrusts should be used only for actual choking cases.

Safe Swimming

Swimming is a lot of fun, but the water can be a dangerous place if you aren't prepared.

Scouting has a checklist called the Safe Swim Defense plan to make sure you are prepared. The plan has eight points.

Safe Swim Defense

1. **An adult is in charge.** Follow the adult's orders.
2. **Physical fitness.** Each swimmer must provide a current health history from his parent, guardian, or doctor.
3. **Safe swim area.** The area is checked for underwater dangers. One area not more than 3½ feet deep is marked off for nonswimmers. Another area is marked for beginners; it can be a little deeper. A third area of deep water is marked for good swimmers.
4. **Lifeguards.** Trained lifeguards are on shore, watching everybody who is in the water.
5. **Lookout.** A lookout is also on shore to direct the lifeguards if a person needs help.
6. **Ability groups.** The leaders divide the swimmers into three groups: (1) *nonswimmers;* (2) *beginners,* who can swim at least 50 feet; and (3) *swimmers,* who can swim 100 yards and float. Each group stays in its own area.
7. **Buddy system.** Each person is paired with another person who has the same swimming ability. They go into the water together, stay together, and come out together.
8. **Discipline.** Everyone agrees to follow water safety rules. Everyone obeys the lifeguards or other supervisors.

The Buddy System

Your den leader or another adult will take care of most of the steps of the Safe Swim Defense plan. But the buddy system depends on YOU!

When you go swimming, you'll have a buddy. If you're a beginner, he'll be a beginner. If you're a swimmer, he'll be a swimmer.

At Scout camp, you and your buddy will check in at the waterfront together. You'll stay together until you check out. When the lifeguard calls "Buddy check!" or "Buddies!" you and your buddy will grasp hands and raise them overhead. Then the lifeguard can make sure all the people in the water are safe.

Left Turn

Right Turn

Slow

Bicycle Safety

Did you notice that requirement 7 talks about "driving" a bicycle? When you are on a bike, you are a driver, just like an adult driving a car.

So you should act like a driver and obey traffic safety rules. Here are the safe driving rules.

1. **Always** wear a safety helmet.

2. **Obey all traffic laws.** Stop at all "Stop" signs. Give signals for turns. Avoid busy streets, if you can.

3. **Observe local laws.** Your community may have rules for registration of bicycles and driving on sidewalks. Learn them and obey them.

4. **Drive with traffic,** not against it. Stay close to the curb.

5. **Watch out** for hazards like potholes and drain grates.

6. **Watch out** for car doors opening or cars pulling into traffic.

7. **Don't carry passengers.** You will have less control of your bike if you have a passenger.

8. **Never hitch a ride** by holding onto a truck, car, or other vehicle.

9. **Be extra careful at intersections.** If traffic is heavy, get off your bike and walk it across the intersection.

10. **Use hand signals** for turning and stopping.

11. **Drive a safe bike.** Keep it in good repair. Don't ride after dark, but have reflectors and lights on your bike in case you have to ride for an emergency reason. In that case, also wear reflective clothing.

12. **Drive "defensively."** That means: Watch out for the other guy. Keep a safe distance from traffic ahead of you. Stay alert. Be ready to stop suddenly.

Home Fire Escape Plan

Suppose you wake up some night and hear your smoke detector or smell smoke. What would you do?

That's easy. Wake the other members of your family and get them out of the house! Then call the fire department.

But what if your family sleeps on the second floor and the fire is coming up the stairway? How would the family get out?

Make a plan now. Discuss it with the adult members of your family.

Figure out **two** possible escape routes for each bedroom. If there is a two-story drop from some bedroom windows, the family may have to buy escape ladders. But that's a lot better than having a family member trapped in a fire because the only way out is blocked by flames.

Make sure your family has a place to meet once they are outside. Then everyone will know when all family members are out and safe.

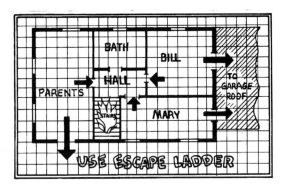

FIRE-ESCAPE PLAN for second floor. Short arrows show usual exits from bedrooms. Long arrows show emergency exits.

ESCAPE LADDER. Folding ladder that is stored under a window.

First Aid Kits

Every home and car should have a first aid kit. Then first aid supplies will be there if they are needed.

Check your family's home or car first aid kit. For requirement 9, you'll explain how the items should be used. If you don't know, ask your Webelos den leader or den chief to show you.

Things that should be in a first aid kit are listed below.

First Aid Kit

■ Tweezers

■ Box of adhesive bandages (different sizes)

■ Twelve each of 3-by-3-inch and 4-by-4-inch sterile pads

■ Roll of 1-inch and roll of 2-inch adhesive tape

■ Scissors

■ Safety pins

- Two 1-inch roller bandages
- Two 2-inch roller bandages
- Three triangular bandages
- Three cravat bandages (a cravat bandage is made by folding a triangular bandage or Scout neckerchief)
- Two 17-inch splints of thin board
- Two 30-inch splints
- Calamine lotion
- Latex gloves
- Mouth-barrier device

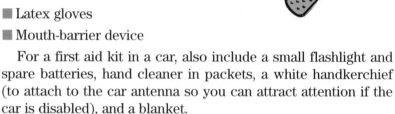

For a first aid kit in a car, also include a small flashlight and spare batteries, hand cleaner in packets, a white handkerchief (to attach to the car antenna so you can attract attention if the car is disabled), and a blanket.

Danger Spots at Home

Some homes are safer than others. In safe homes, toys are not left lying around. Matches and poisons are kept away from small children. Electrical cords are placed such that they don't trip people.

In other words, the family thinks about safety.

Is your family like that? If not, you can help.

Are there danger areas in and around your home? Use the "Home Safety Checklist" on pages 213–214 to find out.

Look around outside, too. Are garden tools stored neatly and safely? Are ladders strong and not wobbly? Are stairs and sidewalks kept free of ice and snow in the winter?

See if you can make your home safer.

Safety in a Car

You may say, "What can I do about safety in a car? I'm not old enough to drive."

That's true. But you *can* do something about car safety. Here are ideas:

■ Always use your seat belt. You are much less likely to get hurt in an accident if you are wearing a seat belt. In some states, wearing a seat belt is the law. What is the law in your state?

■ Don't talk to the driver in heavy traffic. He or she must concentrate on driving.

■ Do talk to the driver when he or she is tired. It will help keep the driver alert. But also remind the driver to stop for a rest and perhaps something refreshing to drink. When a driver dozes off even for a second, an accident can happen.

■ Suggest to the driver that you stop every two hours on a long trip. The driver needs to stretch and relax. Maybe you can take a ball along and play catch at a rest area to help the driver relax.

■ Keep younger children from quarreling or jumping around in the car. Be sure they keep their seat belts fastened or are in their car seats with the harness fastened.

■ Lock the doors. Then younger children won't be able to open them accidentally.

■ Keep hands, head, and feet inside the car—even when it is parked.

■ Don't ride or carry passengers in the bed of a pickup truck.

Readyman Scoreboard

Requirements

Approved by:

1. Explain what first aid is. Tell what you should do after an accident.

   _____

2. Explain how you can get help quickly if there is an emergency in your home. Make a "help list" of people or agencies that can help you if you need it. Post it near a phone or other place with easy access.

   _____

3. Show what to do for these "hurry cases":

   _____

   - Serious bleeding
   - Stopped breathing
   - Internal poisoning
   - Heart attack

4. Show how to treat shock.

   _____

5. Show first aid for the following:

   _____

   - Cuts and scratches
   - Burns and scalds
   - Choking

6. Tell what steps must be taken for a safe swim with your Webelos den, pack, family, or other group. Explain the reasons for the buddy system.

   _____

7. Explain six safety rules you should follow when driving a bicycle.   _____

8. Make a home fire escape plan for your family.   _____

9. Explain how to use each item in a first aid kit.   _____

10. Tell where accidents are most likely to happen inside and around your home.   _____

11. Explain six safety rules you should remember when riding in a car.   _____

12. Attend a first aid demonstration at a Boy Scout troop meeting, a Red Cross center, or other place.   _____

Technology
Activity Badge
Group

Craftsman

Engineer

Handyman

Scientist

Craftsman

Many people use tools every day in their work. Think about the tools used by carpenters, automotive technicians, machinists who make precision metal parts, furniture makers, potters who create vases and bowls.

Other people become experts at using tools so they can enjoy hobbies. For example, a person whose hobby is woodworking might design and build a table for his or her home.

In working on the Craftsman activity badge, you'll become good at handling a variety of tools. You'll use wood to make some of your projects. For others, you'll decide to work with leather, metal, or other materials.

Do These:

1. Explain how to safely handle the tools that you will use for this activity badge.

2. With adult supervision and using hand tools, construct two different wooden objects you and your Webelos den leader agree on, such as the items listed below. Use a coping saw or jigsaw for these projects. Put them together with glue, nails, or screws. Paint or stain them.

Book rack	Napkin holder
Shelf	Animal cutouts
Bulletin board	Garden tool rack
Weather vane	Lid holder
Tie rack	Mailbox
Letter holder	Birdhouse
Notepad holder	Desk nameplate
Toolbox	Letter, bill, and
Towel rack	pencil holder
Recipe holder	Bread box
Lamp stand	Key rack
Kitchen knife rack	Measuring cup rack
Kitchen utensil rack	Measuring spoon rack

3. Make a display stand or box to be used to display a model or an award. Or make a frame for a photo or painting. Use suitable material.

4. Make four useful items using materials other than wood that you and your Webelos den leader agree on, such as clay, plastic, leather, metal, paper, rubber, or rope. These should be challenging items and must involve several operations.

When you pass each requirement, ask your den leader or counselor to initial your Craftsman scoreboard on page 265.

Using Tools Safely

Whether you are working with wood, leather, plastic, or some other material, you will need certain tools. Handle each one as if it could hurt you—because it could!

Tools that cut materials—such as saws, knives, and shears—should be kept sharp. If they are dull, you may have to use too much force and they may slip and cut your hand.

Keep your hands away from saw teeth and knife blades so that if the tool slips, you won't get hurt. Be careful when you're hammering. If you miss the nail head, you sure don't want to hit your thumb!

Practice using your materials and tools until you know how to handle them well.

Protect your tools. When you're through working, put them back in place.

Keep your workshop in order. A clean bench makes a safer place to work.

Choosing Projects

Plans for some projects are shown on these pages. You can find many more in books in your public library. Look under "Crafts" in the library card catalog or computer catalog.

Or try making your own plans. Think about what you want to make. Draw a simple picture of it. Decide how big it should be.

Write the dimensions on the drawing. Keep your costs down by using scrap material if you can.

Then, with adult supervision, go to work!

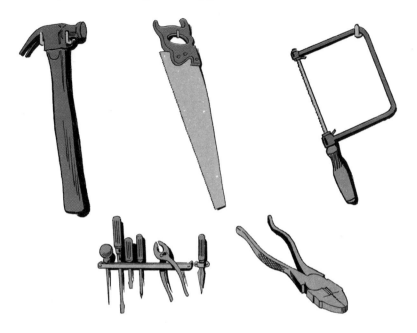

Woodworking Projects

These are some of the tools you need for woodworking projects:

Hammer
Saws (ripsaw, crosscut saw, coping saw)
Pliers
Screwdrivers
Chisels
Awl
Wood clamp

Set of knives
Pocket knife
Whetstone
Sandpaper and sanding block
File and/or rasp
Nails
Drill and drill bits

Weather Vane

Cut the bird's body and legs from thin wood with a coping saw or jigsaw. Bolt the legs on. Fasten the bird to a 1-by-6-by-12-inch board. Fasten the board to the top of a post with washers and a bolt so the board can turn.

Letter Holder

Draw the duck on a 6-by-8-inch piece of ½-inch plywood. Make sure you draw its feet and outspread wings.

Cut them out with a coping saw or a jigsaw. Fasten them to a piece of 1-by-2-by-6-inch wood with glue, nails, or screws.

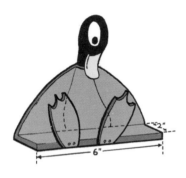

Necktie Rack

To enlarge the pattern for this Scout badge tie rack, use the grid method. With a ruler, make a 12-by-13-inch grid of 1-inch squares on a large sheet of paper.

Draw the badge by copying the badge outline from the small grid to the large one, square by square. Cut out your paper pattern and trace around it on ¼-inch-thick plywood.

Cut the badge shape out with a coping saw or jigsaw. Sand it smooth. Drill holes for ¼-inch dowels 2½ inches long and glue them in. Paint or decorate the rack as you like and fasten a hanger to the back.

Doggie Letter Holder

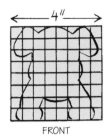

FRONT

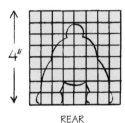

REAR

Enlarge the patterns. (See the grid method explained in the necktie rack instructions above.) Trace them on ¾-inch pine and cut out.

The letter holder is a spiral of coat hanger wire between the doggie pieces. To make the spiral, first straighten a coat hanger. Now wrap the wire as tightly as you can around a soup can, with ½ inch between spirals.

Then use two pliers to bend ½ inch of each end of the wire at right angles to the spirals.

The wire ends are then cemented into small holes drilled into the back of the doggie's front piece and the front of the rear piece. Paint the wood pieces.

Wall Shelf

Draw a half circle with a protractor on a piece of 1-by-4-by-8-inch pine. Cut out with a coping saw.

1"x4"x8"

COPING SAW

PROTRACTOR

Make the brace by sawing diagonally through another piece, 1-by-4-by-6-inches. Sand both pieces smooth.

1"x4"x6" CUT DIAGONALLY

BRADS

Use glue and brads to fasten the brace to the shelf.

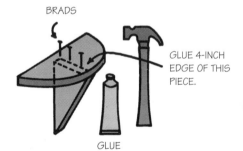

GLUE 4-INCH EDGE OF THIS PIECE.

GLUE

Screw 1-inch angle irons to the bottom of the shelf at the back edge. With adult help, use wall fasteners to attach your shelf to the wall.

1" ANGLE IRONS

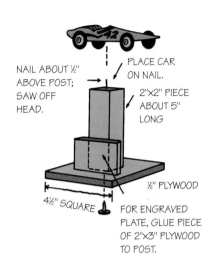

NAIL ABOUT ½"
ABOVE POST;
SAW OFF
HEAD.

PLACE CAR
ON NAIL.

2"×2" PIECE
ABOUT 5"
LONG

½" PLYWOOD

4½" SQUARE

FOR ENGRAVED
PLATE, GLUE PIECE
OF 2"×3" PLYWOOD
TO POST.

Display Stands and Frames

Use any material you like to make a picture frame or a display stand or box.

Maybe you'll decide to make a wooden frame for a painting you made for the Artist activity badge. Or you might make a display stand for your favorite pinewood derby car. One type of stand is shown here.

Leatherworking

There are special tool kits for working with leather. You can buy them at hobby stores, or you can buy the Leathercraft Workshop from your Scouting distributor.

Your leatherworking tools might include some of the following:

Eyelet setter
Lacing fid
Rivet setter
French skiver
Shears
Wing divider
Punch set
Arkansas stone
Tooling board
Skiving knife
Mallet
Thonging chisel
Adjustable creaser
Circle edge slicker

For your first projects, use calfskin leather. It's easy to cut and tool. Look for it at arts and crafts supply stores. Try designing and making simple projects like a key case, eyeglass case, coin purse, or drawstring purse.

Beginning a Project

First make a pattern of the article you plan to make. Draw it on a piece of paper in its exact size. Use a ruler or steel square for straight lines.

Cut out your paper pattern and draw dotted lines where folds will be. Fold the pattern to make sure it looks right.

Make a template by tracing around the paper pattern on a piece of fairly heavy cardboard. Cut the cardboard, following the tracing lines. Then place the template on the piece of leather.

Cutting Leather

Place the leather on a softwood cutting block, with the rough side down. Put your template on the leather and hold it firmly. Draw its outline on the leather with a tracer or awl. Now use a very sharp knife to cut through the leather. Use a steel square or ruler to cut along straight lines.

Tooling Leather

Tooling is the most common way of making designs on leather. A modeling tool is used to press the design into the leather. The leather must be moist. Dampen a sponge with water and hold it on the top side of the leather for about three seconds. Make your design on the leather with the modeling tool. If you don't have one, use an orangewood manicure stick or an awl.

Lacing

To make holes for lacing leather pieces together, use a tool called a drive punch or a large nail. Use a mallet or light hammer to drive the punch or nail. For lacing, you can use a leather thong or plastic laces. The drawings show two common lacing stitches.

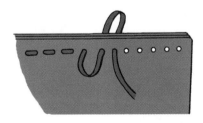

Running Stitch

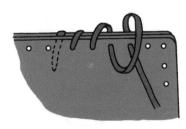

Whipstitch

Clay Projects

Unless you know someone who has a potter's kiln, use oven-firing clay for your clay projects. Regular clay must be fired (baked) in a kiln, which gets much hotter than your kitchen oven. But you can fire oven-firing clay in your kitchen.

Go to a hobby store for oven-firing clay and glazes in powder or liquid form. The glaze, which comes in different colors, will give your projects a shiny finish.

Experiment with two basic methods of working in clay. Use the *coil method* to make bowls, cups, mugs, and other items with circular tops. Try the *slab method* to make boxes and other things with corners.

Coil Method

Suppose you want to make a small bowl. First flatten a big chunk of clay until it is about ½ inch thick. You can do this with a rolling pin. Cut out a circle about 3 inches across. This is the bottom of the bowl.

Coil Method

For the first coil, make a long smooth rope of clay with your hands. It should be just slightly longer than the bottom of the bowl is around—about 10 inches. Coil the rope around the bottom. Cement it to the bottom with *slip*—a thin mixture of clay and water. Smooth the seam with your fingers.

Make more coils and cement them on with slip. Each one should be a little longer than the last so the bowl will slope outward and get wider as you build toward the top.

Use your fingers and a kitchen knife to smooth the sides. Make sure there are no holes in the bowl. Let it dry for an hour or two before decorating, glazing, and firing.

Slab Method

In this method, you make slabs of clay and join them together with slip.

Let's say you are going to make a small box. The sides and bottom will be ⅜ inch thick. Find two flat wooden sticks of that thickness and lay them on your work table with the clay between them. Use a rolling pin, with its edges on the two sticks, to roll out the slab.

Slab Method

Cut out pieces for the bottom, sides, and top. Join the sides and bottom with slip, using your fingers and a kitchen knife to smooth the seams. Let the box dry an hour or two before decorating, glazing, and firing.

Decorating, Glazing, and Firing

Use a pencil, an orangewood manicure stick, and a tongue depressor to press designs into the sides of the bowl or box.

For glazing and firing your projects, follow the directions that came with the glaze and clay.

Craftsman Scoreboard

Requirements	Approved by:

Do These:

1. Explain how to safely handle the tools that you will use for this activity badge. _____

2. With adult supervision and using hand tools, construct two different wooden objects you and your Webelos den leader agree on, such as the items listed below. Use a coping saw or jigsaw for these projects. Put them together with glue, nails, or screws. Paint or stain them. _____

Book rack	Napkin holder
Shelf	Animal cutouts
Bulletin board	Garden tool rack
Weather vane	Lid holder
Tie rack	Mailbox
Letter holder	Birdhouse
Notepad holder	Desk nameplate
Toolbox	Letter, bill, and pencil
Towel rack	holder
Recipe holder	Bread box
Lamp stand	Key rack
Kitchen knife rack	Measuring cup rack
Kitchen utensil rack	Measuring spoon rack

3. Make a display stand or box to be used to display a model or an award. Or make a frame for a photo or painting. Use suitable material. _____

4. Make four useful items using materials other than wood that you and your Webelos den leader agree on, such as clay, plastic, leather, metal, paper, rubber, or rope. These should be challenging items and must involve several operations. _____

Technology Group

Engineer

Engineers designed your school bus, the cars on the road, the road itself, and the bridges you cross. Engineers designed all the different kinds of computers you see at school, in offices, and at home.

Almost anything you use that was manufactured was probably designed by an engineer. Not only that, but engineers designed the machines that workers used to make the product and the factory building where it was made.

Airplanes, space shuttles, space stations—all designed by engineers. Engineers work in many exciting and challenging fields.

When you earn this badge, you can work on engineering projects like bridge models, a catapult, and an electrical circuit.

Do Five of These:

1. List 10 different things engineers do.

2. Visit a construction site. Look at a set of plans. Tell your Webelos den leader about these. (Get permission before you visit.)

3. Visit a civil engineer to understand how to measure the length of a property line. Explain how property lines are determined.

4. Tell about how electricity is generated and then gets to your home.

5. Construct a simple working electrical circuit using a flashlight battery, a switch, and a light.

6. Make drawings of three kinds of bridges and explain their differences. Construct a model bridge of your choice.

7. Make a block and tackle and show how it works.

8. Build a catapult and show how it works.

9. Draw a floor plan of your house. Include doors, windows, and stairways.

10. Explain how engineers use computers.

When you pass each requirement, ask your den leader or counselor to initial your Engineer scoreboard on page 281.

What Engineers Do

Engineering is a specialized profession, which means there are almost as many kinds of engineers as there are engineering jobs to be done. Here are some of the kinds of engineers and a few examples of the work they do:

Civil engineers design projects like bridges, dams, stadiums, highways, and wastewater treatment plants.

Mechanical engineers design automobiles, engines, refrigeration and heating systems, and machines.

Electrical engineers design computers, motors, television sets, telephones, and communications systems.

There are engineers in aerospace work, industry, agriculture, chemistry, and many other areas.

Engineers write the *specifications* for their designs. Specifications are the rules that the project has to follow. They describe how the project is going to perform, what materials go into it, and exactly how the materials are to be put together.

Engineers also may investigate problems like traffic flow, water and air pollution, and river flooding. Then they work on plans to solve the problems.

Visiting a Construction Site

Engineers supervise the work that puts their designs into action. The engineer checks to see that the correct materials are used and the engineering plans—the specifications—are followed.

Good examples are construction jobs like buildings, roads, and dams. With your parent or den, arrange to visit a construction site and talk to an engineer. Ask him or her to show you plans for the job.

Checking Property Lines

In any construction job, whether it's a building, a highway, or an electrical power line, civil engineers have to know where construction will take place in relation to the property lines around it.

Highways and utility projects are constructed on pathways across property that are called *easements*. Engineers have to know where the boundaries of the easements are.

Surveyors use laser equipment to determine the location of the property and easement lines, how long they are, and where corners are. Once the lines are determined, a civil engineer can use the information to draw plans and supervise construction. If you talk with a civil engineer for requirement 3, you'll learn more about this.

Property lines are important to anyone who owns a home, a building, farmland, or a vacant lot. A homeowner who wants to put up a fence around a backyard may have the lot surveyed to find out exactly where the boundary lines are located.

You can use a tape measure or yardstick to measure one of the lot lines around your house or apartment building.

How Electric Power Is Generated and Gets to Your Home

An electric current is created when a magnet is spun rapidly inside a coil of wire. The huge generators in a power plant work on that principle. The turbines that spin the magnet are powered by water, steam, or wind power.

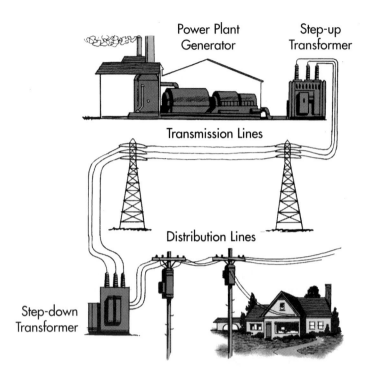

Electricity moves along wires like water running through a pipe. The electricity generated by a power plant moves over wires to a nearby *step-up transformer*. There, the voltage is raised so that the electricity can go efficiently over long distances.

A high-voltage line carries electricity to your town. But the voltage must be reduced by a *step-down transformer* before you can use the electricity in your home.

Electrical Circuits

An electrical circuit is the way electricity moves from an electrical source to the point where it is used. In the house or building where you live, electrical circuits supply electricity to different parts of the building. In lamps and appliances, when a switch is turned to the "on" position, it closes (completes) the circuit and allows electricity to flow to, for instance, the light bulb or the toaster.

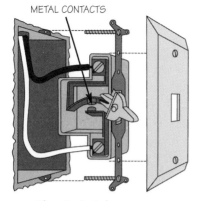

METAL CONTACTS

This switch is in the "off" position. There is a gap in the flow of electricity. When the switch is turned on, the metal contacts come together so the electricity can flow.

Electric Switch

You can make a simple electric circuit. You will need

- A "D" size flashlight battery
- A holder for a small light bulb
- A light bulb that fits the holder
- An on/off switch
- Wire to connect it all together

When the switch is off, the circuit is open, which means there is a gap in the circuit. Electricity cannot flow to the light bulb. When the switch is on, it closes the circuit. The circuit is complete, and electricity reaches the bulb.

Be Safe With Electricity

Even low-voltage electricity is strong enough to kill you. It can give you a hard shock or a bad burn. For your safety's sake:

- Don't touch a switch with wet hands or while standing on a damp floor.

- Don't touch anything electrical while taking a bath.

- Plug only one cord into each electrical outlet. Overloading causes fires.

- Don't put electric wires under rugs and carpets. Walking on wires wears off the insulation. This causes short circuits.

- Newer homes have circuit breakers. But if your home has a fuse box, use the correct size of fuse in it.

- Don't get under a tree during a thunderstorm. Lightning could hit the tree.

- Get out of the swimming pool or lake when you see a storm or lightning, even in the distance.

Learning About Bridges

The best way to learn about bridges is to study the way they are made. Then you can build model bridges, the way civil engineers do. You can use bricks, wooden blocks, and heavy paper.

Start with a *plank bridge.* Set up two bricks. Lay a heavy piece of paper on them to go over "the river" beneath. What happens when you put a toy car on the bridge?

Plank Bridge

What would you do to hold the middle? Putting a wooden block under it helps. This is called a *pier bridge.*

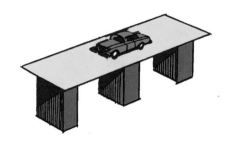

Pier Bridge

Beam Bridge

Take another piece of paper and fold the sides up 1 inch. Set this on the bricks. How much weight does this hold? More than the flat piece of paper? This is called a *beam bridge.*

You may have seen beam bridges on railroads. They hold up a heavy weight over a short distance.

Curve a piece of heavy paper to form an arch. Slip it between two bricks. Set a piece of heavy paper on top of it and the bricks. This is called an *arch bridge.* Does it hold more weight than the others?

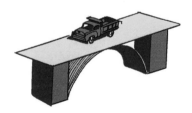

Arch Bridge

Engineers know about shapes and how much weight each one will hold. Make a square out of four drinking straws, fastening the corners with straight pins. Stand it up. Is it rigid? Does it want to fold up? The square will move.

Now make a triangle out of three straws. Does it move out of shape?

In building very long bridges, engineers use a whole row of triangles. These are called *truss bridges*. Railroad bridges over rivers are truss bridges.

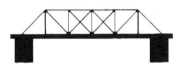

Truss Bridge

Suspension cable bridges are the largest. The Golden Gate Bridge in San Francisco, California, is a suspension bridge.

The Golden Gate Bridge is a suspension bridge.

Technology

Block and Tackle

A block and tackle is used to lift heavy objects easily. A crane is a huge block and tackle.

In a block and tackle, a rope or cable runs over a pulley, which is a small wheel with a grooved rim where the cable runs. The block and tackle is attached to something that must be lifted. A power source pulls the rope and lifts the object. It takes less force to lift this way than it would to try to lift the object without the block and tackle.

Some block and tackles have more than one pulley. Some of the ways a block and tackle can be rigged are shown here.

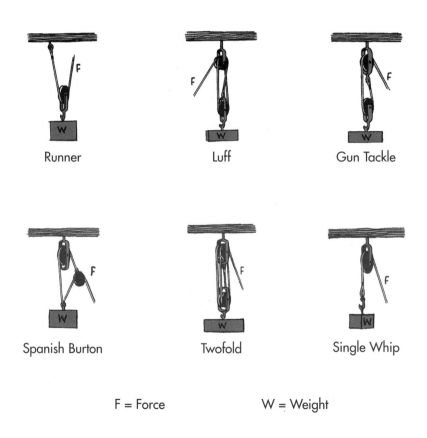

Runner   Luff   Gun Tackle

Spanish Burton   Twofold   Single Whip

F = Force   W = Weight

Making a Single Whip
Block and Tackle

To make a pulley, you need a large spool and a coat hanger. Cut the hanger as shown and bend the ends at right angles through the spool. Then bend down the ends so the hanger won't spread apart. Make sure the spool turns easily.

Testing the Block and Tackle

Use a spring scale to see how much force is needed to lift a weight with and without a block and tackle. If you don't have a spring scale, you can make one as shown.

A cardboard tube from a roll of paper towels or something similar will make a good scale. Suspend rubber band and wire as shown.

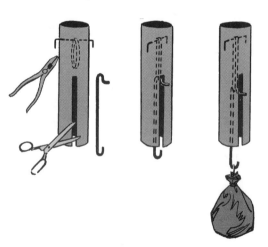

This *runner* block and tackle is lifting several pieces of wood. The boys at either side support the rod to which one end of the block and tackle's rope is attached. The rope goes around the pulley. The other end of the rope is attached to the spring scale, and the boy in the center is holding the scale and lifting, providing the force. The scale measures the force required to lift the object. By attaching the same object directly to the scale, the boys can then measure the force required without a block and tackle.

Making a Catapult

Catapults were once war machines used to throw huge rocks over castle walls. Today, a type of catapult is used to launch planes from aircraft carriers. A slingshot is also a kind of catapult.

Here's a simple catapult you can make. When using it, be sure everyone is out of the way, behind you. Place an object in the can and pull the hinged board downward, stretching the inner tube. When you release the board, the object flies.

Catapult

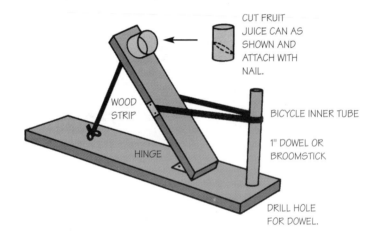

CUT FRUIT JUICE CAN AS SHOWN AND ATTACH WITH NAIL.

WOOD STRIP

BICYCLE INNER TUBE

1" DOWEL OR BROOMSTICK

HINGE

DRILL HOLE FOR DOWEL.

Drawing Floor Plans

An architectural engineer draws plans for buildings and houses. He or she designs the plans to make the best use of standard sizes of building materials, like drywall for the interior walls. The engineer includes specifications for materials, including types of doors and windows.

See if you can draw a floor plan of your house or apartment. You don't have to show measurements on your floor plan, but if the living room is twice as big as the kitchen, your floor plan should show it, so you might want to check measurements in each room.

Show doors, windows, and stairways. Use a ruler to make your plan neat.

Computers in Engineering

Engineers use computers in many ways:

- To make calculations. Many advanced technological problems require a huge number of calculations to be solved. Hundreds of people working on the problem by hand might not be able to do them fast enough.

- To design and draw plans using a computer-aided design (CAD) program. CAD is especially useful to architectural and civil engineers in designing and building complicated bridges and other structures. During the design stage, computers can produce models of the structure that even look three-dimensional on a computer screen. These models can be changed and tested before building ever begins. The computer can analyze things such as the strength and weight of each part of the structure, as well as its cost and availability. For a building, the computer can determine whether there will be enough vertical braces, such as walls and columns, to keep a roof up.

- To calculate and store cost estimates and plan budgets for projects.
- To schedule work.
- To write business letters.

Engineer Scoreboard

Requirements	Approved by:

Do Five of These:

1. List 10 different things engineers do.   _____

2. Visit a construction site. Look at a set of plans. Tell your Webelos den leader about these. (Get permission before you visit.) _____

3. Visit a civil engineer to understand how to measure the length of a property line. Explain how property lines are determined. _____

4. Tell about how electricity is generated and then gets to your home. _____

5. Construct a simple working electrical circuit using a flashlight battery, a switch, and a light. _____

6. Make drawings of three kinds of bridges and explain their differences. Construct a model bridge of your choice. _____

7. Make a block and tackle and show how it works. _____

8. Build a catapult and show how it works. _____

9. Draw a floor plan of your house. Include doors, windows, and stairways. _____

10. Explain how engineers use computers. _____

Handyman

A handyman can do many different jobs. He knows how to take care of a car and a bike. He uses tools to make repairs around the house, and he takes care of the lawn.

When you work on this badge, you can learn a lot about keeping a car, bike, and home in good shape. You can find out how to change a flat tire. You might even build a sawhorse or a step stool.

Keep adding to this knowledge after you earn the badge. Your handyman skills will always be useful to you and your family.

Do Six of These:

1. With adult supervision, wash a car.

2. Help an adult change a tire on a car.

3. With adult supervision, replace a bulb in the taillight, turn signal, or parking light or replace a headlight on a car.

4. With adult supervision, show how to check the oil level and tire pressure of a car.

5. Make a repair to a bicycle, such as tightening the chain, fixing a flat tire, or adjusting the seat or handlebars.

6. Properly lubricate the chain on a bicycle.

7. Properly inflate the tires on a bicycle.

8. Replace a light bulb in a fixture or a lamp.

9. With adult supervision, arrange a storage area for household cleaners and other dangerous materials where small children cannot get them.

10. Build a sawhorse or stool to be used around your home.

11. Help take care of the lawn.

12. Arrange a storage area for hand tools or lawn and garden tools.

13. Clean and properly store hand tools or lawn and garden tools in their storage areas.

14. Mark hand tools or lawn and garden tools for identification.

When you pass each requirement, ask an adult member of your family to initial your Handyman scoreboard on page 297.

Taking Care of a Car

In just a few years you'll be old enough to drive a car. Now is the time to start learning how to take care of one.

Washing a Car

Use an automatic shut-off nozzle on the hose so you don't waste water while you are washing the car.

Use products specifically designed for washing your car. Use a sponge or clean cloth for a scrubber. Check the car owner's manual for any instructions on caring for the finish.

Close the car windows so wash water won't drip inside. Rinse the car with plain water. Start washing the top of the car and work down so the suds and dirty water won't streak areas you have already washed. Do a small area—about 3 feet square—at a time. Then rinse by spraying.

You can let the car drip dry, but wiping it dry with a dry, clean cloth prevents water spots.

Changing a Tire

Don't try to change a car tire unless an adult is with you.

First, set the parking brake as tight as you can. If the car has an automatic transmission, put it in "park." If it has a manual transmission, put it in first gear. Put wedges in front and back of the wheel diagonally opposite the tire you are going to change. These steps will keep the car from moving forward or backward when you jack it up.

Before using the jack, use the sharp end of the lug wrench (found with the jack) to pry off the wheel cover. You'll see the nuts that hold the wheel on the axle. With the other end of the wrench, loosen the nuts one turn. If they are tight, you may need the adult's help.

You'll find instructions for using the car's jack in the instruction manual. Follow the instructions exactly. If the jack is not placed properly under the car, you could damage the car when you jack it up, or the car could fall off the jack and injure you.

Use the jack to lift the car so that the flat tire just clears the ground. Remove the nuts and pull the wheel off. Slip the spare tire wheel on over the bolts. Screw the nuts on until all of them are fairly tight. Carefully lower the jack until it is free of the car. Then, with the lug wrench, tighten one nut as tight as you can make it. Next, tighten the nut opposite the first. Then tighten all the others. Finally, go around the circle again, tightening each nut as hard as you can. Ask the adult to check.

Fit the wheel cover back into its brackets and push it into place. Put the jack, lug wrench, and flat tire back in the trunk of the car.

The job is done, but remind the car's owner to have the flat tire fixed!

Replacing a Taillight or Headlight

Each car model is different, so it's a good idea to have an adult advise you how to replace a taillight or headlight. On many cars the rear lights can be replaced from inside the trunk. See the owner's manual on how to change a taillight, because taillight bulbs and installation methods aren't the same for all cars.

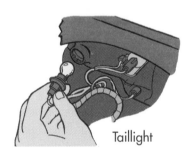

Taillight

Headlights take a little more work and may require special tools. Because headlights and headlight bulbs aren't the same for all cars, follow the directions in the owner's manual and have an adult advise you on how to change a headlight.

SOCKET

Headlight

Checking Oil and Tire Pressure

Oil allows the parts of the car's engine to move easily and helps keep the car's engine from over-heating. It is important to have enough oil in the engine at all times.

Dipstick

You can check the oil by using a metal rod called a *dipstick*. **Ask an adult to help you find the oil dipstick in the engine.**

While the engine is cool, pull out the oil dipstick and wipe it clean with a rag. Then put it back, all the way in. Pull it out again and look at the markings.

If the oil level is below the "add" line, the car needs oil. Put the dipstick back in. Tell the owner that the car needs oil.

Tire Gauge

You need a tire gauge to check tire pressure. **When the tires are cool,** take the cap off the tire's valve stem. Push the tire gauge hard against the valve. The gauge's scale will show the tire's pressure. The recommended pressure is shown on a sticker usually attached to the edge of the car door. You can also find the recommended pressure in the owner's manual. Check all tires, including the spare.

If any of the tires need more air, tell the car's owner.

Handyman

Taking Care of a Bicycle

A bicycle is a lot simpler to maintain than a car. But it is a machine, too, so it needs to be taken care of just as a car does.

Adjusting a Bike Chain

If the chain needs tightening, turn the bicycle upside down. Loosen the two axle nuts on the rear wheel with a wrench. A combination or socket wrench is best so that you don't wear down the nuts over time. If the bicycle has a coaster brake, loosen the brake arm mounting nuts, too.

Now pull the wheel back until the chain has about ½ inch of play in its center. Tighten the axle nut on the chain side. Make sure that the wheel is centered between the chain stays. Then tighten the other axle nut and the coaster brake arm mounting nuts. Don't try to adjust the chain on a multispeed bike that has a derailleur.

Fixing a Flat

To fix a flat tire, you need a tire repair kit. Some kits have a scraper or sandpaper, patches, and cement. Other kits have patches that don't need cement.

Take the wheel off the bicycle, and then take off the tire and tube. Taking off the tire can be tricky. You might have to use tools called *tire levers*. Ask an adult to help you the first time if you have trouble.

If you can't see where the hole in the tube is, pump air into the tube. Dunk it into a tub of water. Bubbles will show where the air is escaping. Dry off the area around the hole.

Use the scraper or sandpaper to rough up the tube around the hole. If your repair kit has cement, put a light coating of cement around the hole and quickly wipe it off. Then put on another coat of cement and let it get tacky. If you have glueless patches, you don't need to use any cement.

Remove the coating from a patch and smooth the patch over the hole. Press the patch hard to spread the cement evenly and make a tight seal.

Put the tube back in the tire and position the tire carefully on the wheel before you inflate it.

Adjusting the Seat and Handlebars

To adjust the seat (also called the saddle) or handlebars of your bike, all you need is the right wrench. For some bikes, you'll need a combination wrench, and for others, an Allen wrench.

To change the height of the seat, loosen the bolt that keeps the seat post tight in the frame and then raise and lower the seat post to the height you need. Make sure that at least 2 inches of the seat post is in the frame.

You can raise and lower the handlebars on your bike and also change the position of the handlebars. Look at your bike and find the bolts that control these adjustments. Loosen the bolts to make the adjustments.

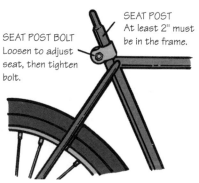

SEAT POST
At least 2" must be in the frame.

SEAT POST BOLT
Loosen to adjust seat, then tighten bolt.

Lubricating a Bicycle

Oil prevents rust and helps to keep a bicycle running smoothly.

To lubricate the chain, turn the bicycle upside down. Use the pedals to make the crank turn, and then drip lightweight oil on the chain. The oil will spread over the chain as you turn the crank.

When all the links of the chain have a light coating of oil, the job is done. Wipe any extra oil from the chain and sprocket with a clean rag.

Inflating the Tires

A bicycle's tires should be kept at the correct pressure. The pressure may be stamped on the side of the tire. If it isn't, check the bicycle owner's manual.

Use a bicycle tire gauge to check the pressure. (Many bike tires require higher pressure than a car tire gauge can read.) You can inflate tires with a hand pump. Keep checking the pressure until it is right.

Handyman Around the House

You can make life easier for your family by helping with minor repairs and other jobs. Requirements 8, 9, and 10 cover some ways you can help.

Replacing a Light Bulb

This is just about the simplest job there is.

But you can learn an important lesson as you do it. That lesson is: Whenever you are working on an electrical appliance, **first turn off the switch if it has one, and then pull the plug or turn off the circuit breaker.**

Wait for the old bulb to cool if it has just burned out. Then all you have to do is screw out the old bulb and screw in the new one. Use the correct wattage bulb for the fixture. Now put the plug back in the outlet or turn on the circuit breaker. Turn on the switch to test the light.

Storing Dangerous Materials

Household cleaning materials are full of poisons. Little kids don't know that. If they get the chance, they will play with poisons and may even try to drink them.

So if you have a little brother or sister, check to see whether cleaning supplies are in a safe storage area. If not, you might arrange to store them out of the reach of small children.

Or you could buy a small lock and install it on the present storage area. Directions for installing the lock will be on the package.

Woodworking Jobs

If you like working with wood, try making a sawhorse or stool. Either one will be useful around your house.

The carpenter's best friend is the sawhorse—or better, two sawhorses. Using sawhorses, a carpenter has his or her work at a comfortable height for sawing, planing, and nailing boards.

Easy-to-Make Sawhorse

The easiest sawhorse uses two steel brackets. You can buy them at a hardware store. Use two-by-four lumber for the legs and crosspiece. Cut four legs, each 2 feet long. Cut a crosspiece about 30 inches long.

Fit the legs and crosspiece into the steel brackets, and you have a strong sawhorse.

1. Clamp bracket to crosspiece.

2. Insert legs in bracket slots.

3. Spread legs, forcing bracket teeth to bite into the wood.

4. Tighten wing nut.

5. Ready to use.

All-Wood Sawhorse

The main cross-piece is a two-by-four, cut 30 inches long. Set it on edge and nail a 30-inch one-by-four to its top. This will be the top surface of the sawhorse. Turn it over and nail another 30-inch one-by-four to the bottom.

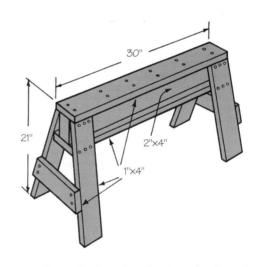

Cut the four legs from one-by-fours. Each should be 21 inches long. Nail the legs to the two-by-four crosspiece, just under the top, and again to the edge of the bottom one-by-four board, as shown.

Cut the braces to fit. Nail on the braces, and the job is done.

Making a Stool

To make a stool, you need three pieces of ⅝-inch wood and two pieces of ¾-inch wood. See the measurements for the pieces in the drawings.

Measure and cut the top from ⅝-inch wood. For the legs, clamp two pieces of ¾-inch wood together, mark where you'll cut, and saw them out. This will make the legs exactly the same, so the stool won't wobble.

Cut the braces from ⅝-inch wood. Nail the stool together with finishing nails. Note that the legs are set in from the ends of the top. Measure carefully before you drive the top nails into the legs to make sure they go into the legs.

Countersink the top nails; that is, use another nail to tap them just below the surface. Fill the nail holes with wood putty.

Sand the stool all over and paint it a color you like.

Legs are nailed to top, 2" in from each end.

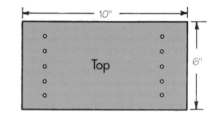

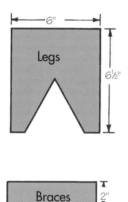

Cut braces to fit after legs are nailed to top. They will be about 6" long.

Handyman Around the Yard

If your home has a lawn, you can help take care of it.

If the grass isn't too long, don't rake up the clippings. They will rot and enrich the soil.

If the clippings are very long, you may have to rake them up because they could damage the grass by cutting off sunlight. Put them on a compost pile. If you don't have a compost pile, dispose of the clippings by whatever method allowed by law in your community.

Taking Care of Tools

Your family may already have a storage area for hand tools and lawn and garden tools. Perhaps you can make it neater.

For hand tools, you can build a rack from pegboard. Use special pegboard hangers to store saws, hammers, augers, and other tools.

For lawn and garden tools like rakes, hoes, and trowels, do this: Nail a length of one-by-four to a wall in a convenient place. Tap two long nails into the board to support each tool.

Cleaning Tools, Putting Them Away, and Marking Them

Whenever you want to use a tool, your job goes much faster if the tool is clean and in its place. After you use tools, clean them: Carefully remove sawdust from woodworking tools; clean dirt off gardening tools. If your family's tools aren't ready to use, spend a little time cleaning them and storing them for the next use.

Mark tools with waterproof ink for identification. Or use a plastic tape machine to put your family's name on tools.

Handyman Scoreboard

Requirements   **Approved by:**

Do Six of These:

1. With adult supervision, wash a car.   _____

2. Help an adult change a tire on a car.   _____

3. With adult supervision, replace a bulb in
   the taillight, turn signal, or parking light
   or replace a headlight on a car.   _____

4. With adult supervision, show how to
   check the oil level and tire pressure of a
   car.   _____

5. Make a repair to a bicycle, such as tightening the chain, fixing a flat tire, or adjust-
   ing the seat or handlebars.   _____

6. Properly lubricate the chain on a bicycle.   _____

7. Properly inflate the tires on a bicycle.   _____

8. Replace a light bulb in a fixture or a lamp.   _____

9. With adult supervision, arrange a storage
   area for household cleaners and other
   dangerous materials where small children
   cannot get them.   _____

10. Build a sawhorse or stool to be used
    around your home.   _____

11. Help take care of the lawn.   _____

12. Arrange a storage area for hand tools or
    lawn and garden tools.   _____

13. Clean and properly store hand tools or
    lawn and garden tools in their storage
    areas.   _____

14. Mark hand tools or lawn and garden tools
    for identification.   _____

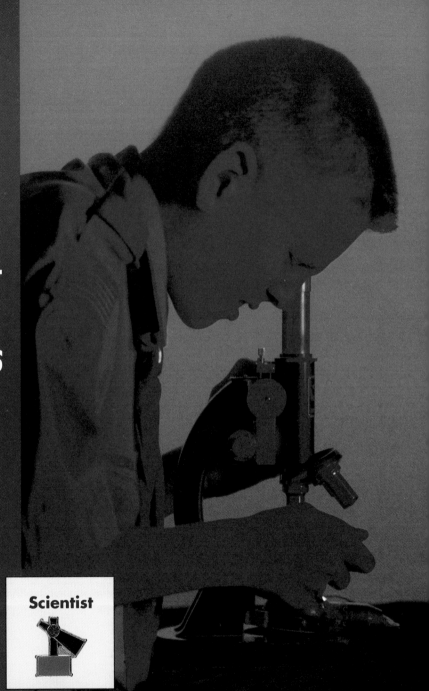

Technology Group

Scientist

Scientists know about laws of nature that explain much about the world and the universe. They continue to learn by experimenting, and they make discoveries.

They take nothing for granted. They may think an idea is true, but they test it over and over to prove it. When you earn the Scientist activity badge, you'll do scientific experiments and test some famous scientific laws. You'll explore ideas about how airplanes fly and the way changes in atmospheric pressure can move objects. You'll also experience the strange tricks your eyes and your brain can play on you.

Do These:

1. **Read Bernoulli's principle. Show how it works.**
2. **Read Pascal's law. Tell about some inventions that use Pascal's law.**
3. **Read Newton's first law of motion. Show in three different ways how inertia works.**

And Do Six of These:

4. Show the effects of atmospheric pressure.
5. Show the effects of air pressure.
6. Show the effects of water pressure. This may be combined with atmospheric pressure or with air pressure.
7. Build and launch a model rocket with adult supervision. (NOTE: You must be at least 10 years old to work with a model rocket kit sold in hobby stores.)
8. Explain what causes fog. Show how this works.
9. Explain how crystals are formed. Make some.
10. Explain how you use your center of gravity to keep your balance. Show three different balancing tricks.
11. Show in three different ways how your eyes work together.
12. Show what is meant by an optical illusion.

When you pass each requirement, ask your den leader or counselor to initial your Scientist scoreboard on page 326.

Physics

Until the beginning of the 20th century, the science of physics was divided into the studies of sound, light, heat, electricity and magnetism, and mechanics (the study of motion and the forces that cause it).

Since then, physicists have explored many new and exciting areas. Some of these fields are called quantum mechanics, nuclear physics, and astrophysics. These terms may sound complicated, but the basic ideas in physics explain everyday events you may take for granted—like why you can ride a bike without tipping over and why an airplane can fly.

Keep reading to learn about several laws of physics and experiments you can do to prove those laws.

Bernoulli's Principle

In 1738 a Swiss scientist named Daniel Bernoulli discovered a fact known as Bernoulli's principle, which is:

**The pressure of a moving gas decreases
as its speed increases.**

Bernoulli's principle is used to explain how an airplane is able to fly.

Air is a gas. Air moves over and underneath the wings of an airplane as it travels. An airplane wing is curved on top and flat on the bottom. Because of that, air travels a longer distance *over* the wing in the same amount of time that air moves *under* the wing, which is a shorter distance.

This means that the air over the wing travels at a greater speed, causing a lower pressure (Bernoulli's principle at work). The air under the wing travels in a straight line, more slowly, so its pressure stays high. The plane is lifted because of this difference in pressure: Lower pressure over the wing and higher pressure under the wing causes *lift.*

Air moves quickly, so pressure is low.

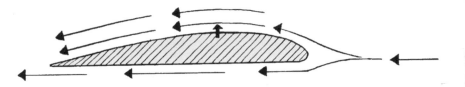

Air moves more slowly, so pressure stays high.

Another way to explain it is that the molecules of the faster air spread out, so they put less pressure on the top of the wing.

A *molecule* is the smallest possible quantity of a substance that still shows what the substance is made of. A molecule is composed of one or more atoms. For instance, a molecule of water is made up of two atoms of hydrogen and one atom of oxygen.

Testing Bernoulli's Principle

These two fascinating experiments with Bernoulli's principle are for requirement 1.

1. Push a short pin through the middle of a 3-inch cardboard square.

2. Put the pin into the hole in a thread spool or toy spool, making sure the pin doesn't stick out the open end.

3. Put the spool to your mouth and blow steadily. The cardboard will stay on the spool. The harder you blow, the tighter it will hold.

The air stream (your breath) is moving. It makes a low-pressure area between the cardboard and the bottom of the spool. The air on the other side of the cardboard has more pressure, so it pushes the cardboard against the spool.

Hold a lighted match behind a business card and blow hard against the card. The flame will move toward you. Why?

Pascal's Law

A French physicist named Blaise Pascal discovered a fact about liquids in 1647. If a liquid is in a closed container, pressure in every direction will be the same. When pressure is added to the top, pressure will increase equally throughout the container.

Pascal's discovery led to the invention of the *hydraulic press*, which is used in manufacturing to form three-dimensional objects from sheets of metal or plastic. This is the way a hydraulic press works: It has two connected cylinders filled with oil—a smaller cylinder and a larger one. Each cylinder has a movable piston. When pressure is applied to the smaller piston, it creates extra pressure throughout the oil in both cylinders.

This causes the piston in the larger cylinder to move, operating the press. A small amount of force on the small piston leads to a stronger force on the large piston, because it has a larger area.

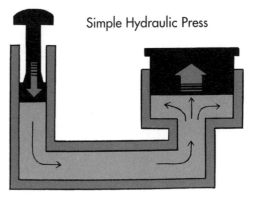

Simple Hydraulic Press

Pascal's law is used today in the large hydraulic jack a mechanic slides under a car when a tire needs to be changed. When the mechanic presses down on the jack handle, he's putting pressure on the fluid in the jack. That creates enough force to lift the car.

Pascal's law is also at work in a car's hydraulic brakes. A small amount of pressure on the brake pedal puts increased pressure on the brake fluid. This in turn activates the car's brakes, slowing or stopping the car.

Other examples of devices that use hydraulics are a fork lift, wing flaps on a plane, and a barber's chair.

Inertia

Sir Isaac Newton, an English mathematician and physicist, discovered many laws of physics. In 1687, his book *Mathematical Principles of Natural Philosophy* included his three laws of motion.

The first law of motion says that a thing at rest tends to remain at rest until an outside force moves it. The law also says that a thing in motion continues to move at a constant speed in a straight line, unless an outside force acts on it.

The law describes *inertia*. Inertia is what causes an object to resist any change in motion.

These experiments may seem like magic tricks, but they demonstrate inertia, and you can use them for requirement 3:

Set a coin on a card on the top of a jar. Snap the edge of the card. The card will fly out because of the force you are using to move it, and the coin will drop into the jar because of inertia.

Make a stack of nickels. Try to snap a penny along the table at the bottom coin. If you hit the target just right, the bottom nickel will fly out; the others remain in a stack. Why?

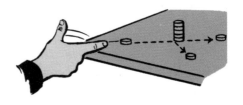

Set a glass of water on the end of a long strip of paper. (Use a plastic glass, just in case. Or you can use a book instead of a glass of water.) Pull the paper slowly. The glass moves with it. Give the paper a sudden jerk. The glass stands still.

Spin a fresh egg on its side. It will stop soon. Spin a hard-boiled egg. It will spin for a much longer time. When you spin a fresh egg, you spin the outside. The white and yolk inside are loose and tend to remain at rest, slowing down the fresh egg. When you spin the hard-boiled egg, you spin the whole egg, because cooking has made the yolk and white solid. They move right along with the shell.

Swing a pail of water back and forth at arm's length. (Don't fill the pail so full that it's too heavy for you.) After a few times, swing it over your head in a full circle. Tell what happens. Do you know why?

Remember, a moving object tends to travel in a straight line unless an outside force acts on it. You're the outside force. Your hold on the bucket and your arm action provide *centripetal force*. You're constantly changing the direction of the bucket, away from straight line travel, and making it go in a circle. Centripetal force makes an object travel a circular route.

Some road curves are banked (tilted toward the inside of the curve) to help cars stay on the road. You'll also see banked curves on bobsled tracks, velodromes (bicycle tracks), and roller coasters. That tilt provides centripetal force that causes circular travel.

Atmospheric Pressure

We live under a blanket of air called the earth's atmosphere. It is many miles deep.

At sea level the atmosphere exerts a pressure of almost 15 pounds per square inch on every surface. A mile above sea level, the blanket of air is thinner, so the atmospheric pressure is less.

Experiments With Atmospheric Pressure

More magic tricks? There's a scientific explanation behind each one. The experiments in this section will demonstrate requirement 4.

Here's one you can do with an egg and a glass bottle with an opening slightly smaller than the egg.

1. Cook the egg in boiling water for 10 minutes.
2. Put it in cold water. Take off the shell.
3. Fold a small piece of newspaper three times in the same direction.
4. Light it. Drop it into the bottle. Quickly put the egg in the top of the bottle.
5. The egg will bounce up and down. Then it will slip neatly into the bottle.

Air molecules are constantly moving, but heat makes them move faster and spread apart. The burning paper heats the air in the bottle and expands it, pushing most of it out. The expanding air coming out of the bottle makes the egg bounce. As the air left in the bottle cools, the inside air pressure drops. The outside atmospheric pressure pushes the egg into the bottle.

Here's another experiment with atmospheric pressure. You need a glass bottle, a shallow pan, and a candle.

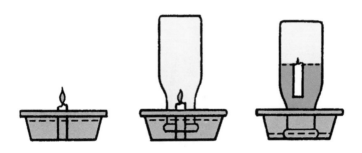

1. Pour the water from a half-filled bottle into a pan. Set a 2-inch-high candle in the pan and light it.
2. Hold the empty bottle over the candle with the top a little below the water. The water will bubble. Hold the bottle until the bubbling stops.
3. Lower the bottle. The candle and water will rise up in the bottle.

The candle flame heats the air in the bottle and expands it, pushing part of it out and making the water bubble. The air pressure inside the bottle drops. Outside the bottle, the higher atmospheric pressure on the water's surface pushes the water and the candle up into the bottle. The flame goes out when it burns up all of the oxygen in the bottle.

For the next experiment, you'll need a cork, a toothpick, a small piece of paper for a sail, and glue to make a small cork boat. You'll also need a glass that will fit over the boat and a larger container for the water. (You can do this experiment with or without the cork boat. The boat makes it more fun and easier to see the water line inside the small glass.)

1. Make a cork boat as shown. Float it.
2. Put a glass over it, putting one edge in the water first, and slowly turn the glass bottom up.
3. Raise the glass, but keep the top under water.

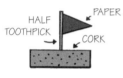

When you lift the glass, the air trapped inside it can't compete with the outside force of atmospheric pressure on the water surface in the large container.

Have an adult supervise this next experiment. You'll need a very *clean*, empty screw-top gallon can and a metal pail larger than the can.

To be sure the can is clean, rinse it at least three times and let it stand open for 24 hours.

1. Fill the pail with cold water.
2. Pour a glass of water into the can. *Leave the top off.* Put the open can on a stove. Boil the water. Let it steam for a minute or more, but don't let it boil dry.
3. Use a hot pad to take the can off the stove. Screw on the cap. Turn the can over and place it, top down, into the pail of water. The can will be crushed.

The steam drives nearly all the air out. The water cools the steam, leaving the can almost empty of air and creating a partial vacuum (a space in which there is very low pressure). The higher outside atmospheric pressure crushes the can.

The Effects of Air Pressure

If we compress air (put pressure on it), it becomes more forceful and we can use it in machines. For example, a jackhammer that is used to break up pavement uses compressed air. A tire pump compresses air, and bicycle tires use compressed air to give you a smooth ride.

Experiments With Air Pressure

Air pressure can do amazing things! These experiments go with requirement 5. For the first one, you'll need a pop bottle and a small piece of newspaper.

1. Make a ball of a 1-inch-square piece of newspaper.
2. Lay the pop bottle on its side on a table. Put the ball in the neck of the bottle.
3. Blow into the bottle. The ball will come *out* of the bottle.

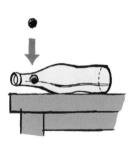

You might expect that blowing on the ball will make it move to the back of the bottle. But what really happens is this: The air you blow into the bottle increases the air pressure, which drives the ball outward.

For the next experiment, you need books and a hot water bottle.

1. On the edge of a table, place several heavy books on top of an empty hot-water bottle.
2. Hold the opening of the bottle tightly against your mouth. Blow hard into the bottle. Your breath will lift the books.

All you need is a balloon and a glass for the next experiment.

1. Put a balloon into a glass. Have the bottom of the balloon touching the bottom of the glass.
2. Blow up the balloon. Hold it shut. You can lift the glass by the neck of the balloon.

The air pressure inside the balloon holds the balloon against the glass.

Water Pressure

This experiment goes with requirement 6. You'll need two large juice cans and something to punch holes in them. The tops of the cans should be open.

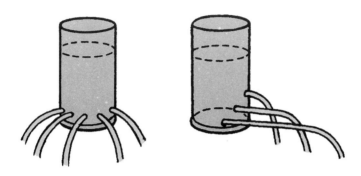

1. Punch five holes near the bottom of a tall juice can. Make the holes about ½ to ¾ inch apart.
2. Fill the can with water. Notice that all the water streams are the same length.
3. Take the other can and punch three holes at different levels (but not one above the other). Fill the can with water. Now notice that the water streams are different lengths.

The amount of water pressure depends on the depth below the surface of the water. In the first can, the water pressure on the holes was equal, since they all were at the same level. The streams of water looked the same. In the second can, the top hole had the least water pressure, and the lowest hole had the most. The lowest stream, with the most pressure, went farthest.

When a dam is built on a river, it is thickest at the bottom, because that's where the water pressure is greatest.

Water Pressure and Atmospheric Pressure

When you read about the water pressure experiment, did you wonder if atmospheric pressure was at work too? It was, because the surface of the water was open to the air. Now try this. You'll need another can, this one with a tight-fitting lid.

1. Use a can with a lid that can be taken off. Punch a nail hole in the lid. Make another hole near the bottom of the can on the side.
2. Fill the can with water. Put the lid on.
3. Turn the can upside down. Water runs out the hole in the lid. Why? The weight of the water plus atmospheric pressure (air coming in the hole in the can's side, above the water) causes water to run out.
4. Put your finger over the hole in the side and the water stops. Remove your finger and it starts.

Your finger stops the air coming in, so there is no pressure of the atmosphere above the water. The upward force of atmosphere on the water in the bottom hole keeps the water from running out.

Here's another experiment that shows how atmospheric pressure works against water pressure:

1. Slip a balloon onto a faucet. Fill it, supporting the weight with your hand.
2. Hold the neck of the balloon tightly and remove it from the faucet. Set the balloon in a bucket of water or in a sink with water in it. Let go of the neck of the balloon. Atmospheric pressure pushing on the surface of the water around the balloon forces a fountain of water out.

Water Pressure and Air Pressure

Because of a scientific invention, divers can work on the bottom of a river, lake, or sea. They use a *diving bell.* Diving bells are used today to help with the underwater work needed in building things such as bridges, piers, and jetties.

Air is fed into the bell through a hose. Even though the bottom of the diving bell is open, air pressure keeps the water out. For an idea of how a diving bell works, you'll need a bottle cap, a bucket, a glass, and water. The glass is your diving bell. This is another experiment you can choose for requirement 6.

1. Float a bottle cap in a bucket full of water.
2. Place a dry glass straight down over the cap. Push the glass down halfway. The cap floats. Where is the water level inside the glass?
3. Push the diving bell (glass) to the bottom. The cap rests on the bottom.
4. Raise the glass carefully. The cap will float again. Watch the water level inside the glass as you bring it slowly up.

Though you are not feeding more air into the glass, the amount of air in it when you touch it to the water remains the same. When you push the glass down, you are compressing the air in it and providing the pressure to push the water out of the way.

Action-Reaction

You've read about Isaac Newton and his first law of motion early in this chapter. Newton made many other discoveries. His third law of motion says that every action has an equal and opposite reaction. This principle explains how a rocket is propelled skyward.

Try this simple demonstration for yourself.

If you decide to buy and build a model rocket kit for requirement 7, you must be at least 10 years old and have an adult helping you during construction and launching. Follow the kit directions and observe all safety rules.

REACTION

(THRUST)

ACTION

Blow up a balloon and hold the opening closed. This is like a rocket that hasn't been ignited yet. The energy is stored in the form of compressed air in the balloon.

Release the balloon, and the stored air rushes out of the opening. This is the *action*. The *reaction* is a force called *thrust*. Thrust causes the balloon to move in the opposite direction from the rushing air.

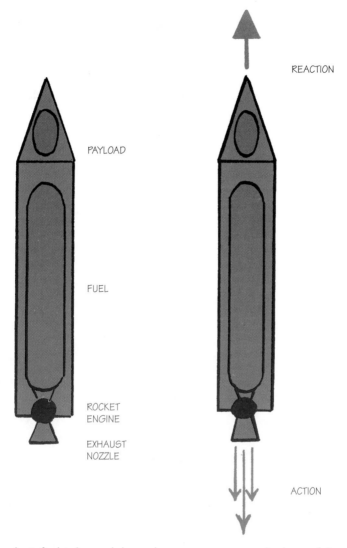

REACTION

PAYLOAD

FUEL

ROCKET
ENGINE

EXHAUST
NOZZLE

ACTION

As the rocket's fuel is burned, hot exhaust gasses are pushed out of the exhaust nozzle at very high speed. The escaping exhaust gasses are the action.

That action causes an equal but opposite reaction. The thrust propels the rocket through the air. If the rocket burned fuel even more quickly, both the action and the reaction would be greater.

Hot exhaust gasses escape through the exhaust nozzle.

More Fun With Science

Fog, crystals, gravity, optical illusions—there's just no end to the experiments you could do in all the scientific fields. Here are a few more ideas that will help you complete your Scientist activity badge.

Fog

Did you know that air has water in it? The water is in the form of molecules so small you can't see them.

If cool air moves in after a warm day, the invisible molecules are drawn together into tiny droplets of water. Billions of these droplets make up fog.

Making Fog

1. Fill a bottle with hot water. Then pour out most of the water. Leave about 1 inch in the bottom.
2. Hold the bottle to the light. Notice the streams of vapor rising from it.
3. Hold an ice cube in the bottle opening. Hold the bottle toward the light. Notice the thin streams of vapor moving down into the bottle. This is fog.

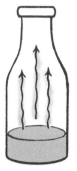

1. Put about 1 inch of cold water in a quart-sized bottle.
2. Cover the opening with your hand. Shake hard to soak the air in the bottle. Pour out the water. Hold the bottle upside down.
3. Light a wooden match. Quickly blow it out. Put the smoking head into the opening of the bottle. The smoke will help the water vapor change into water drops.
4. Set the bottle in a good light. Place your mouth on the bottle opening. Press down and blow hard—you'll then see clear air in the bottle.
5. Raise your head. The fog forms again.

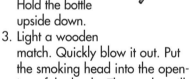
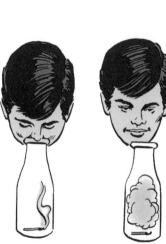

Blowing helps heat the air. This evaporates the fog. When you raise your head, the compressed air expands and cools. Cooling condenses water vapor into tiny water drops you can see, so the fog forms in the bottle again.

Crystals

When some liquids become solid, they form tiny shapes called crystals. Each crystal formed by one liquid is the same shape. Many minerals are made up of crystals.

Quartz Crystal

Crystal Candy

Here's a great experiment— you can eat it when it's finished! You'll need sugar, water, a saucepan, a spoon for stirring, clean white string, a pencil, and a glass or jar.

Bring 1 cup of water to boil in a saucepan. Turn off the heat and add 2 cups of sugar. Stir until the sugar is dissolved. Let it cool. Then pour the solution into a tall glass or a glass jar.

Tie a clean white string to a pencil. Moisten the string in water and drag it through dry sugar so some sugar crystals stick to it. Hang the string in the glass. Store it in a cool place. In a few days you'll see crystals forming on the sides of the glass. By your next den meeting, big hard crystals will have formed on the string. Look at them through a magnifying glass. Then—enjoy!

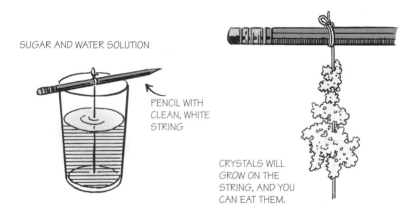

SUGAR AND WATER SOLUTION

PENCIL WITH CLEAN, WHITE STRING

CRYSTALS WILL GROW ON THE STRING, AND YOU CAN EAT THEM.

Center of Gravity

Gravity is the force that holds objects to the earth. The same force holds the moon and planets in their orbits. Sir Isaac Newton's law of universal gravitation explained this in 1687.

Did you ever sit still on a bike with your feet on the pedals and try to keep your balance? You had to keep shifting your weight, right?

Why? Because each time you moved, your *center of gravity*—the point in your body where your weight is concentrated—shifted a little. (A person's center of gravity is usually somewhere behind the navel.)

Normally, when you stand or walk, you unconsciously keep your center of gravity over your feet, which are your base. But if you try to walk along a straight line on the floor, you'll find yourself moving your arms to adjust your center of gravity and keep your balance.

Try these experiments to see what happens when your center of gravity is a bit beyond your control.

Sit in a chair with your feet on the floor and keep your arms folded across your chest. See if you can stand up, but obey this rule: You may not lean forward. Your center of gravity remains too far back to allow you to stand. Now try to stand up by leaning forward first. This allows you to adjust your center of gravity and move it over your feet.

Place a chair against the wall. Bend over it with your head touching the wall. Move your feet back. Your legs, from ankles to hips, should slant toward the wall. Lift the chair. Try to stand straight without moving your feet.

Stand with one shoulder, arm, leg, and foot close against a wall. Try to bring your outside foot up to touch the one next to the wall. Stop at the point where you feel yourself losing your balance. The wall is in your way, so you can't move your body that direction to adjust your center of gravity and keep your balance.

Cut a bird out of a 6-by-6-inch piece of light cardboard. Glue or tape a penny at the front end of each wing. The middle of each penny should be just in front of the bird's beak. Set the beak on the end of your finger or put it on the corner of a table or a book. It won't fall. Where do you think its center of gravity is?

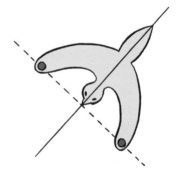

Optical Illusions

How Your Eyes Work Together

Your eyes are wonderful instruments. They are like amazing cameras that can work together.

Each of your eyes focuses a picture of what you are seeing on the retina that lines the eye. The optic nerve carries these two pictures to the brain. Then your brain makes one picture out of the two.

Sometimes your eyes and brain can trick you. Using what it already understands about the world, your brain does the best it can with the images it receives. It might make you believe you're seeing something impossible! Try these easy experiments that show how the eyes work.

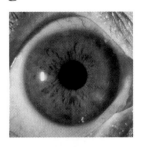

Our eyes and the lens of a camera are similar. Both focus light rays to produce images.

Roll a sheet of paper into a tube. Hold the edge of your hand against the side of the tube. With one eye, look at a distant object through the tube. Look at your hand with the other eye. There seems to be a hole in your hand. What do you think is happening?

One eye sees the distant object through the paper tube, and the other eye sees your hand. Your brain combines the two images in one view.

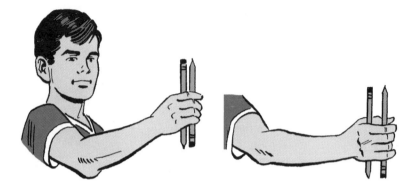

Hold two pencils, as shown, at arm's length. Look past the pencils at the far corner of the room. You'll see two sets of pencils. Do this again with the pencils held about 1 inch apart. You'll see four pencils.

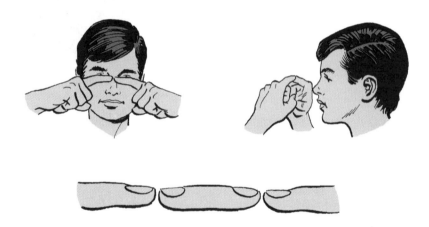

Place the tips of two fingers together about 6 inches from your eyes. Look past them at the far corner of the room and you'll see a small sausage. Pull the fingers apart slowly. The sausage will seem to hang in the air.

Light and Dark

The pupils of your eyes adjust for the level of light that is available.

Stand in a corner of the room, facing the corner, with your back to the light. Look in a mirror. Notice the size of the opening in the pupil of each eye. The openings will be large.

Turn around with your face toward the light. Look in the mirror again. The pupils will be smaller.

Look at something far away. Cup your hands into tubes. Look through them as you would through field glasses. You see more clearly because your pupils get bigger. They receive more light from the faraway objects when they are protected from other light.

Brain Teasers

In some of the optical illusions below, you might be fooled about measurements, sizes, and distance. When your brain tries to make sense out of what your eyes are seeing, it uses what it has already learned about how things usually look. That doesn't mean it's always right!

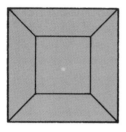

Draw a ½-inch square inside a 1-inch square. Connect the corners. Look at it steadily. The inside square seems to move closer, then farther away.

Draw a box as shown. Look at it steadily. Sometimes it seems you're looking at the top of the box. Sometimes it seems to be the bottom.

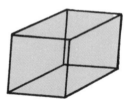

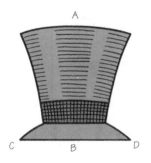

Is the high silk hat longer from A to B than from C to D? Measure it.

Does it look like you could put a dime on top of this box so the coin won't touch the edges? Try it.

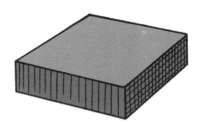

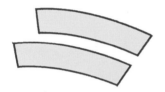

Which of the two designs at left is longer? Better get your ruler.

Which of the dotted circles is larger?

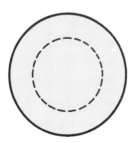

Scientist Scoreboard

Requirements	Approved by:

Do These:

1. Read Bernoulli's principle. Show how it works. _____

2. Read Pascal's law. Tell about some inventions that use Pascal's law. _____

3. Read Newton's first law of motion. Show in three different ways how inertia works. _____

And Do Six of These:

4. Show the effects of atmospheric pressure. _____

5. Show the effects of air pressure. _____

6. Show the effects of water pressure. This may be combined with atmospheric pressure or with air pressure. _____

7. Build and launch a model rocket with adult supervision. (NOTE: You must be at least 10 years old to work with a model rocket kit sold in hobby stores.) _____

8. Explain what causes fog. Show how this works. _____

9. Explain how crystals are formed. Make some. _____

10. Explain how you use your center of gravity to keep your balance. Show three different balancing tricks. _____

11. Show in three different ways how your eyes work together. _____

12. Show what is meant by an optical illusion. _____

Outdoor Activity Badge Group

Forester

Geologist

Naturalist

Outdoorsman

Outdoor Group

Forester

Trees and other forest plants are important parts of the interconnected life on Earth. A forester's work—taking care of trees and managing forest land—is important to the well-being of the planet. You'll learn why when you earn the Forester activity badge.

Wherever you live, on a farm, in a small town, in a large city—or even in the middle of a forest—you can learn about identifying trees and planting new trees.

You might visit a forest with your Webelos den. Take your time and notice everything—all kinds of trees and other plants, animals, birds, and insects. The forest is a fascinating place.

Do Five of These:

1. **Make a map of the United States. Show the types of forests growing in different parts of the country. Name some kinds of trees that grow in these forests. For each type of forest, give one or more examples of uses for the wood of its trees.**

2. **Draw a picture to show the plant and tree layers of a forest in your area. Label the different layers. (If you don't live in an area that has forests, choose an area that does and draw a picture of that forest.)**

3. **Identify six forest trees common to the area where you live. Tell how both wildlife and humans use them. (If you don't live in a region that has forests, read about one type of forest and name six of its trees and their uses.)**

4. **Identify six forest plants (other than trees) that are useful to wildlife. Tell which animals use them and for what purposes.**

5. **Draw a picture showing**
   - **how water and minerals in the soil help a tree grow**
   - **how the tree uses sunlight to help it grow**

6. Make a poster showing how a tree's growth rings tell its life history.

7. Collect pieces of three kinds of wood used for building houses.

8. Plant 20 forest tree seedlings. Tell how you planted them and what you did to take care of them after planting.

9. Describe the harm wildfires can cause. Tell how you can help prevent wildfire.

10. Draw your own urban forestry plan for adding trees to a street, yard, or park near your home. Show what types of trees you would like to see planted.

When you pass each requirement, ask your den leader or counselor to initial your Forester scoreboard on pages 346–347.

Forest Regions of the United States

Most trees grow best in certain kinds of places. Each type of tree needs a certain range of climate, rainfall, and soil. The United States has several different kinds of forests.

West coast forest: Mild climate, lots of rain. Some of the trees are Douglas fir, ponderosa pine, redwood, giant sequoia.

Western forest: Chiefly on mountain slopes. Cold winters, short summers, dryness in summer in the southern part. Typical trees are ponderosa pine, blue spruce, western larch, quaking aspen. Pinyon pine in the southwest.

Northern forest: Low temperatures, short growing season. Common trees are eastern white pine, northern white cedar, white and black spruces, paper birch, sugar maple, northern red oak.

Central hardwood forest: Climate varies from north to south. Rich soils. Good rainfall, usually. Some of the trees are red, white, and black oak; black walnut; sycamore; sweetgum; silver maple; poplar; hickory. Hardwood trees lose their leaves in the fall. Some conifers (trees that have cones) also grow in this region.

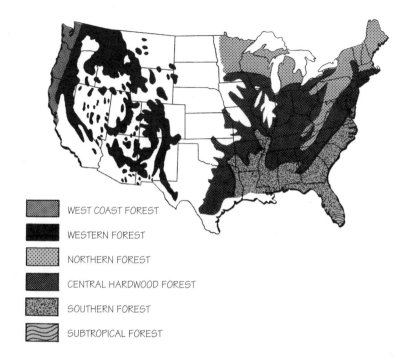

WEST COAST FOREST

WESTERN FOREST

NORTHERN FOREST

CENTRAL HARDWOOD FOREST

SOUTHERN FOREST

SUBTROPICAL FOREST

Southern forest: Drier soils, but usually enough rainfall. Typical trees are shortleaf and longleaf pines, magnolia, red and white oak, pecan, poplar, overcup oak, holly. In swamps, bald cypress and gums.

Subtropical forest: Warm climate and humid (damp). Common trees are West Indies mahogany, mangroves, palms.

What Is a Riparian Forest?

Forests along streams and wetlands are called *riparian forests.* They are very much influenced by how close they are to water and have unique vegetation compared with areas farther away from water.

The plant life in the rich soil and the aquatic life in the water attract more kinds of birds, insects, and small animals to the riparian forest, compared with other kinds of forests.

The combination of forest and water attracts some species of birds that migrate in the fall and spring and is important to their survival.

Forest Structure

Did you know a forest has *layers*? Here are the five basic forest layers, from top to bottom.

The canopy: The canopy of a forest is made up of the tops of the tallest trees. It's like the roof of the forest. This layer gets the most sunlight, so it often produces the most food for wildlife. Birds, squirrels, reptiles, and insects live here.

The understory: Shorter trees grow in the understory of the forest. They get less sunlight, but they also produce food and habitat for animals, birds, and insects.

The shrub layer: Shrubs are woody plants, smaller than trees, that have more than one stem. Mammals, birds, and insects live and feed in the shrub layer.

The herb layer: These plants are small and have softer stems that are not woody. Depending on the type of forest and the amount of sunlight at this level, you'd find ferns, grasses, and wildflowers here. Insects, mice, other small animals, and snakes live here.

Large animals like deer and bears depend on the food in the understory, shrub layer, and herb layer.

The forest floor: This bottom layer collects dead leaves and plants, fallen trees, animal droppings, dead animals—and returns them to the soil in a process called *decomposition.* Earthworms, fungi, and insects, along with bacteria and other microscopic organisms, gradually break down the materials. The plants of the forest absorb the nutrients released by decomposition.

Look for plants in the different forest layers in your area (or in a forest area in your state). What kinds of trees are the tallest? Which trees are in the understory? In an eastern hardwood forest, the tallest trees might be oak and hickory. The understory

Forester

could contain flowering dogwood, redbud, sassafras, and sumac. The shrub layer might have blackberry and wild grape. In a western conifer forest, the tallest trees might be Douglas fir, western hemlock, and western red cedar. The understory might have Pacific yew, dogwood, and ocean spray. The shrub layer might have salal and sword fern. The forest you study could have entirely different trees and plants.

Forest Trees

Foresters learn everything about the many kinds of trees, smaller plants, and animals that grow and live in the forests they manage. A few of the forest trees that grow in the United States are shown on these pages.

Douglas Fir
Pacific Northwest coast and Rocky Mountains
Height: 100–250 feet
Used for lumber, plywood, paper.

Sweetgum
Southeastern states and north to Connecticut, New York, Ohio, Illinois, Missouri, Oklahoma
Height: 80–120 feet
Used for veneer, furniture, cabinets, and woodwork. (*Veneer* is a thin layer of wood used to make furniture surfaces.)

Eastern White Pine
Northeastern states
Height: 50–100 feet
Used for cabinets, interior lumber, woodenware.

Ponderosa Pine
All western states, into southern Canada and
northern Mexico
Height: 60–200 feet
Used for lumber, fences, railroad ties; very impor-
tant for millwork.

Shagbark Hickory
Eastern half of the United States
Height: 60–80 feet
Used for furniture, wall paneling, tool handles,
cooking fuel; provides nuts for wildlife.

Walnut
Eastern half of the United States
Height: 80–100 feet
Used for furniture, gunstocks, doors, and cabinets;
wildlife and humans eat the nuts.

White Oak
Eastern half of the United States
Height: 60–120 feet
Used for lumber, furniture, boats, fuel wood; the
acorns are important food for wildlife.

Hemlock
Northeast (eastern hemlock)
Far west (western and mountain hemlocks)
Height: 60–100 feet (mountain hemlock);
125–200 feet (western hemlock)
Used for lumber, pulpwood for paper, and rail-
road ties.

Longleaf Pine
Southeastern coastal states
Height: 100–120 feet
Once used for turpentines and resins; now used
for lumber and framing.

Animals and Humans Depend on Forests

Many kinds of trees are used for building materials and wood for furniture. Foresters know which types of trees are best for building and which are more useful for making paper—or which are important for *both* building and making paper.

Trees like walnut and pecan supply nuts to use in baking cookies and pies. Wild plums and other fruits grow on forest trees. People often pick wild blackberries, huckleberries, and gooseberries, which grow on shrubs in the shrub layer.

Animals find even more to eat in the forest than humans do. Think about seeds, acorns, grasses, tree leaves—do you know which animals eat them?

Here are a few more ways wildlife and humans use forest plants.

Wildlife uses:

- Bluebirds, catbirds, and mockingbirds eat the red berries of the holly tree.
- Deer eat tree bark, leaving marks. Deer also eat tree leaves, stems, and other green plants.
- Bears mark their territory by clawing and biting tree trunks. Mountain lions sharpen their claws on trees.
- Moose, elk, and deer use tree trunks or flexible saplings to rub the velvet off their antlers.
- Beavers eat the bark and cut down trees to build dams and homes for themselves.

Human uses:

- Hickory and white ash are used to make baseball bats and tool handles.
- Western red cedar is used to make porches, decks, and shingles for roofs.
- Mesquite and hickory chips on cooking fires flavor food.

- Candles are made from the waxy covering of the southern bayberry fruit.
- Maple syrup is made from the sap of sugar maples harvested in the early spring.

Identifying Forest Trees and Plants

A forest is a community of plants, from the tallest trees down to the smallest mosses and lichens that you have to kneel on the ground to see.

When you visit a wooded area or forest, take along a tree field guide. A wildflower guide is handy, too. Your public library may have these books.

Take time to look closely at everything. Use a magnifying glass to study tiny details.

When you're looking at trees, check for:

- Type of leaf. Feel it. Is it smooth or rough? Notice the shape.
- Leaf edges—smooth or toothed?
- Type of bark—smooth or rough, peeling, light or dark?
- Unusual features—thorns, flowers, berries. Some trees will have more than one leaf shape. The sassafras has three leaf shapes.
- With conifers, notice the length, shape, and grouping of the needles. Spruce needles are sharp and short, with four sides, and they grow separately on the twigs. Pine needles grow in bundles, so count the number in a bundle for a clue to the kind of pine it is. Needles of a longleaf pine could be 18 inches long, but jack pine needles are only about 1 inch long. The size and type of cone will also provide clues to the identity of the tree.

The tree supports much life. Look for woodpecker holes, insects hiding under the bark, mistletoe rooted in the branches, fungi growing on the bark, and the nests of birds and squirrels. Move slowly and quietly so you can have a chance to see birds, squirrels, and other animals.

How a Tree Grows

The tree grows in its roots, trunk, and crown (its top, where all the branches and leaves are). The tree needs food to grow, and its roots and leaves play a part in the process of making food.

Roots: Roots anchor the tree in the earth. They soak up the water, minerals, and nitrogen from the soil that the leaves need to make food for the tree. A layer of growth cells at root tips makes new roots each year. Tree roots help slow erosion by holding soil in place.

Trunk: The trunk is a pathway for water and minerals to move from the soil upward to the leaves. It grows outward each year. (See "The Inside Story of a Tree," page 340.) As the trunk grows taller, the crown of the tree grows higher in search of more sunlight. In trees used for lumber, the trunk produces most of the useful wood.

Crown: The crown is the upper part of the tree, including the branches and leaves. The leaves take in sunlight and use it to make food for the tree in a process called *photosynthesis* (discussed on the next page).

The crown of the tree grows each year by adding a new growth of leaves and twigs. This growth comes from young cells in buds on the twigs.

Tree Bud

Photosynthesis

Trees, like all plants with green leaves, use sunlight to make food from air and water, in a chemical process called *photosynthesis*. The food *(carbohydrate)* is made in the leaves.

Carbon dioxide from the air comes through pores in

Chlorophyll captures the sun's energy.

Carbon dioxide from the air.

Oxygen and moisture are released into the air.

Water and minerals from the roots.

the leaves. Water and minerals come up through the roots in tubelike pathways in the tree to the veins in the leaves. (You can see these tubes on the branch and in the stem when you detach a leaf.)

Chlorophyll is what makes a leaf green. It also captures the sun's energy and uses it to process carbon dioxide and water, making liquid sugar. This flows to every living part of the tree, nourishing it and helping it grow.

Some of the oxygen taken from the water is left over. The tree doesn't need all the leftover oxygen, so the leaves release excess oxygen and also water, keeping the air around the trees damp and cool.

Forester

The Inside Story of a Tree

Inner Bark: Carries food made in the leaves down to the branches, trunk, and roots. It consists of hollow tubes.

Fire Scar: A tree can be damaged by fire even if it is not burned down. Disease and insects can enter through fire scars.

Outer Bark: Protects the tree from injuries.

Thinning: At this point, nearby trees were cut down, giving the tree more light. There were 20 years of growth before thinning, and 10 years of growth after.

Sapwood: Carries sap from roots to leaves.

Cambium: This thin layer of cells between bark and wood is where the trunk grows. Each year it forms a ring of new wood toward the inside of the trunk and new inner bark toward the outside of the trunk.

Heartwood: Originally sapwood, inactive; gives strength to a tree.

Collecting Wood Samples

Many kinds of wood are used in building houses. In any house, you are likely to find oak, pine, and cedar as part of the structure, decoration, or furniture.

You may be able to get scraps of these woods and others by visiting a lumberyard.

Show the grain from four different angles by cutting each sample as shown here. Sand each surface with sandpaper. You may want to lacquer or varnish half of each surface. This shows what the wood looks like when it's finished.

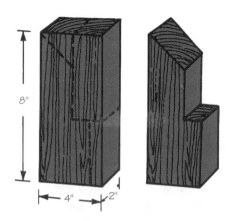

Tree Planting

Planting new trees is the key to *sustainable forestry*. Sustainable forestry means that people in the future will have the same abundant forests that we enjoy today.

■ Carry seedlings in a bucket or box. Keep the roots damp.

■ Plant them at least 6 feet apart.

■ Dig holes just deep enough to hold the roots. Loosen the sides and bottom of the hole so that tiny roots can push into the soil. The roots should not be stuffed into the hole, or the tree's chances of surviving are low.

■ A seedling should be planted so that its old ground line is about ¼ inch below the new ground level. (The *ground line* is the dark mark on the trunk.)

■ A seedling should be planted with its trunk straight up and the hole filled with soil even with the ground. The soil should not be sunk in or mounded up above the ground.

- Press the soil down firmly around the roots to prevent air pockets. If you don't, the roots will dry out and the tree will probably die.
- A newly planted seedling needs lots of water, so soak the soil around the seedling with water, and then soak it again.
- Cover the ground around the base of the seedling with several inches of *mulch*—composted leaves, wood chips, grass cuttings, straw, or sawdust. This holds in moisture and helps make the soil richer for the new tree.

Fire in the Forest

Fire can both benefit and destroy a forest. A cool fire burning slowly along the ground does not hurt the trees. By burning away excess brush, the fire provides nutrients and space for new trees to grow. A new, young forest then provides habitat for many animals and birds.

But a hot wildfire burns high into the tree crowns and can injure and kill many trees. A wildfire in a forest can do much

Fall Color

Why do some hardwood tree leaves change color and fall off the tree? Chlorophyll production stops in the fall, revealing the yellow and orange pigments that were hidden by the green of the chlorophyll. Reds and purplish colors also develop in leaves rich in sugar, in trees like hard maples, dogwoods, and sweetgums.

As winter approaches, days grow shorter. The place where the leaf stem is connected to the branch weakens. Wind and frost can cause the connections to break, and the leaves fall.

more than destroy trees. It also destroys food and cover for wildlife. Sometimes it destroys the animals themselves. And, as more people build their homes near or in forests, more and more homes are at risk of being destroyed by wildfire.

Wildfire can burn the plant cover that protects the soil and sometimes might cause erosion. When soil and ashes wash into streams and lakes, good fishing may be spoiled. Campsites and other recreation areas may be destroyed by fire.

You can help prevent wildfire in these ways:

■ Be extremely careful with any fire you build in the outdoors.

■ Always build your fire in a safe place and watch it at all times.

■ Don't leave a fire until it is out and *cold*. If you can still feel heat through the ashes, the fire is not completely out. (Be careful not to burn your hands!)

■ If you see a fire, report it immediately to the nearest fire warden or fire department.

Because some kinds of fires can help the forest, foresters sometimes intentionally set controlled fires (called *prescribed fires*) or allow a "natural fire" caused by lightning to burn in order to reduce the buildup of deadwood or leaves on the forest floor. When this material gets too deep, a wildfire will burn hotter, increasing the destruction.

Foresters also use prescribed fires to maintain savannas, which are grasslands with scattered trees and shrubs. Fires help control the invasion of too many trees into the grassland.

The lodgepole pine, which grows in the west from Alaska to Baja California, actually needs fire to release its seeds. Its cones stay closed and attached to the tree for years. When a ground fire comes through the forest, the heat causes the cones to open and release the seeds.

Urban Forestry

Foresters work in cities, too. That's called urban forestry. These foresters know what kinds of trees grow well in a city environment.

Planting trees in cities helps in these ways:

- New trees beautify streets and show that people care about the way their city looks. People enjoy walking along tree-lined, shady sidewalks. Trees in front of businesses make the property more attractive to customers.

- Flowering trees put on a show in the spring. Fall leaf colors brighten the city in autumn.

- Adding trees in parks creates shady places to play and picnic.

- Shade trees can be located to shade pavement and buildings, cooling them in summer and cutting down on air-conditioning costs.

- A grove of trees can shelter an area from winter winds.

- Trees provide habitat and food for birds and other wildlife in the city.

- Trees purify air by taking in carbon dioxide and releasing oxygen.

Urban foresters plan tree-planting projects, decide what kinds of trees to plant, and supervise crews of workers who plant and care for new trees. The foresters also may advise volunteer groups working on community tree-planting projects.

Forester Scoreboard

Requirements	Approved by:

Do Five of These:

1. Make a map of the United States. Show the types of forests growing in different parts of the country. Name some kinds of trees that grow in these forests. For each type of forest, give one or more examples of uses for the wood of its trees. _____

2. Draw a picture to show the plant and tree layers of a forest in your area. Label the different layers. (If you don't live in an area that has forests, choose an area that does and draw a picture of that forest.) _____

3. Identify six forest trees common to the area where you live. Tell how both wildlife and humans use them. (If you don't live in a region that has forests, read about one type of forest and name six of its trees and their uses.) _____

4. Identify six forest plants (other than trees) that are useful to wildlife. Tell which animals use them and for what purposes. _____

5. Draw a picture showing

   • how water and minerals in the soil help a tree grow

   • how the tree uses sunlight to help it grow

6. Make a poster showing how a tree's growth rings tell its life history. _____

7. Collect pieces of three kinds of wood used for building houses. _____

8. Plant 20 forest tree seedlings. Tell how you planted them and what you did to take care of them after planting. _____

9. Describe the harm wildfires can cause. Tell how you can help prevent wildfire. _____

10. Draw your own urban forestry plan for adding trees to a street, yard, or park near your home. Show what types of trees you would like to see planted. _____

Outdoor Group

Geologist

A geologist is a person who studies the history of the earth and its life. In this case, the history books are rocks. Geologists are interested in learning how the earth is made.

Geologists study rock formations at the tops of mountains and deep in the earth's crust. They investigate earthquakes, volcanoes, and geysers. They know about the uses of rocks and minerals. Some geologists search for mineral deposits like gold, diamonds, coal, and oil.

In earning this badge, you'll find out how the earth is formed and what is in it. You'll find out what fossils are. You'll learn what they can tell us about the earth millions of years ago.

Do Five of These:

1. Collect five geologic specimens that have important uses.

2. Rocks and minerals are used in metals, glass, jewelry, road-building products, and fertilizer. Give examples of minerals used in these products.

3. Make a scale of mineral hardness for objects found at home. Show how to use the scale by finding the relative hardness of three samples.

4. List some of the geologic materials used in building your home.

5. Make a drawing that shows the cause of a volcano, a geyser, or an earthquake.

6. Explain one way in which mountains are formed.

7. Describe what a fossil is. How is it used to tell how old a formation is? Find two examples of fossils in your area.

When you pass each requirement, ask your den leader or counselor to initial your Geologist scoreboard on page 368.

Rocks and Pebbles

Your own backyard and neighborhood are good places to begin collecting rocks. Use a guide to rocks and minerals to help you identify the rocks you pick up. (See more about collecting on pages 355–357.)

Rhyolite

While you're examining a rock, think about the rock you can't see and pick up. It's under your feet, under your yard, and it runs deep into the planet. It's the earth's *crust*.

Shale layer on sandstone

Granite

The Earth's Crust and Deeper

The earth's crust is up to 65 miles thick and is made up of many kinds of rock, formed in layers at different times. In places, the layers are broken or have been folded, pushed up, or dropped down in blocks. In some places, the crust is fractured along a line called a *fault*. (See page 362.) Some faults run for hundreds of miles.

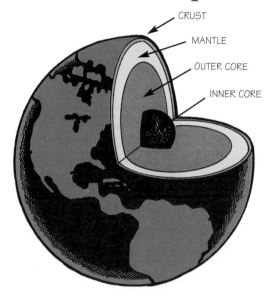

CRUST
MANTLE
OUTER CORE
INNER CORE

When you see mountain peaks, rock cliffs along rivers, or layers of rock where a highway has been cut through, you're seeing the upper parts of the earth's crust.

Below the crust is the *mantle*, which is about 1,750 miles deep. The upper part of the mantle (the *asthenosphere*) is partly molten (melted). Below that the mantle is solid.

Below the mantle is the *outer core*, which is iron and nickel melted together in a hot liquid.

The *inner core*, at the center of the planet, is a solid ball of iron and nickel.

Three Kinds of Rock

All rocks belong to one of the three main groups making up the earth's crust: igneous, sedimentary, and metamorphic rocks.

Igneous Rock

Igneous rock is any rock made by the cooling of magma or lava. Magma is molten material that flows under the earth's crust. Sometimes it finds a weak spot and breaks through to form great areas of rock called flood basalts, or it may erupt as a volcano. Besides basalt, examples of igneous rock are granite and obsidian.

The Tooth of Time at Philmont Scout Ranch is an example of igneous rock formed by volcanic action 22 to 40 million years ago.

Sedimentary Rock

Sediment is gravel, sand, clay, or soil that settles out of water in riverbeds, ponds, lakes, and oceans. Sediment may contain shells and skeletons. Sedimentary rock is formed in layers, like a giant cake, after sediment has been under great pressure for millions of years. If the sediment was originally sand, it becomes sandstone. Clay turns into shale. Shells and skeletons make limestone. Small pebbles and sand form conglomerate.

Metamorphic Rock

Metamorphic rock has been through a process much like baking. (*Meta* means changed, and *morphic* means form.) The change is caused by intense heat and great pressure deep in the earth. Under these conditions, sedimentary limestone becomes marble. Sedimentary sandstone turns into quartzite. Igneous granite changes into gneiss (pronounced "nice").

How Rocks Break Down

Wind, water, heat, and cold are all strong forces in the world. They slowly break down any rock, no matter how hard it is. The result is sand, gravel, clay, and soil.

Lichens growing on rock also break it down, slowly loosening rock particles.

When material from decayed plants and animals mixes with the broken-down rock, soil forms. Rock is always being broken down, very slowly.

Useful Minerals

The earth contains useful minerals. Some, like silica (sand), are easy to see and collect. Others, like iron and zinc, are found in rocks. They must be removed from the rock by a process called *smelting* or *refining*.

There are three classes of useful minerals—metals, nonmetallic minerals, and fuels. Here are some examples.

Metals	Nonmetallic Minerals		Fuels
	Used in build-ing materials and supplies	Precious and semiprecious stones	
Iron	Gypsum	Turquoise	Coal
Tin	Potash	Topaz	Natural gas
Platinum	Limestone	Garnet	Petroleum
Zinc	Sand	Tourmaline	Uranium (used for nuclear fuel)
Mercury	Borax	Diamond	
Aluminum	Talc	Zircon	
Lead	Quartz	Sapphire	
Gold		Ruby	
Uranium			
Copper			
Silver			
Magnesium			

Precious and Semiprecious Stones

Collecting Specimens

One way to begin a collection of geologic specimens is to visit a business that sells building stone or one that makes gravestones. These businesses might have small scraps of marble, granite, sandstone, limestone, pumice, shale, or slate that they will give you.

Or, go on a field trip. If possible, go with a collector who knows a lot about rocks (called a *rock hound*). A rock hound will know which rocks contain useful materials.

Look for minerals in gravel or sand pits, road cuts, diggings, mountains, hills, and stream banks. But stay away from dangerous areas like quarries, mine dump heaps, and old mines. Always have an adult with you. Be careful when climbing on rocks or cliffs.

Watch out for snakes. They may crawl under rocks, so learn to poke around a rock with a stick before reaching under it.

Keep your rock samples small. Small ones are easier to carry and easier to care for.

Collecting rocks is not allowed in national parks and in many state parks. Ask permission before you collect anywhere.

Geologist's Equipment

- Safety glasses to protect your eyes.
- A pocket magnifier for seeing things up close.
- Geologist's hammer for pulling rocks out of hillsides and breaking them open.
- Cold chisel, ½-inch to 1-inch wide, for chipping stone with a hammer and for digging things loose.
- Small notebook and pencil for recording where and when you found a sample. Number each sample in the notebook.
- Clear plastic food storage bags. Write the number of the rock sample on paper and slip it into the bag with the rock sample.
- Heavy gloves for rough work.
- A small day pack for carrying equipment and rocks.

Your Collection

You can display your rock collection by putting specimens in egg cartons, or you can make dividers for boxes.

On each specimen, paint a spot of quick-drying white enamel. When it is dry, write a number on the spot with a dark felt-tip pen. For each specimen, keep a card with that number. The card should tell what the specimen is and where and when you found it.

Specimen Boxes

Egg Carton

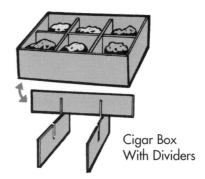

Cigar Box
With Dividers

Identifying Rocks and Minerals

Rocks and minerals are often hard to identify. You can get help by borrowing a field guide to rocks and minerals from a library. Or arrange to show your specimens to a high school science teacher. He or she may be able to help identify them.

Geologists use the following tests to identify minerals.

Color Clue: Scratch the specimen on a plate of unglazed porcelain or the back of a piece of tile. The color that appears helps to identify it.

Luster Clue: How does the specimen look when light is reflected from it? Is it shiny, dull, or greasy?

Cleavage Clue: How does it split or break up? Does it turn into powder? Split in layers? If it breaks into crystals, how many sides does a crystal have?

Chemical Clue: Does it contain limestone? If a drop of vinegar bubbles on it, the answer is yes.

Hardness Clue: How hard is it? See the hardness scale.

Geologist

Hardness Scale for Minerals

Scale No.	Mineral Example	Scratch Test
1	Talc	Easily with fingernail
2	Gypsum	Barely with fingernail
3	Calcite	Barely with copper penny
4	Fluorite	Easily with knife blade
5	Apatite	Barely with knife blade
6	Feldspar	Not by blade; easily with glass
7	Quartz	Easily marks steel and hard glass
8	Topaz	Harder than common minerals
9	Corundum	Scratches topaz
10	Diamond	Scratches corundum; hardest mineral

Geologic Materials in Construction

Here are some of the geologic materials used in construction. Maybe you can add others.

Ore	Metal	Use
Hematite Limonite Magnetite	Iron	Beams, girders, posts, nails, machines, screws
Azurite Malachite Chalcocite	Copper	Electric wiring, gutters, roofing, pipes
Sphalerite	Zinc	Galvanizing pipe, sheet metal
Bauxite	Aluminum	Siding, windows, doors, roofs
Quartz	Silicon	Glass
Kernite Borax	Boron	Glass
Limestone	Calcium	Cement, building stone

Volcanoes

Volcanoes are simply vents in the ground formed by the pressure of magma building up. They come in many sizes and shapes. The streams of melted rock that pour out of the earth during some volcanic eruptions are called *lava*.

Lava changes the earth's shape as it flows and cools. In time, it may build up into a mountain peak with a vent up the center. From this chimney comes smoke, steam, and gas mixed with melted minerals.

As lava pours out, it spreads over the country-side and keeps building

Mount St. Helens in Washington state erupted in 1980.

up. Geologists say that in some places this mineral rock may be thousands of feet deep.

Cool lava becomes igneous rock. The foaming surface of lava forms lightweight pumice stone, which is used as an abrasive cleanser or polish.

Geologist

Capulin Volcano

Capulin Volcano, an extinct volcano in northeastern New Mexico, is more than 1,000 feet high from its base to the crater rim. Long ago, wagon trains traveling west used it as a landmark. From its rim you can see parts of five states: New Mexico, Oklahoma, Texas, Kansas, and Colorado.

Capulin Volcano National Monument is not far from Philmont Scout Ranch. If you visit Philmont, maybe you'll have a chance to see Capulin Volcano, too.

Capulin Volcano is one of the United States' largest recent cinder cones. But that's "recent" in geologic terms: Geologists estimate that it was active about 7,000 years ago. The cone is also one of the most perfectly shaped. The rim is 1 mile around, and the center is 415 feet below the rim.

Geysers

Geysers form when underground water meets hot gases and molten rock deep in the earth. This water is partly changed into steam by the red-hot magma. The steam gathers in the geyser's tube. When enough pressure builds, a column of steam and boiling water erupts into the air.

Old Faithful geyser is in Yellowstone National Park. It shoots 100 to 150 feet into the air. Until 1959, this occurred about every 70 minutes. Since then, its timing has been affected by several earthquakes, making it less predictable.

Old Faithful geyser in Yellowstone National Park

In some geysers, the steam pours out in a steady cloud.

Underground hot water and steam are also present in areas around geysers called *geothermal fields*. In some places, steam from the geothermal field is piped to power plants and used to make electricity, but this often kills the nearby geysers.

In some geysers there is so much water it isn't turned into steam. This heated water flows out as a hot spring. Because the water is hot, it dissolves minerals from the rocks it passes over. Some of these mineral springs have become health resorts.

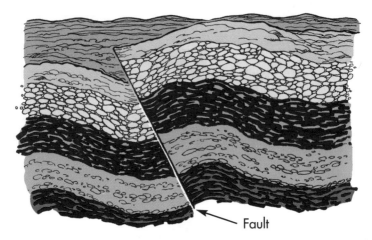

Fault

A fault is a fracture in the earth's crust. Earthquakes may occur along a fault.

Earthquakes

The earth's rock crust is not in one piece like an unbroken shell around the planet. It's made up of parts called *plates.* The plates that are mostly land are called continental plates, and the plates under oceans are called oceanic plates.

The plates are huge, and they are moving all the time. They move slowly, perhaps 1 inch a year, but they have great force.

Most earthquakes occur along plate boundaries, when the edges of two plates slide into each other or past each other. Far below the surface, the rocks are strained to the limit by this pressure and finally break up, sending out vibrations called *seismic waves.* The seismic waves reach the surface, causing anything from a short, light shaking to violent tremors that can wreck a city.

In California, many earthquakes have happened along the San Andreas fault. The San Andreas fault lies over the place where the North American plate meets the Pacific plate.

An earthquake may happen near the surface of the earth, or it may be as much as 400 miles down. Scientists use a machine called a *seismograph* to measure the force of vibrations in the earth's crust.

How Mountains Are Formed

CRUSTAL UPLIFT
Rocky Mountains

VOLCANIC ACTION
Mt. Rainier

EROSION
Buttes and mesas

Mountains have been formed over millions of years. There are three basic ways this has been done.

First, mountains are formed when the plates in the earth's crust collide. Over a very long time, the crust will fold or arch up, resulting in mountains caused by *crustal uplift*. The Rocky Mountains were formed this way.

In the Great Basin area of the western United States, which includes most of Nevada and parts of its neighboring states, the crust was pushed upward and then pulled apart. Huge sections of the crust, called fault blocks, dropped downward, making broad valleys between mountain ranges.

Volcanic action also makes mountains, like you read on page 359. This action happens along the moving edges of the plates. Mount Rainier in Washington state is an example of a mountain made out of cooled lava and volcanic debris.

Finally, *erosion* makes mountains, usually lower ones. Softer rocks erode, or get worn away by wind and water, more quickly than harder rocks. This results in certain kinds of mountains, such as the flat-topped mesas or buttes in parts of the western and southwestern United States. Also, parts of the Ozark Mountains in Arkansas and Missouri were created by the forces of erosion.

Fossils Are Fun!

You may find fossils while you are looking for rock specimens. If you do, why not collect them, too?

A fossil is a trace of animal or plant life from millions of years ago that has hardened in rock. Sedimentary rock usually contains fossils. A fossil may be a print of a shell or the skeleton of a fish or bird. It may be a dinosaur's track or a leaf or flower print.

Would you believe that fossils from the sea can be found in a desert? It's true. And fossils have been discovered on top of mountains! This means that the spot where they were found was once an ocean floor.

Certain plants and animals live in hot climates, but their fossils have been found in cold countries. This means that these areas were not always cold. Geologists study the rock layer in which the fossils were found. Then they can tell when the country was warm and for how long.

Fossils show us what plants and trees lived millions of years ago and where. They show the changes that have happened through the years.

An unusual type of fossil is petrified wood or bone. A chemical known as silica replaced each cell of the original matter. Slowly the material turned to stone. Today it looks just as it did millions of years ago.

You probably can find fossils in your own neighborhood. Look in diggings, road cuts, or stream banks. Look wherever cuts have been made through layers of sedimentary rock.

If you don't know a good place to hunt for fossils, ask your teacher or write to a college geology department in your state.

Geologist in the City

Is it hard to find rocks in the heart of a huge city? They're all around you. You're walking on rock. You're looking at rock. When you go inside downtown office buildings and department stores, you're entering enclosures built of rock.

A city may have more rock samples than any plot of ground out in the countryside. You can hunt for them, even if you can't take them home.

Here are a few places to look for some types of rocks in the city:

Granite. This strong igneous rock is used often in city buildings. Look for it on the outside of buildings. It can be gray, pink, or a deeper rose color. It has a speckled pattern. The darkest flecks are mica crystals, and the glasslike areas are quartz. The feldspar in it is smooth. You can find both rough and polished granite in buildings.

Sandstone. In eastern cities, many older homes, called *brownstones*, were built of brick and then covered with brown sandstone blocks.

Slate. This metamorphic rock, changed by heat and pressure, was once clay. It can be split into slabs. You might find an old sidewalk made of gray slate. Chalkboards in schools used to be made of smooth black slate. Some roofs are made of slate.

Marble. Look for marble in the lobbies of office buildings and banks. A streaky, swirling pattern of mixed color and a smooth, shiny surface will be the main clues. Marble comes in many different colors. The main color might be black, gray, green, pink, or white.

You can find marble in museums and parks, too. Pure white marble is often used for sculptures, statues, and monuments.

Geologist Scoreboard

Requirements   **Approved by:**

Do Five of These:

1. Collect five geologic specimens that have important uses.   _____

2. Rocks and minerals are used in metals, glass, jewelry, road-building products, and fertilizer. Give examples of minerals used in these products.   _____

3. Make a scale of mineral hardness for objects found at home. Show how to use the scale by finding the relative hardness of three samples.   _____

4. List some of the geologic materials used in building your home.   _____

5. Make a drawing that shows the cause of a volcano, a geyser, or an earthquake.   _____

6. Explain one way in which mountains are formed.   _____

7. Describe what a fossil is. How is it used to tell how old a formation is? Find two examples of fossils in your area.   _____

On to Naturalist!

Outdoor Group

Naturalist

If you like watching wildlife, you're already a naturalist. A naturalist studies living creatures and plants in the wild. When you visit a nature center to learn about birds, reptiles, mammals, trees, and wildflowers, your guide is a naturalist.

For this badge, you might keep an insect zoo, watch tadpoles change into frogs, or make a terrarium for wild plants. Perhaps your den will visit a real zoo or take a nature walk in the woods.

Naturalists have a great love for nature. They notice details that other people miss. They know that the well-being of all living things is interconnected.

Do Four of These:

1. Keep an "insect zoo" that you have collected. You might have crickets, ants, or grasshoppers. Study them for a while and then release them.

2. Set up an aquarium or terrarium. Keep it for at least a month.

3. Visit a museum of natural history, nature center, or zoo with your family, den, or pack. Tell what you saw.

4. Watch for birds in your yard, neighborhood, or town for one week. Identify the birds you see and write down where and when you saw them.

5. Learn about the bird flyways closest to your home. Find out which birds use these flyways.

6. Learn to identify poisonous plants and venomous reptiles found in your area.

7. Watch six wild animals (snakes, turtles, fish, birds, or mammals) in the wild. Describe the kind of place (forest, field, marsh, yard, or park) where you saw them. Tell what they were doing.

8. Give examples of
    • A producer, a consumer, and a decomposer in the food chain of an ecosystem

- **One way humans have changed the balance of nature**
- **How you can help protect the balance of nature**

When you pass each requirement, ask your den leader or counselor to initial your Naturalist scoreboard on page 393.

Your Insect Zoo

Keeping an insect allows you to study it closely and get to know what it does. Get a book from the library about the insect you keep.

It will need your care each day. Consider it a visitor and release it back to its natural outdoor habitat after a while.

Summer is the best time to keep an insect zoo because insects are most active then. Here are tips on finding and caring for different insects.

Crickets

Sink a small plastic jar or can into the ground so its rim is level with the surface. Put a sweet, gooey mixture in the jar. It might be a mixture of two parts molasses and one part water or a mashed pulp of overripe fruit.

The sweet smell will attract crickets and beetles, and they will tumble in.

Or you can look for crick- ets under rocks and logs. You have to be quick to catch a cricket. Crickets don't bite, but they do jump.

Cricket home

You can use a large, wide-mouthed plastic jar as a cricket home. Have an adult help you punch air holes in the jar lid, or if the lid is too hard, make a lid out of fiberglass screenwire and put a rubber band around it.

Put 1 inch of moist soil in the bottom. (Soil from the place you found the cricket should be good.) Put in a bottle cap for drinking water and a rock or small piece of wood. Crickets like to crawl underneath rocks or other objects.

Don't place the jar where it will get direct sunlight, as it will heat up inside and the cricket may die.

Food: Try lettuce, a small wedge of raw potato, or a bit of dry dog or cat food—fresh food each day. Keep the house clean by removing leftover food and droppings.

Expect some chirping! Your cricket guest may keep you awake or sing you to sleep.

Ants

To capture ants you need a 2-foot-square piece of white cloth or paper, two large-mouth bottles with lids, a piece of cardboard, and a trowel. Now find an anthill or ant nest under rocks. **Caution:** Don't try to collect fire ants or other stinging ants. Stay away from them.

Stir the anthill gently with your trowel. When the ants come out to investigate, use the cardboard to guide them into one jar. Put some dirt from the anthill in with

them. Some ants may be carrying white objects, which are the larvae and pupae, two stages of ant development. Collect some of these too.

Now find the colony's queen— if you can. Some ant queens live very deep in the ground, and when the nest is disturbed, the other ants carry her off to safety. That is

because the queen produces all of the colony's young. She will be larger than the other ants. As you look for the queen, spread the dirt on the white cloth, and she should show up against the white background.

Put the queen into the second bottle and add some dirt.

Ant house

You can use a wide-mouthed jar with screenwire (if the holes are small enough to keep ants from climbing out) or cheesecloth on top to let in air. Put your ant colony in it, including the queen, along with

the dirt from the anthill. Add ordinary soil until the jar is about two-thirds full. Keep the soil moist, but not wet, by putting in a few drops of water when it looks dry. Fill a bottle cap with water for the ants to drink.

Keep the house covered when you aren't watching the ants at work. Ants like to work in the dark. You can cover it with black paper or cloth held on by rubber bands. Handle the house with care, and don't jar or jiggle it.

Food: Small bits of sugar, peanuts, apples, and bananas every few days. Remove uneaten food each time you put in new food.

Praying Mantises, Grasshoppers, and Walkingsticks

Praying mantises and grasshoppers are usually found on grass and in grain fields. Look for walkingsticks on trees. Sometimes you can pick up these insects with your fingers, but a collecting net like the one shown on the next page is useful.

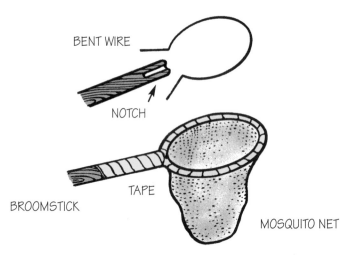

BENT WIRE

NOTCH

BROOMSTICK

TAPE

MOSQUITO NET

You can also catch many types of insects by using a stick to shake a bush so they will fall off. Hold an umbrella upside down under the bush or spread a large cloth on the ground to catch them. To catch night-flying moths and other insects, hang up an old sheet and shine a flashlight on it. The insects will be attracted to the light and land on the sheet.

Cage for a praying mantis

You'll need metal screening and a large round tin can with a plastic lid. The screening will be the top of the cage. Cut the screening so it is 12 inches high and long enough to go around the can and overlap 1 inch. Make a tube from the screening, to fit inside the can. Lace it together with wire.

Set the wire tube in the can. Fill the bottom of the can with plaster of paris. Push a branch into the plaster of paris before it hardens. The can's plastic lid goes on top of the screen tube.

Food: Flies, small insects, tiny bits of raw liver, chopped meat. The mantis prefers live food.

Water: Put in a bottle cap.

Note: In some states it is against the law to confine a praying mantis. Make sure you check your state's laws.

Grasshoppers and walkingsticks

Cover the bottom of a plastic jar with 1 inch of soil. Cover this with grass sod. (Water the grass occasionally.) Punch air holes in the cover.

Food: Grass for grasshoppers. Walkingsticks eat the leaves of oak, locust, cherry, and walnut trees. Supply water, too.

Moths and Butterflies

These amazing insects have four stages in their lives.

1. **Egg.** Egg masses are on the undersides of leaves or grass blades.
2. **Larva.** A larva (caterpillar) emerges from the egg.
3. **Pupa.** During this stage, the larva develops into an insect with wings. There is a difference between moths and butterflies in the pupal stage:

   ■ A typical moth caterpillar spins a soft silky covering around itself and becomes dormant (goes to sleep). The covering is called a *cocoon*. (See page 379.) Some cocoons have twigs or leaves attached to the outside.

Naturalist

■ A butterfly larva doesn't spin a cocoon (except for a few kinds of butterflies, like the skippers). The butterfly's body changes, forming a firm outer case called the *chrysalis*. It is also dormant.

4. **Moth or butterfly.** In the spring or summer, an adult moth or butterfly emerges. Butterflies come out more quickly than moths.

Monarch Butterfly

Collecting moth and butterfly larvae

Many larvae blend in with their surroundings, so look closely to find a green larva on a leaf. Other larvae may have bold patterns, like the monarch butterfly larva with its black, yellow, and white stripes. Some larvae have hairs or spines sticking out. Be careful, because in some species the hairs can irritate your skin or the spines can sting.

Use a wide-mouthed jar with a screw top. Punch air holes in the top. Put in a branch or twig and some leaves of the tree or shrub on which you found the larva. Keep a fresh supply of the same leaves in the jar until the larva stops eating. Then it will enter the pupal stage (cocoon or chrysalis). Later it will emerge as a butterfly or moth. Be prepared to release it at that time.

Starting with a cocoon or chrysalis

Look for the cocoons of moths and the chrysalises of butterflies in early spring before trees and shrubs have leaves. You'll find them hanging from branches or twigs. Cut away part of the twig.

Keep the cocoon in clean, covered jar. Punch air holes in the cover. Soon you'll see a miracle—a moth or butterfly emerging. Release the butterfly or moth very soon so that it can find the food it needs.

Moth Cocoon

Aquariums

Perhaps you already have an aquarium for tropical fish at home. Even if you do, it's fun to make one for fish or water animals you have collected from a stream or pond.

JOINTED HANDLE, 4½' TO 5½' LONG

DIP NET, ½" MESH

BAIT CAN OR JAR FULL OF POND WATER FOR
COLLECTING TADPOLES

Use a fish bowl or a square-sided aquarium. Make a dip net to catch small fish along the edge of a pond and put them in your aquarium with water from the pond.

Tadpoles

In the spring, you can catch tadpoles in ponds and watch them grow into frogs or toads in your aquarium. Prepare your aquarium by putting a layer of sand and rocks on the bottom. Plant a few aquatic plants in the sand. You can buy them at tropical fish stores. Fill the aquarium with water from a pond. Put in some rocks—they'll be needed later.

Catch two or three tadpoles and put them in. As the tadpoles grow, you'll see the first hint of legs. Feed the tadpoles soft insects, earthworms, grasshoppers, flies, and crickets.

Tadpole's Growth

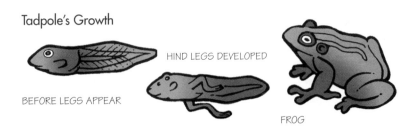

HIND LEGS DEVELOPED

BEFORE LEGS APPEAR

FROG

380

Watch for the legs to appear, because when your tadpoles start looking like frogs or toads, they can no longer breathe in the water. Lower the water level so they can climb out on the rocks. Feed the maturing frogs or toads mealworms, which you can buy at pet shops.

Make a support for your terrarium. Use lathing strips and nail them to a wood block.

Terrariums

One kind of terrarium is a small garden of plants in a big bottle or jar with the lid on it. You can also turn an aquarium into a terrarium.

The terrarium shown here is simple. You seal it up, and it will support plant life for two or three months.

Use a wide-mouthed gallon jar and build a base to fit it. Put in ½ inch of sand or fine gravel. Sprinkle ½ inch of charcoal chips over that. On top of the charcoal, put 2 cups of rich soil. If the soil in your area is poor, use potting soil from a garden center.

Plant small tropical plants that thrive in low light and high humidity, like aluminum plant, flame violet, and artillery plant. Ask about small tropical plants at a garden center.

Mist the plants lightly with water before screwing on the lid. You shouldn't need to water them again because the moisture will circulate in the closed jar.

Keep the terrarium where it will get indirect sunlight each day. Don't put it in direct sunlight because the container will heat up too much.

If you want a cactus terrarium, it should have a wide open top so moisture gets out instead of staying inside. (Cactus plants can't take high humidity.) Or you can plant cacti in a dish garden. Any container two or three inches deep will work. Use soil recommended for the cactus plants you choose.

Handle the plants carefully so the spines don't stick your hands.

Cacti need water, but not too often. Give them bright indirect light, and turn the container so all the plants get light.

Don't fertilize any terrarium plants, or they may outgrow their containers.

Visiting Nature Centers

If your area has a museum of natural history, a nature center, or a zoo, visit it. At a natural history museum, you'll see many wonderful exhibits about nature. The museum will have displays of birds and mammals that are hard to spot in the wild.

The museum may also have skeletons and likenesses of creatures that lived thousands of years ago.

A nature center has indoor exhibits and an outdoor area where you can hike and see trees and plants that grow wild in the area.

At a zoo you can get a fairly close view of many animals and birds from all over the world, some that are rarely seen by humans. A day at a nature center or zoo is a lot of fun.

Bird Feeders

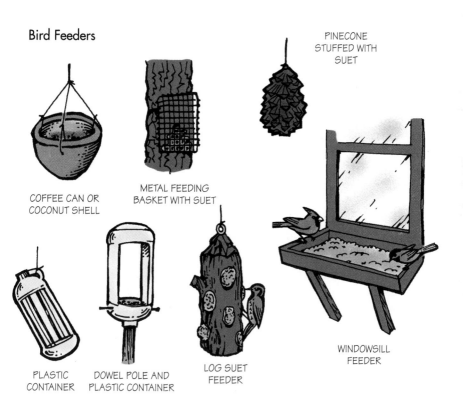

PINECONE STUFFED WITH SUET

COFFEE CAN OR COCONUT SHELL

METAL FEEDING BASKET WITH SUET

PLASTIC CONTAINER

DOWEL POLE AND PLASTIC CONTAINER

LOG SUET FEEDER

WINDOWSILL FEEDER

Bird Watching

An easy way to watch birds is to bring them to your yard by setting out a bird feeder. You may also build a bird nesting box and put it near your window for a close-up view of birds.

Some simple bird feeders are shown on the previous page. The log, pinecone, and basket are for feeding suet (hard fat from beef or mutton) or peanut butter.

Fill other types of feeders with seed that is sold as food for birds. Some birds may like small pieces of fruit or bread crumbs. See what kind of birds come to your feeder.

Borrow a field guide to birds from a library so you can identify the birds you see. Keep a record of the birds for at least one week.

Here are some things to notice about birds:

- **Marks.** The chickadee's black cap and bib, the downy woodpecker's red spot on the back of the head. Marks help you remember the bird.

- **Wings.** Pointed, rounded?

- **Tail.** Long or short? Rounded, square, or forked?

- **Bill.** Short bills are good for cracking seeds. Long pointed bills are good for digging in bark for insects.

- **Toes.** Most birds have four toes—three pointing forward and one back; but tree-climbing woodpeckers have two forward, two back.

- **Flight and behavior.** The starling flies straight as an arrow, but the goldfinch dips up and down. The nuthatch hops down trees headfirst.

- **Song.** In spring, the black-capped chickadee's song sounds like "Fee-bee." The song sparrow gives three sharp whistles, and then a chirp. If you can imitate the sound, it may draw a bird closer; so can kissing the back of your hand to make a chirp.

Bird Flyways

Some birds, like starlings, blue jays, sparrows, and nighthawks, stay in one area all their lives. Other kinds of birds migrate, flying south each fall to warmer places to spend the winter. They return to nest and live in their northern homes each spring.

Many birds that migrate use regular main routes. These routes are called *flyways*. The map shows the four main flyways in North America.

You don't have to live on a flyway to see birds moving in the spring and fall. Some will pass over your town. But most flocks of birds, like geese and ducks, use the flyways. These are their highways between winter and summer homes.

Poisonous Plants

As a naturalist and camper, you should know the poisonous plants in your area. Avoid them!

Three common poisonous plants are shown here. If you touch them, your skin may get red and itchy. If you think you have touched a poisonous plant, wash the spot with soap and water.

Notice that poison oak and poison ivy have three leaflets on the end of stems. They all also have white or whitish fruit. That's why Scouts say, "Leaflets three, let it be; berries white, poisonous sight."

Poison Oak

Poison Sumac

Poison Ivy

Venomous Reptiles

Snakes and other reptiles will usually do their best to stay out of your way. But if you stumble over one, it may bite.

Most snakes and reptiles don't have poison in their bite. The few that do are listed here.

Gila monster: This lizard grows to about 2 feet long. The lighter part of the pattern is white or yellow. It is found in parts of Nevada and Utah and down into Mexico.

Coral snake: Grows to about 2 feet long. It is ringed with red, yellow, and black bands. (The red and yellow bands touch—remember the saying "red on yellow kill a fellow.") Most coral snake species are found in Central and South America, but two are found in the United States. The harlequin or bead coral snake is found in some southeastern states, and the Arizona coral snake is found in southern New Mexico and Arizona.

Eastern diamondback rattlesnake: Sometimes grows to 7 feet in length. It is found along the Atlantic coast from North Carolina to Florida and west to Louisiana. It is never more than 100 miles from the coast.

Western diamondback rattlesnake: Often grows to 7 feet in length. It lives in the southwestern United States, from Missouri and eastern Texas to southeastern California.

Timber rattlesnake: Is less than 6 feet in length. It ranges from Maine to Texas, but its numbers are now greatly reduced.

Prairie rattlesnake: About 3 feet in length. Sometimes it grows to 5 feet. It lives in the western half of the United States.

Sidewinder or horned rattlesnake: Found in the deserts of the Southwest.

Water moccasin (cottonmouth): Found in or near water from southeastern Virginia to Florida. It can be seen westward to east Texas and north as far as southwestern Illinois. It sometimes grows as long as 6 feet.

Copperhead: Not often longer than 4 feet, it lives in most southeastern states. It can be found as far north as Massachusetts and Pennsylvania and westward to Illinois and Texas.

Watching Animals in the Wild

Take a nature hike with your family or den and see how many wild creatures you can spot. Look for birds, snakes, turtles, fish, and mammals.

Be as quiet as you can. Animals will hide if they see, hear, or smell you. Here are a few tips.

Mammals: Look for rabbits, squirrels, woodchucks, mice, and other small animals. In muddy spots around streams, you may see tracks. See if you can identify the animal that made the tracks.

Turtles: Look around ponds and streams. Some kinds of turtles will bite, so approach them with care.

Snakes: Look under logs, leaf piles, rocks, and sawdust piles. Be careful. Don't handle the snake unless an expert tells you it is not venomous. Don't harm the snake.

Fish: It is very hard to spot fish unless they are in shallow water. That is because the light bounces off the water, making it hard to see far down.

To see better under water, make the waterscope shown here. Use it by lying on your stomach on a low dock. Put the end of the waterscope into the water and look through the top.

Waterscope

WATER-PROOF TAPE

TIN CANS WIRED AND TAPED TOGETHER

FOR SAFETY, PUT TAPE ALONG THE VIEWING EDGES.

PLASTIC OR GLASS DISH OR JAR

Ecosystems

An ecosystem is a community of plants and animals living in an environment that supplies what they need for life.

There are many types of ecosystems. For example, a forest, a desert, and a wetland each contain different combinations of plants, animals, soils, and water sources.

In an ecosystem, plants and animals depend on their environment and on each other. Energy and food flow through the community in a *food chain*.

The sun: Without the sun, there would be no life on earth. The sun's energy flows through a cycle in the ecosystem. Plants are the first to use this energy.

Producers: All green plants—trees, shrubs, grasses, flowers, etc.—use the sun's energy to grow. Plants also take up nutrients and minerals from the soil. The plants produce leaves, bark, fruits, nuts, and seeds that many animals eat.

Consumers are animals that use the stored energy, nutrients, and minerals in their food to grow and to maintain their health.

■ **Primary consumers:** Plant-eating animals are called herbivores. They're the primary consumers in the ecosystem because they're the first to benefit by eating the producers. Examples: Rabbits, squirrels, deer, seed-eating birds, grasshoppers. On farms, cattle are primary consumers.

- **Secondary consumers:** Animals that eat other animals are meat-eaters or *carnivores*. In an ecosystem, they're secondary consumers, because they benefit from the energy and nutrients stored in their prey (the plant-eaters). Examples: Hawks and owls eat mice and rabbits. A mountain lion hunts deer and smaller animals.

- Some consumers eat both plants and animals. They're called *omnivores*. The gray fox hunts rabbits, mice, voles, birds, and insects, but it also eats blackberries, grapes, persimmons, and grass. Humans who eat meat and plants, such as fruits, vegetables, and grain products, are omnivores too.

Decomposers: These are the fungi, lichens, bacteria, and insects that break down dead plants and animals. This returns organic matter and minerals to the soil, making them available to trees and other plants—the producers. Nature is a good recycler.

The Balance of Nature

When you figure out the food chain in an ecosystem, you can see how the animals, plants, and their habitat are connected. The

Naturalist

ecosystem is in balance when all the necessary parts of its community are present. Animals are able to find food and have healthy young.

Nature is out of balance when there is not enough habitat and food for animals to survive. After some natural events, like a forest fire started by lightning, the original ecosystem may slowly recover. Nature eventually adjusts the balance.

The needs and plans of humans often alter the balance of nature quickly and permanently. When people clear forest and brush and turn it into agricultural land, much of the animal life may disappear from the area, except for animals that can adapt to the farming environment. When a huge shopping center is built and surrounded by a paved parking lot, animals can't adapt to that environment. Pollution of air or water can damage or wipe out an ecosystem.

Losing one link of the food chain can upset the balance, too. Because wolves were seen as a threat to livestock, people killed them. Without these predators, the population of white-tailed deer increased tremendously, but their wild habitat decreased. Deer adapt well to environments like new housing developments. Some people enjoy watching deer near their homes, but others consider deer a nuisance when they graze in flower beds and destroy young trees by eating the bark.

You and the Balance of Nature

You are part of an ecosystem too, whether you live in wilderness or in a city. What can you do to protect the balance of nature?

You can help in small ways. When you want to see what lives under a rock, lift it carefully and replace it gently, so you don't destroy the creatures and their habitat. If you plant a garden of flowers that bees and butterflies like, you'll provide food for them. Can you think of other small ways you can help?

You can help in larger ways by joining local efforts to solve water and air pollution problems. Or your den can plant trees or clean up a stream.

Can you think of other ways to protect the balance of nature?

Naturalist Scoreboard

Requirements	Approved by:

Do Four of These:

1. Keep an "insect zoo" that you have collected. You might have crickets, ants, or grasshoppers. Study them for a while and then release them. _____

2. Set up an aquarium or terrarium. Keep it for at least a month. _____

3. Visit a museum of natural history, nature center, or zoo with your family, den, or pack. Tell what you saw. _____

4. Watch for birds in your yard, neighborhood, or town for one week. Identify the birds you see and write down where and when you saw them. _____

5. Learn about the bird flyways closest to your home. Find out which birds use these flyways. _____

6. Learn to identify poisonous plants and venomous reptiles found in your area. _____

7. Watch six wild animals (snakes, turtles, fish, birds, or mammals) in the wild. Describe the kind of place (forest, field, marsh, yard, or park) where you saw them. Tell what they were doing. _____

8. Give examples of _____

   - A producer, a consumer, and a decomposer in the food chain of an ecosystem

   - One way humans have changed the balance of nature

   - How you can help protect the balance of nature

Outdoor Group

Outdoorsman

To go camping, you need skills that will help you feel at home in the outdoors. When you earn the Outdoorsman activity badge, you'll learn about building campfires, cooking, setting up tents, making outdoor beds, tying knots, and many other skills.

You'll have a chance to use your new camping skills with a friend, your family, or your Webelos den. You may visit a Boy Scout troop activity to learn how Boy Scouts use their outdoor skills.

The outdoors is calling you. Have fun!

Do Five of These:

1. Show your ability to tie the following knots:
   - Square knot
   - Bowline
   - Clove hitch
   - Two half hitches
   - Taut-line hitch

2. Pitch a tent using two half hitches and a taut-line hitch. Make a ground bed. Sleep in your tent for at least one night, if your parent allows you to do this.

3. With your adult partner, take part in a Webelos overnighter or camp overnight with a Boy Scout troop.

4. Help with a two-night campout away from home with your family. Or go on two one-night campouts with your family.

5. With your family or Webelos den, plan and take part in an evening outdoor activity that includes a campfire.

6. Help cook your own lunch or supper outdoors with a parent or another adult. Clean up afterward.

7. Know and practice the rules of outdoor fire safety.

8. Visit a nearby Boy Scout camp with your den.

When you pass each requirement, ask your den leader or counselor to initial your Outdoorsman scoreboard on page 412.

Whipping a Rope

Ropes are made of twisted fibers. When a rope is cut, the fibers separate. You can whip the ends in place with string so the rope won't unravel.

Cut off the part that has already unraveled. Take a piece of strong string, dental floss, or thin twine at least 2 feet long. Make it into a loop and place it at one end of the rope, with one end of the string pointing in the same direction as the rope end and the other end of the string pointing the opposite way.

Wrap the string tightly around the rope starting ¼ inch from the rope end. When the whipping is as wide as the rope is thick, pull out the string ends hard and trim them off.

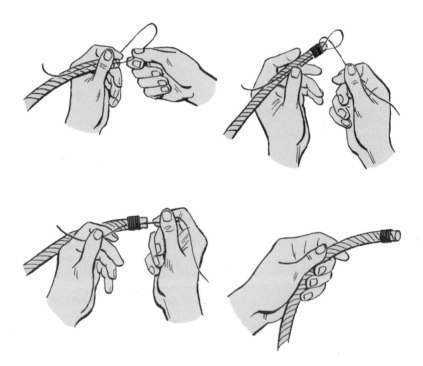

Camp Knots

You'll use rope for many purposes when you go camping. Practice these knots. They'll come in handy in different situations.

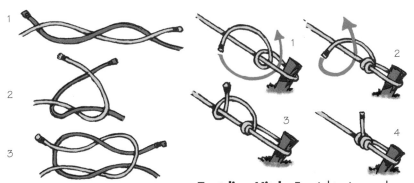

Square Knot: For tying two ropes together and for tying bandages in first aid.

Taut-line Hitch: For tightening and loosening a rope easily and for use on tent guy lines. Tighten or loosen it by pushing the hitch up or down.

Clove Hitch: For tying a rope to a tree or post.

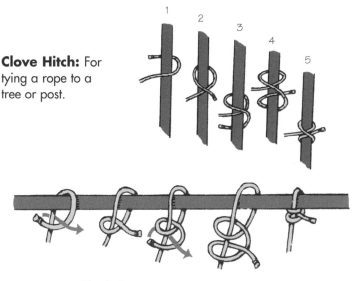

Two Half Hitches: For tying a rope to a post or ring. It is strong but is easy to loosen.

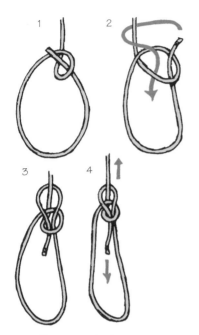

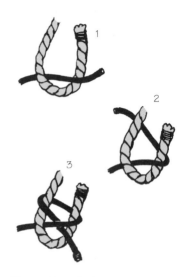

Sheet Bend: For tying two ropes together, especially when one is thicker than the other.

Bowline: Used when you want a loop that will not slip or close up. It is often used in rescue work.

Camping Out in a Yard

Camping is living outdoors. You can learn how to camp by starting with backyard camping. Most good campers practice skills close to home first.

With a parent's permission, set up a camp in your own backyard if you have one or in a friend's backyard. Requirement 2 says spend at least one night there, if you can. If you're not allowed to sleep outside, you can still practice setting up a camp.

You'll make your own simple tent and a comfortable bed on the ground.

With adult supervision, and only if the laws where you live allow it, you can build a safe fire, cook your meals, and clean up afterward. (See the Outdoor Code on pages 424–425.)

Homemade Tent

If your family doesn't own a tent, you can make one that won't cost much money. It will do for mild weather. You'll need a sheet of heavy-duty builder's plastic—about 8 by 9 feet. Tie a rope between two trees or posts, using clove hitches or two half hitches.

Drape the plastic over the rope and spread it like a tent. Hammer four stakes in the ground near each edge. Hold a stone under each corner of the sheet and tie a knot around it and the sheet. Then tie the rope to the stakes, and your sheet won't fly away. Be sure to leave both ends of your homemade tent open for ventilation, and make the tent wide enough for two people.

This tent will be fine for an overnight campout with a friend or parent.

Envelope Bed

You'll sleep on the ground for your backyard campout. Be comfortable. Feel the ground all around with your hands and remove all sticks and stones.

Spread your groundsheet—a piece of plastic that helps keep your bedding dry. An old shower curtain works fine.

If you have an air mattress, put it on the groundsheet. If you don't, use pieces of your clothing for padding under your head, the small of your back, and your knees.

To make your envelope bed, you need two blankets. Make it like this:

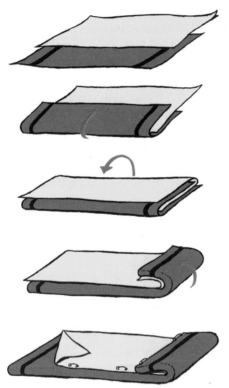

1. Lay the first blanket on the ground. Put the second blanket half on and half off the first one.

2. Fold the first blanket over the second. Leave half of the second showing.

3. Fold the remaining half of the second blanket over the first. This gives you two thicknesses over you and under you.

4. Fold the bottom of the blankets up.

5. Fasten the blanket envelope with big blanket pins up both sides and at the bottom.

Camping Away From Home

Your Webelos den may have overnighters. Webelos Scouts and their adult partners camp out for one or two nights.

You may also have campouts with a Boy Scout troop. Perhaps your family goes camping, too.

No matter how you camp, you'll have a great time—if you are prepared.

Packing for a Campout

If you have a regular Scout pack, use that. If not, you can pack a laundry bag or suitcase.

Here's what you and your adult partner will need for a Webelos campout:

- Two waterproof groundsheets
- Two sleeping bags, or two blankets each, to make blanket beds
- Changes of underwear
- Changes of socks
- Pajamas, if you use them
- Knives, forks, spoons
- Plates, bowls, cups
- Cooking pot or pan
- Pliers for dipping dishes in hot rinse water
- Plastic sheet to air-dry dishes on
- Saw for fuel wood
- Matches in waterproof container
- Charcoal or camp stove if not using wood fire .
- Food for all camp meals
- A cooler to keep perishable foods cold
- Trash bag
- One or two flashlights with fresh batteries
- Toothbrushes and toothpaste
- Toilet paper
- Sweaters or jackets
- Ponchos or raincoats
- Bar soap
- Towels
- Extra pants and shirts, if rain is likely
- Extra pair of shoes
- Whistle
- *Webelos Scout Book*
- Bible, testament, or prayer book

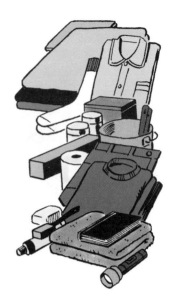

You may have to bring a tent, too, unless a Boy Scout troop is letting the den use its tents.

Wear your Webelos Scout uniform in camp.

Activities in Camp

At a den or troop overnighter, the leaders will suggest activities, such as working on outdoor activity badges, learning Scout skills, and playing outdoor games.

In the evening you may have a campfire program, with songs, skits, and other fun. Join in with your friends.

Be Safe and Comfortable

Here are tips to keep you safe and comfortable when you camp with your den or your family.

Snakes: Snakes are not likely to bother you if you don't bother them. Stay away from them.

Insects: A good bug spray keeps most of them away. Spray on exposed skin and also around your ankles and on your socks. Don't spray inside the tent because this may destroy the water-proofing.

Black Bear

Poisonous plants: Learn to recognize poison ivy, poison oak, and poison sumac (see page 386) and stay away from them. Never eat anything from the woods unless you know exactly what it is.

Animals: Animals can be drawn to your camp by the food you throw away or leave out. Bears are the most dangerous camp raiders and roadside beggars. **You must remember that they are not tame. Never let anyone get near them.**

Mice, chipmunks, raccoons, opossums, porcupines, and skunks add to the adventure of camping. Watch them and enjoy them, but **don't try to catch or pet them.**

Swimming: Always swim with an adult and use the buddy system (see page 242). Watch for drop-offs or holes and swift currents. Don't swim in polluted water! Don't get too much sun or get too tired. Use a sunscreen lotion to protect your skin.

Getting lost: Anyone can get lost, even adults. But some things can help you to not get lost or to keep you safer if you do:

- Always stay with a buddy.
- Let people know when you leave and where you are going.
- Carry a plastic trash bag poncho in case of rain.
- Carry a whistle to signal for help.

If you think you are lost, sit down in an open area. Relax. Blow your whistle every so often. Stay put.

Cooking in Camp

You and your adult partner may be expected to bring your own food to a den campout, unless the whole den cooks together. Choose foods that are easy to fix—and that you love to eat.

For most meals you'll need a fire. You may build it with wood or charcoal or use a camp stove. If you have a choice, use wood, because fire making is a skill you need to learn.

Building a Wood Fire

If your campsite already has a fireplace, use it. If it doesn't, you must make a safe fire site. Clear a circle 10 feet across, taking out anything that could burn—twigs, leaves, dry grass, pine needles. Your fire will be in the center of the circle. (See the illustration on the next page.) Have a pot of water nearby for emergencies and to extinguish the fire.

You will need three kinds of materials to make your fire:

Tinder: Stuff that flares up quickly when you touch a lighted match to it. It must be dry. Look for dead twigs on standing trees and tiny dry twigs on the ground. Dry weed tops are good, too.

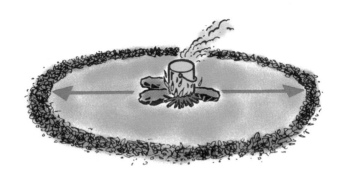

Kindling: Small branches about as thick as your thumb and 6 to 10 inches long. Snap dead branches off standing trees and pick up dry branches on the ground. They will catch the flame from the tinder.

Fuel wood: Larger dead branches you find on the ground. You may need a saw to cut them into pieces about a foot long. They provide the heat for cooking.

You don't need a big fire for cooking on a campout. Five to 10 pieces of fuel wood should be plenty.

Outdoor Fire Safety Rules

1. Follow all rules of your campsite.

2. Clear all burnable materials from your 10-foot fire circle. Don't build the fire under overhanging branches of trees or shrubs or near roots of trees.

3. Never leave your fire unattended.

4. Have a pot or bucket of water nearby in case sparks start a fire away from the fire circle.

5. When you are finished cooking, make sure the fire is **DEAD OUT.** Spread the coals and ashes and sprinkle them with water. Stir and sprinkle until the site is cold. Feel it with your hand to make sure.

Making Your Fire Lay

Put your tinder in the center of the fire circle. Then arrange kindling in one of the ways shown here, so that the flames from the tinder will catch the kindling quickly.

When the kindling is burning, add a couple of pieces of fuel wood. As the fuel wood burns down to coals, add more fuel.

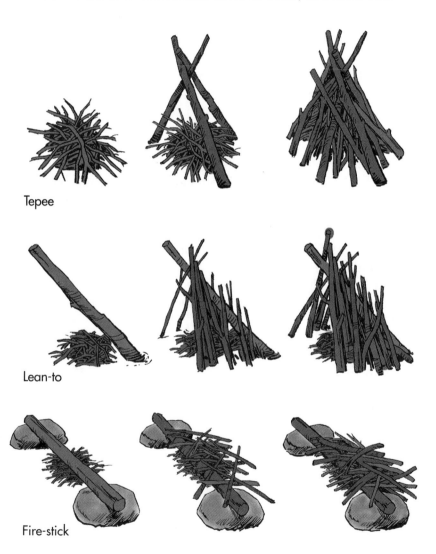

Tepee

Lean-to

Fire-stick

You can use logs or big flat rocks to hold your pots and pans. Don't use sandstone or wet rocks. They may explode if they get hot.

Rock Fireplace

What to Cook

Keep meals simple on your first few campouts. Consider cooking hamburgers, hot dogs, bacon and eggs, or canned food like spaghetti, beans, and vegetables.

You might prepare a supper dish in aluminum foil at home before you go to camp. Here's how to do it:

You need an 18-by-24-inch sheet of heavy-duty aluminum foil, or two sheets of regular foil.

Use a piece of meat about the size of your hand. It could be ground beef, steak, chicken, or fish. Flatten ground beef. Lay the meat near the center of the foil. Slice a small onion and cut a small potato in thin slices and arrange them over the meat. Add peas, beans, or thinly sliced carrots.

Now fold the foil into a package. Join the edges and fold them over tightly so steam can't escape.

Take the foil dinners to camp in a cooler so the food won't spoil. About a half-hour before supper, lay the packages directly on the coals of the fire. Turn them over after 15 minutes and cook them another 10 minutes. Dinner should be ready. Eat it from the foil.

Note: To protect against food poisoning, always wash your hands before you handle food. Wash all vegetables and fruits. Make sure that food packets stay cool in the cooler and that food is thoroughly cooked before you eat it.

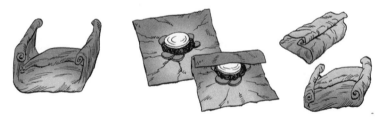

Cleanup

Every Scout camper learns to wash dishes and clean up after eating. Do your part in the cleanup job.

Make sure your cooking fire is **DEAD OUT.** Pick up garbage and trash and put it in a garbage bag to take out of the campsite.

Put all leftover food, milk, and other drinks back in the camp cooler or food box.

Visit a Scout Camp

One of your Webelos overnighters may be held at a Boy Scout camp. If not, ask your den leader to take the den to camp for a visit.

When you become a Boy Scout, you'll go to Scout camp often. Now is a good time to see what Scout camp has to offer. You'll have a great time there!

Hiking With Your Den

As a Webelos Scout you may go on nature hikes, rock hunts, and other outdoor activities.

Never go hiking alone. Go with your den leader and den chief. Start with a short hike. Take it easy and pay careful attention to your surroundings. Stop to look at trees and plants. Try to name as many kinds as you can. Look at the houses and buildings. Count the different kinds of birds you see.

When you sit down for a rest, look around. Find grasses that aren't the same. Count the different bugs you find. You'll enjoy your hike more if you notice everything. Some people hike as if they were walking through a tunnel. They never see a thing.

Watch for signs and landmarks so you can find your way back.

Your First Hike

For your first hike, choose a destination about a mile from your starting place. It may be a park, high hill, pond, or lake. Perhaps a grove of trees or a picnic area is nearby. Out and back would be a 2-mile trip—a pretty good start. Set your own pace.

Hike for 15 minutes. Rest for 5 minutes. Then try a 20-minute walk and a 10-minute rest. Stay together. Try different speeds until you find the pace that's best for all the hikers.

Walk a little every week. Go farther each time. This makes you stronger.

Face traffic when walking along a road. This means walking on the left side. Walk single file when the whole den goes. Don't hike at night. If for some reason you are ever out walking at night, carry a flashlight and wear white or reflective clothing.

What to Wear

The Webelos Scout uniform is ideal for hiking. Take along a raincoat or poncho in case it rains.

Shoes: You depend on your shoes to get you to your destination and back. Choose them carefully. Take good care of them. A hightop shoe or boot is best because it keeps out gravel and sand.

It's very important that your hiking shoes fit well. If they don't, you'll be sure to get blisters. The shoes should be fairly tight around your heel. There should be room to wiggle your toes.

- Never go hiking in new shoes. Break them in first by wearing them part of every day for a week or more.

- To keep leather shoes soft and partly waterproof, rub them with saddle soap. Do this before and after every hike.

- When leather shoes get wet, wipe them with paper or old socks. Dry them slowly, away from direct heat.

Socks: Socks are almost as important as shoes. They soak up moisture. They also cushion your feet. Socks made of wool, polypropylene, or a wool/nylon blend work well. Take an extra pair on a hike. Then you can put on clean socks before you start back. This dry pair will feel great. Don't use socks with holes or holes that have been darned. They start blisters.

Sun Safety

Too much sun can be dangerous. Follow these tips from the American Academy of Dermatology to stay safe in the sun:

- Try to stay out of the sun between 10 A.M. and 4 P.M. when the sun's rays are the strongest.

- Use lots of sunscreen with a sun protection factor (SPF) of at least 15. Put on more every two hours when you're outdoors, even on cloudy days.

- Wear protective, tightly woven clothing, such as a long-sleeved shirt and pants.

- Wear a 4-inch-wide broad-brimmed hat and sunglasses with lenses that protect you against the sun's ultraviolet rays (called UV protection).

- Stay in the shade whenever you can.

- Stay away from reflective surfaces, which can reflect up to 85 percent of the sun's damaging rays.

Outdoorsman Scoreboard

Requirements   **Approved by:**

Do Five of These:

1. Show your ability to tie the following knots: _____
   - Square knot
   - Bowline
   - Clove hitch
   - Two half hitches
   - Taut-line hitch

2. Pitch a tent using two half hitches and a taut-line hitch. Make a ground bed. Sleep in your tent for at least one night, if your parent allows you to do this.   _____

3. With your adult partner, take part in a Webelos overnighter or camp overnight with a Boy Scout troop.   _____

4. Help with a two-night campout away from home with your family. Or go on two one-night campouts with your family.   _____

5. With your family or Webelos den, plan and take part in an evening outdoor activity that includes a campfire.   _____

6. Help cook your own lunch or supper outdoors with a parent or another adult. Clean up afterward.   _____

7. Know and practice the rules of outdoor fire safety.   _____

8. Visit a nearby Boy Scout camp with your den.   _____

Rank Advancement and Special Awards

Earning the Webelos Badge

The Webelos badge is the fourth rank in Cub Scouting (higher than Bobcat, Wolf, and Bear). You can start working on it as soon as you join a Webelos den. To earn the Webelos badge, you must be active in your den at least three months and complete the require-ments. The requirements are listed on the scoreboard on the following pages.

You'll be proud to reach Webelos rank and receive your badge at a pack meeting.

Webelos Badge Scoreboard

Requirements   **Approved by:**

1. Have an adult member of your family read the Webelos Scout Parent Guide that comes with this book (See pages 444–460) and sign here. _____

2. Be an active member of your Webelos den for three months. (Active means having good attendance, paying den dues, working on den projects.) _____

3. Know and explain the meaning of the Webelos badge. _____

4. Point out the three special parts of the Webelos Scout uniform. Tell when to wear the uniform and when not to wear it. _____

5. Earn the Fitness activity badge and two other activity badges from different activity badge groups. _____

6. Plan and lead a flag ceremony in your den. _____

7. Show that you know and understand the requirements to be a Boy Scout.

  ■ Understand and intend to live by the

      Scout Oath _____

      Scout Law _____

      Scout motto _____

      Scout slogan _____

  ■ Know the following and when to use them:

      Scout salute _____

      Scout sign _____

      Scout handclasp _____

  ■ Understand and agree to follow the Outdoor Code. _____

(Continued on next page)

Webelos Badge   **415**

8. Complete one of the following:

a. Earn the religious emblem of your faith* _____

OR

b. Do two of these:†

■ Attend the church, synagogue, mosque, or other religious organization of your choice; talk with your religious leader about your beliefs; and tell your family and Webelos den leader what you learned. _____

■ Tell how your religious beliefs fit in with the Scout Oath and Scout Law. Discuss this question with your family and Webelos den leader: What character-building traits do your beliefs and the Scout Oath and Scout Law have in common? _____

■ With your religious leader, discuss and write down two things you think will help you draw nearer to God. Do these things. _____

(1) _____

_____

(2) _____

_____

* If you earned your faith's religious emblem when you were a Wolf or Bear Cub Scout, you must do two of the other religious requirements listed under (b). Webelos religious emblems are listed on pages 434–435.

† Completion of requirement (b) does not qualify a youth to receive the religious emblem of his faith.

- Pray to God or meditate reverently each day as taught by your family and by your church, synagogue, or religious group. Do this for at least one month. _____

- Under the direction of your religious leader, do an act of service for someone else. Talk about your service with your family and Webelos den leader. Tell them how it made you feel. _____

- List at least two ways you believe you have lived according to your religious beliefs. _____

(1) _____

_____

(2) _____

_____

The Meaning of the Webelos Badge

The Webelos badge has a Webelos emblem on it, which contains a blue *W*, the word *Webelos*, and a small Scout badge at the bottom. It means you are on the Webelos trail that leads from Cub Scouting to Boy Scouting.

The Parts of Your Uniform

Webelos Scouts may wear either the blue uniform they wore as Cub Scouts or the tan shirt and olive green trousers they will wear as Boy Scouts. You and your family decide which one you will wear.

With either basic uniform, Webelos Scouts wear the Webelos cap, Webelos neckerchief, and Webelos neckerchief slide.

When to Wear the Uniform

Wear your uniform

■ To all den meetings and pack meetings

■ On campouts and other den activities

■ At den service projects

■ During Scouting's Anniversary Week in February

The Webelos uniform may *not* be worn

■ When you are involved in any distinctly political activity

■ When you are appearing on the stage professionally

■ When you are participating in demonstrations not authorized by the Boy Scouts of America

Planning and Leading a Flag Ceremony

For Webelos badge requirement 6, you must plan and lead a den flag ceremony using the U.S. flag. Here are some ideas:

■ Have the Webelos Scouts give the Cub Scout salute and repeat the Pledge of Allegiance to the flag.

■ Parade the U.S. flag and the den flag past the line of Webelos Scouts, who stand at attention and salute.

■ Plan a ceremony on the history of the flag. Each boy in the den can make and color a different paper flag to show how our present flag developed out of earlier flags.

■ Have the Webelos Scouts march past the flag, giving the proper salute.

Understanding the Requirements for Joining Boy Scouts

Working on the Webelos badge helps you find out about values important to Boy Scouts and things they know, including the Scout Oath and Law. By practicing the Boy Scout salute, sign, and handclasp now for requirement 7, you'll already know them when you become a Boy Scout.

The Scout Oath

On my honor I will do my best to do my duty to God and my country and to obey the Scout Law; to help other people at all times; to keep myself physically strong, mentally awake, and morally straight.

The Meaning of the Scout Oath

When you say "On my honor," that's like saying "I promise." It also means you are the kind of person who always tries to do what is right and you can be trusted to keep this promise. No one can take your honor from you, but you can throw it away by breaking your promise and doing what you know is wrong.

Notice that the Scout Oath has three basic parts. Let's look at what they mean.

TO DO MY DUTY TO GOD AND MY COUNTRY AND TO OBEY THE SCOUT LAW

Your family and religious leaders teach you to know and serve God. By following these teachings, you do your duty to God.

Men and women of the past worked to make America great, and many gave their lives for their country. By being a good family member and a good citizen, by working for your country's good and obeying its laws, you do your duty to your country.

Obeying the Scout Law means living by its 12 points. The Scout Law is explained below.

TO HELP OTHER PEOPLE AT ALL TIMES

Many people need help. A cheery smile and a helping hand make life easier for others. By doing a Good Turn daily and helping when you're needed, you prove yourself a Scout and do your part to make this a better world.

TO KEEP MYSELF PHYSICALLY STRONG, MENTALLY AWAKE, AND MORALLY STRAIGHT

Keeping yourself physically strong means taking good care of your body. Eat the right foods and build your strength. **Staying mentally awake** means learn all you can, be curious, and ask questions. Being **morally straight** means to live your life with honesty, to be clean in your speech and actions, and to be a person of strong character.

The Scout Law

A Scout is trustworthy, loyal, helpful, friendly, courteous, kind, obedient, cheerful, thrifty, brave, clean, and reverent.

The Meaning of the Scout Law

The Scout Law has 12 points. Each is a goal for every Scout. He does his best to live up to the Law. It is not always easy to do, but a Scout always tries.

A Scout is TRUSTWORTHY.

A Scout tells the truth and keeps his promises. Honesty is part of his code of conduct. People can depend on him.

A Scout is LOYAL.

A Scout is true to his family, friends, Scout leaders, school, nation, and the community of the world.

A Scout is HELPFUL.

A Scout is concerned about other people. He willingly helps others without pay or other reward.

A Scout is FRIENDLY.

A Scout is a friend to all. He is a brother to other Scouts and all the people of the world. He seeks to understand others. He respects those with ideas and customs different from his own.

A Scout is COURTEOUS.

A Scout is polite to everyone. He knows that good manners make it easier for people to get along together.

A Scout is KIND.

A Scout understands that there is strength in being gentle. He treats others as he wants to be treated. He is never cruel to living things.

A Scout is OBEDIENT.

A Scout follows the rules of his family, school, and troop. He obeys the laws of his community and country. If he thinks some rules and laws are unfair, he tries to change them in an orderly manner, rather than disobeying them.

A Scout is CHEERFUL.

A Scout looks for the bright side of things. He cheerfully does tasks that come his way. He tries to make others happy.

A Scout is THRIFTY.

A Scout works to pay his way and to help others. He saves for the future. He protects and conserves natural resources. He carefully uses time and property.

A Scout is BRAVE.

A Scout can face danger even if he is afraid. He has the courage to stand for what he thinks is right even if others laugh at him or threaten him.

A Scout is CLEAN.

A Scout keeps his body and mind fit and clean. He admires those who believe in living by these same ideals. He helps keep his home and community clean.

A Scout is REVERENT.

A Scout is reverent toward God. He is faithful in his religious duties. He respects the beliefs of others.

The Scout Motto

The Scout motto is "Be Prepared." Someone once asked Robert Baden-Powell, the founder of Scouting, "Be prepared for what?" Baden-Powell replied, "Why, for any old thing." That's the idea. The Scout motto means you are always ready to do your duty and to face danger, if necessary, to help others.

The Scout Slogan

The Scout slogan is "Do a Good Turn Daily." This doesn't mean you're supposed to do one Good Turn during the day and then stop. It means you do *at least* one Good Turn a day. It means looking for chances to help and then helping quietly, without boasting about it.

Always remember that a Good Turn is an *extra* act of kindness—something you go out of your way to do.

The Scout Sign

The Scout sign identifies you as a Scout anywhere in the world. Use it whenever you give the Scout Oath or Scout Law.

The three upraised fingers stand for the three parts of the Scout Oath. The thumb and little finger touch. They stand for the bond between all Scouts.

The Scout Salute

The Scout salute signifies respect and courtesy. You use it to salute the flag of the United States of America. During some ceremonies, you may also salute your Webelos den leaders or Boy Scout leaders.

To give the Scout salute, place the fingers of your right hand as you do for the Scout sign. Bring the hand smartly up to your head, palm facing down, until your forefinger touches the edge of your cap above the right eye. If you aren't wearing a cap, touch your forehead above the right eye. When the salute is completed, snap your hand down quickly to your side.

The Scout Handclasp

To give the Scout handclasp, use your left hand instead of the right. The Scout handclasp is a token of friendship. That's why you use your left hand—it's the one nearest your heart.

Outdoor Code

As an American, I will do my best to—

BE CLEAN IN MY OUTDOOR MANNERS.
I will treat the outdoors as a heritage.
I will take care of it for myself and
others. I will keep my trash and
garbage out of lakes, streams,
fields, woods, and roadways.

BE CAREFUL WITH FIRE.
I will prevent wildfire. I will build my
fires only where they are appropriate.
When I have finished using a fire,
I will make sure it is cold out.
I will leave a clean fire ring, or
remove all evidence of my fire.

BE CONSIDERATE IN THE OUTDOORS.
I will treat public and private property
with respect. I will use low-impact
methods of hiking and camping.

BE CONSERVATION-MINDED.
I will learn how to practice good
conservation of soil, waters, forests,
minerals, grasslands, wildlife,
and energy. I will urge others
to do the same.

BOY SCOUTS OF AMERICA

Rank Advancement

The Outdoor Code

As a Webelos Scout, you'll hike and camp out. As a Boy Scout, you'll be outdoors a lot more often. The Outdoor Code is a guide all Scouts use. Read it with your den leader and discuss what it means.

Outdoor Code

As an American, I will do my best to—be clean in my outdoor manners, be careful with fire, be considerate in the outdoors, and be conservation-minded.

Be clean in my outdoor manners: I will treat the outdoors as a heritage. I will take care of it for myself and others. I will keep my trash and garbage out of lakes, streams, fields, woods, and roadways.

Be careful with fire: I will prevent wildfire. I will build my fires only where they are appropriate. When I have finished using fire, I will make sure it is cold-out. I will leave a clean fire ring or remove all evidence of my fire.

Be considerate in the outdoors: I will treat public and private property with respect. I will use low-impact methods of hiking and camping.

Be conservation-minded. I will learn how to practice good conservation of soil, waters, forests, minerals, grasslands, wildlife, and energy. I will urge others to do the same.

The Scouting way is to leave no trace of your presence in the outdoors. Always take good care of nature.

Earning the Religious Emblem of Your Faith

If you decide to earn the religious emblem of your faith for requirement 8, you'll find information about that starting on page 434.

Earning the Compass Points Emblem

After you've earned the Webelos badge, you can earn the compass points emblem. It is awarded after you earn seven activity badges: four more in addition to the three you earned for the Webelos badge. Wear your compass points emblem attached to the button on the right pocket of your Webelos uniform shirt.

After you earn the compass points emblem, you'll receive a metal compass point for each four additional activity badges you earn. Pin these compass points on the emblem in the "E," "W," or "S" positions, in any order you choose.

You can earn the emblem and all three compass points by completing 19 activity badges, including the three required for the Webelos badge.

Compass Points Emblem Scoreboard

Webelos badge awarded on (date): _____

Activity badges earned for the Webelos badge:
(Earn Fitness and two others.)   1 _____Fitness_____

2 _____

3 _____

Activity badges earned for the compass points emblem: (After you earn the Webelos badge, earn four additional activity badges.)   1 _____

2 _____

3 _____

4 _____

Compass Points Scoreboard

Earn a *compass point* for each additional *four* activity badges you complete:

E

1 _____
2 _____
3 _____
4 _____

W

1 _____
2 _____
3 _____
4 _____

S

1 _____
2 _____
3 _____
4 _____

Earning the Arrow of Light Award

After you have earned the Webelos badge, you can continue working on the requirements for the Arrow of Light Award, which is Cub Scouting's

highest award. This award tells everyone you're ready to be a Boy Scout.

The Arrow of Light Award displays an American Indian sign for the sun and, below it, an arrow. The seven rays of the sun stand for each day of the week. They remind you to do your best every day as you follow the arrow that leads to Boy Scouting.

It will be a proud day for you when you receive the Arrow of Light Award. It is the only Cub Scout badge you can wear on your Boy Scout uniform.

The requirements are listed on the scoreboard on the following pages.

Arrow of Light Award Scoreboard

Requirements   **Approved by:**

1. Be active in your Webelos den for at least six months since completing the fourth grade (or for at least six months since becoming 10 years old), and earn the Webelos badge. _____

2. Show your knowledge of the requirements to become a Boy Scout by doing all of these:

   ■ Repeat from memory and explain in your own words the Scout Oath or Promise and the 12 points of the Scout Law. Tell how you have practiced them in your everyday life. _____

   ■ Give and explain the Scout motto, slogan, sign, salute, and handclasp. _____

   ■ Understand the significance of the First Class Scout badge. Describe its parts and tell what each stands for. _____

   ■ Tell how a Boy Scout uniform is different from a Webelos Scout uniform. _____

   ■ Tie the joining knot (square knot). _____

3. Earn five more activity badges in addition to the three you already earned for the Webelos badge. The total of eight activity badges must include:

   ■ Fitness (already earned for the Webelos badge) _____

   ■ Citizen _____

   ■ Readyman _____

   ■ At least one from the Outdoor Group _____

   ■ At least one from the Mental Skills Group _____

   ■ At least one from the Technology Group _____

   ■ Two more of your choice _____

See page 22 for the activity badge groups.

4. With your Webelos den, visit at least

   ■ one Boy Scout troop meeting,   _____

   ■ and one Boy Scout–oriented outdoor
     activity.   _____

5. Participate in a Webelos overnight campout
   or day hike.   _____

6. After you have completed all five of the
   above requirements, and after a talk with
   your Webelos den leader, arrange to visit,
   with your parent or guardian, a meeting of a
   Boy Scout troop you think you might like to
   join. Have a conference with the Scoutmaster. Complete and turn in a "Join Boy Scouting" application to the Scoutmaster during
   the conference.   _____

Working on the Arrow
of Light Award

You must have eight activity
badges to earn the Arrow of Light
Award. Three of them *must* be
Fitness (which you already
earned for the Webelos badge),
Citizen, and Readyman. Of the

other five, at least one must be from the Mental Skills Group, one
from the Outdoor Group, and one from the Technology Group.
Activity badge groups are shown on page 22.

Remember, the three activity badges you earned for the Webelos badge count in the total.

The other requirements should be easy, if you're active in your
den. Be sure to attend Webelos campouts and other den activities. Be sure to go along when your den visits a Boy Scout troop
meeting or other Boy Scout event.

Remember, the three activity badges you earned for the Webelos badge count in the total.

The other requirements should be easy, if you're active in your den. Be sure to attend Webelos campouts and other den activities. Be sure to go along when your den visits a Boy Scout troop meeting or other Boy Scout event.

The First Class Scout Badge

The First Class Scout badge is shown here.

The three-point design of the top part of the badge is like the north point of the compass sailors used long ago. These three points, like the three fingers in the Scout sign, stand for the three parts of the Scout Oath.

The main part of the badge shows that a Scout is able to point the right way in life as truly as the compass points north in the field.

The two stars on the right and left top points symbolize Scouting's ideals of truth and knowledge. Stars guide us by night and remind us of the Scout's outdoor life.

The eagle with the shield is the national emblem of the United States of America. It stands for freedom and readiness to defend that freedom.

The scroll with the Scout motto is turned up at the ends to suggest a Scout's smile as he does his duty.

The knot attached to the bottom of the scroll reminds you that as a Boy Scout, you promise to do a Good Turn for someone every day.

The Boy Scout Uniform

The basic Boy Scout uniform is a tan shirt and olive green trousers. The shirt may have either short or long sleeves. For summer you may wear the short-sleeved shirt, olive green shorts, and long (or short) socks.

Your hat will depend on the style worn by the troop you join. It may be a base-ball-style cap or a broad-brimmed campaign hat.

Each troop has its own neckerchief design. Yours will be the one worn by your new troop.

Some of the insignia on your Boy Scout shirt are like those on your Webelos uniform. But on your right sleeve, you'll wear your patrol emblem. On your left

shirt pocket, you'll wear the highest Boy Scout rank you've earned (not all your ranks, as you did in Cub Scouts). Your Arrow of Light Award goes at the bottom of the left pocket. You'll wear red epaulets that attach to the shirt at the shoulder.

Wear your Boy Scout uniform with pride. It shows you are a good citizen and are ready and willing to help other people.

Your Religious Duties

Webelos badge requirement 8 concerns your religious duties. Many religious faiths have special emblems for Webelos Scouts that you can earn by doing certain requirements.

If you earned your faith's religious emblem when you were a Wolf or Bear Cub Scout, you must do two of the other religious requirements listed on page 416.

Religious Emblems for Webelos Scouts

Talk to your pack leaders or local council to find out how to contact the religious organizations listed below about religious emblems for Webelos Scouts.

If your faith isn't listed, it didn't have a religious emblem program for Webelos Scouts at the time this book was published.

Religious Organization	Webelos Scout Emblem
Armenian: Diocese of the Armenian Church of America (Eastern Diocese)	Saint Gregory
Association of Unity Churches	God in Me

Baha'i	Unity of Mankind
Baptist	God and Family
Buddhist	Metta
Christian Church (Disciples of Christ)	God and Family
Churches of Christ	Joyful Servant
Church of Jesus Christ of Latter-day Saints (LDS)	Faith in God
Eastern Orthodox	Chi Rho
Eastern-Rite Catholic Churches	Parvuli Dei
Episcopal	God and Family
First Church of Christ, Scientist (Christian Science)	God and Country
Hindu	Dharma
Islamic	Bismillah
Jewish	Aleph
Lutheran	God and Family
Meher Baba	Love for God
Polish National Catholic	Love of God *(Milosc Boga)*
Presbyterian Church (U.S.A.)	God and Family
Prostestant (Available to any Christian denomination.)	God and Family
Religious Society of Friends (Quakers)	That of God
Reorganized Church of Jesus Christ of Latter Day Saints	Light of the World
Roman Catholic	Parvuli Dei
The Salvation Army	Silver Crest, God and Family
United Church of Christ	God and Family
United Methodist	God and Family

Religious Emblems

Cub Scout World Conservation Award

As a Webelos Scout, you can earn the Cub Scout World Conservation Award. This is a special international award. (You may earn it only once while you are in Cub Scouting.) Use this scoreboard to keep track of your progress.

World Conservation Award Scoreboard

Webelos leader initials

1. Earned the Forester activity badge. _____

2. Earned the Naturalist activity badge. _____

3. Earned the Outdoorsman activity badge. _____

4. Participated in a den or pack conservation project. _____

Qualified to receive the World Conservation Award:

Date _____

Webelos leader signature _____

The Cub Scout Academics and Sports Program

If you were a Cub Scout before joining your Webelos den, you already may know about earning belt loops and pins in the Cub Scout Academics and Sports program. You can earn them by learning about and playing sports like basketball or soccer, or by investigating an academic area like math or art.

bicycling

You can earn some of these awards along with your pack or den. You can earn some on your own, or with your family or in your community.

The requirements for each subject are listed in *Cub Scout Academics and Sports Program Guide*, which is available from your den leader or your local council service center.

music

You can earn:

Belt loops for learning about and participating in an Academics or Sports area.

Academics and Sports pins by earning the belt loop and then completing additional requirements that have you explore more about the academic or sport area you are working on.

You can wear the belt loop on your uniform belt. Wear the pin on your ordinary clothes.

Some activity badges in this book ask you to earn a belt loop or pin: **Sportsman** requires two individual sports belt loops and two team sports belt loops. **Athlete** requires the Physical Fitness Sports pin. **Aquanaut** gives you a choice of earning the Swimming belt loop.

On to the Adventure of Boy Scouting!

Adventure! That's what Boy Scouting is. You're standing at the doorway to the most exciting adventures you can imagine.

Step into the world of Boy Scouting, and you'll hike along trails, canoe across misty lakes, and camp under the open sky. Smell fresh rain in the woods and fill your mouth with the taste of wild strawberries. At the end of a patrol bike hike, plunge into a cool mountain lake. Cook your meals over a camp stove.

Travel the back country without leaving a trace and live well with only what you carry in your pockets and pack. Observe wildlife close up and study nature all around you.

Sound inviting? As a Boy Scout, you can do all this and more.

Scouting is also a doorway to friendship. Boys you know might be joining your troop, and you'll meet a lot of other Scouts along the way. Scouting is a worldwide brotherhood many millions strong. Almost anywhere you go, you'll find Scouts excited about the same activities you enjoy.

Want to learn skills you can use outdoors? Scouts know how to find their way with a map and compass, how to stay warm and dry in stormy weather, and how to give proper first aid. When you master important Scouting skills, you can teach others what you know. Everyone helping everyone else—that's part of Scouting, too.

People have always relied on Scouts to **Be Prepared** in times of need. Your troop leaders will show you meaningful ways to help your family, community, nation, and world. The acts of kindness you perform every day will improve the lives of others. In an emergency, you'll be ready to do whatever the situation requires.

Outdoor adventures, service projects, leadership in your patrol and troop—Scouting will give you experiences and responsibilities that will help you mature. The Scout Oath and the Scout Law provide the guidelines you need to become a strong, confident adult. The knowledge and attitudes you develop as a Scout will be with you the rest of your life.

And Scouting is fun. You can look around during Scouting activities and see everyone sharing and learning.

Are you ready to get in on all the fun that Scouts have? Do you want to enjoy the adventures and friendship of a troop and patrol? It's all up to you!

Becoming a Boy Scout

In order to become a Boy Scout, you must:

■ Be a boy who has completed the fifth grade or who has earned the Arrow of Light Award, or be 11 years old but not yet 18.

■ Find a Boy Scout troop you want to join.

■ Complete the requirements to join the Boy Scouts. (You already learned most of these to earn the Arrow of Light Award!)

Troops Visited

Troop	Location	Date	Time	Leader	Phone

Scoutmaster's conference to complete requirements needed to join Boy Scouts was held on (date)_____

I received my Webelos Arrow of Light Award on _____

My graduation ceremony was conducted on _____

Webelos Advancement Tracking Chart

Aquanaut

Do all (two)
___1___2

Do any three
___3___4___5___6___7___8

Artist

Do any five
___1___2___3___4___5___6___7___8

Athlete

Do all (two)
___1___2

Do any five
___3___4___5___6___7___8___9

Citizen

Do all (seven)
___1___2___3___4___5___6___7

Do any two
___8___9___10___11___12___13___14___15___16

Communicator

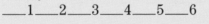

Do any seven
___1___2___3___4___5___6
___7___8___9___10___11___12___13___14

Craftsman

Do all (four)

___1 ___2 ___3 ___4

Engineer

Do any five

___1 ___2 ___3 ___4 ___5 ___6 ___7 ___8 ___9 ___10

Family Member

Do all (six)

___1 ___2 ___3 ___4 ___5 ___6

Do any two

___7 ___8 ___9 ___10 ___11 ___12

Fitness

Do any six

___1 ___2 ___3 ___4 ___5 ___6 ___7

Forester

Do any five

___1 ___2 ___3 ___4 ___5 ___6 ___7 ___8 ___9 ___10

Geologist

Do any five

___1 ___2 ___3 ___4 ___5 ___6 ___7

Handyman

Do any six

___1 ___2 ___3 ___4 ___5 ___6 ___7
___8 ___9 ___10 ___11 ___12 ___13 ___14

Naturalist

Do any four

___1 ___2 ___3 ___4 ___5 ___6 ___7 ___8

Outdoorsman

Do any five

___1 ___2 ___3 ___4 ___5 ___6 ___7 ___8

Readyman

Do all (six)

___1 ___2 ___3 ___4 ___5 ___6

Do any two

___7 ___8 ___9 ___10 ___11 ___12

Scholar

Do any three

___1 ___2 ___3 ___4

Do any three

___5 ___6 ___7 ___8 ___9

Scientist

Do all three

___1 ___2 ___3

Do any six

___4 ___5 ___6 ___7 ___8 ___9 ___10 ___11 ___12

Showman

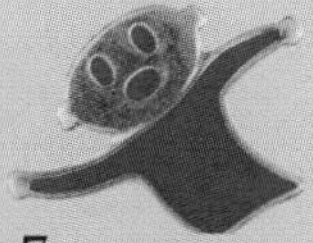

Select four from **one** category

Puppetry   1___2___3___4___5___6

Music   1___2___3___4___5___6___7

Drama   1___2___3___4___5___6___7___8

Sportsman

Do all (four)

___1___2___3___4

Traveler

Do any five

___1___2___3___4___5___6___7

Webelos Scout Parent Guide

Parents, Guardians, or Family Members:

This is your part of the *Webelos Scout Book*. It tells what this advanced program of Cub Scouting is all about, how it operates, and how you can help your boy as he enters the exciting, challenging Webelos Scouting program.

Welcome to Webelos Scouting

Webelos Scouting will be a new world of adventure for your boy: a way to learn new skills, to enjoy lots of outdoor activities, and most of all, to have fun.

This guide will give you a head start on understanding how Webelos Scouting works, and you'll find out how you can help your boy and his Webelos den.

> After you've read this guide, be sure to sign your name beside Webelos badge requirement 1 on page 415 of your boy's *Webelos Scout Book* (under "Approved by"). This will help him earn the Webelos badge.

What Is Webelos Scouting?

Webelos Scouting is the advanced part of the Cub Scouting program of the Boy Scouts of America. Webelos Scouts are older than boys in the Tiger Cub, Wolf, and Bear levels of Cub Scouting.

If a boy has completed third grade, or if he has not completed third grade but is 10 years old, he's the right age for Webelos Scouting.

Most Webelos Scouts are in this program for about 18 months. Webelos Scouting is a transitional program that shifts the emphasis from the home-centered activities of Wolf and Bear Cub Scouts to group-centered activities. This is preparation for the great adventure of Boy Scouting.

After your boy's Webelos experience, at age 11 or when he has completed fifth grade, he'll be ready for more independence and adventure.

The Webelos Scouting program will provide your boy with a variety of new experiences that will help him assume responsibilities and gain maturity, knowledge, and skills.

Webelos Scouting Can Help You

As a parent or guardian, you want the best for your boy. You want a close relationship with him, and you want to help him grow physically, mentally, and morally.

Webelos Scouting is designed to assist you. The program is geared to your boy's developing abilities and changing interests. You'll find yourself growing closer to him as you encourage him in his Webelos advancement and when you take a turn assisting with den activities.

Join him in the adventure of Webelos Scouting.

Advancement

Much of your boy's progress will take place through activities centered around his *advancement.* He'll advance in Webelos Scouting by earning activity badges and other awards.

Each of the 20 activity badges focuses on a different subject in the areas of physical skills, mental skills, community, technology, and the outdoors. Athlete, Scholar, Citizen, Craftsman, Sportsman—these are just a few of the badges. The entire den works on one badge each month, mostly in their meetings.

Your boy may learn the backstroke for the Aquanaut badge, practice first aid skills for the Readyman badge, or learn about the minerals that make up the earth's crust for the Geologist badge. Each badge presents an array of hands-on activities and fascinating information that will enrich his life.

He also may earn the Webelos badge, which has its own set of requirements. Later, he'll be eligible to work on Cub Scouting's highest award, the Arrow of Light.

Your boy will keep track of his badges and awards on a chart in the back of his *Webelos Scout Book* (see pages 440–443).

The name *Webelos* comes from "*WE*'ll *BE LO*yal *S*couts." Pronounce it WEE-buh-lows.

If Your Boy Is New in Scouting

If your boy has not been in the Cub Scout program before joining Webelos Scouts, he should complete the Bobcat rank requirements on page 6 of his *Webelos Scout Book* as quickly as he can. All boys in Cub Scouting earn this rank first.

He may need your help to fully understand the Cub Scout Promise and Law of the Pack. When he has passed the Bobcat requirements to your satisfaction, he'll receive his Bobcat badge at a pack meeting.

Then he'll be ready to start on his adventures in Webelos Scouting.

Purposes of Webelos Scouting

While Webelos Scouting's activities are tailored to your boy's age group, its main purposes are the same as those for Cub Scouting at younger levels:

- Positively influence character development and encourage spiritual growth
- Help boys develop habits and attitudes of good citizenship
- Encourage good sportsmanship and pride in growing strong in mind and body
- Improve understanding within the family
- Strengthen boys' ability to get along with other boys and to respect other people
- Foster a sense of personal achievement by helping boys develop new interests and skills
- Show boys how to be helpful and to do their best
- Provide fun and exciting new things for boys to do
- Prepare boys to become Boy Scouts

Where Webelos Scouting Fits In

If you're new to Cub Scouting, this will help you understand how it's set up. Your boy belongs to a small group called a Webelos *den*. The den is part of a larger Cub Scout *pack* that includes younger boys in the Tiger Cub program and in the Wolf and Bear Cub Scout dens.

The pack is chartered to a community organization, such as a school, a church or other religious institution, a service club, or other group interested in helping youth. It's called the *chartered organization* because it holds a charter from the Boy Scouts of America that allows it to use the Scouting program.

In addition to their den meetings, Webelos Scouts take part in monthly pack meetings led by an adult volunteer called the *Cubmaster*. Parents can serve on the *pack committee*, which plans pack activities.

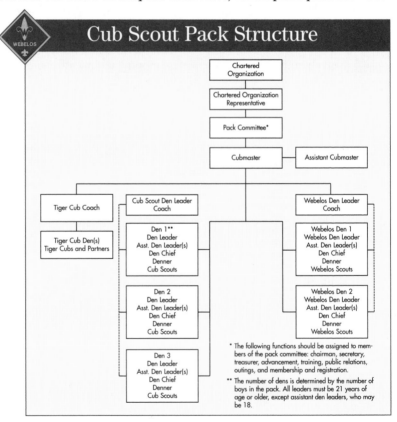

Cub Scout Pack Structure

Chartered Organization

Chartered Organization Representative

Pack Committee*

Cubmaster — Assistant Cubmaster

Tiger Cub Coach

Cub Scout Den Leader Coach

Webelos Den Leader Coach

Tiger Cub Den(s)
Tiger Cubs and Partners

Den 1**
Den Leader
Asst. Den Leader(s)
Den Chief
Denner
Cub Scouts

Webelos Den 1
Webelos Den Leader
Asst. Den Leader(s)
Den Chief
Denner
Webelos Scouts

Den 2
Den Leader
Asst. Den Leader(s)
Den Chief
Denner
Cub Scouts

Webelos Den 2
Webelos Den Leader
Asst. Den Leader(s)
Den Chief
Denner
Webelos Scouts

Den 3
Den Leader
Asst. Den Leader(s)
Den Chief
Denner
Cub Scouts

* The following functions should be assigned to members of the pack committee: chairman, secretary, treasurer, advancement, training, public relations, outings, and membership and registration.

** The number of dens is determined by the number of boys in the pack. All leaders must be 21 years of age or older, except assistant den leaders, who may be 18.

The Webelos Experience:
Advanced Cub Scouting

If your boy has been a Cub Scout, he already knows a little about Webelos Scouting from his Cub Scouting experiences. He may be surprised, though, to see how different it is. You'll find that your part in his Webelos experience is different, too.

What's ahead for him now? Well, he's growing up. He's probably taller and more mature than the younger Cub Scouts. He wants more grown-up activities, more responsibility, more independence.

You'll still be involved in his Cub Scouting activities, but it will be different from your role when he was a Wolf or Bear Cub Scout. In the Webelos den, the emphasis is on having fewer Cub Scouting activities to do at home and more to do with the den.

The Webelos experience is different in many ways from the experience of Cub Scouting for younger boys:

■ Webelos Scouts don't do achievements and electives as Wolf and Bear Cub Scouts do. Webelos Scouts work on *activity badges.*

■ The Webelos den uses activity badges as their monthly program themes.

■ When a Wolf or Bear Cub Scout passes requirements, he goes to a parent or guardian who signs his book. When a Webelos Scout passes requirements, he takes his book to the Webelos den leader or an adult the leader designates. (The adult, in many cases, is a Webelos parent.)

■ Webelos Scouts are encouraged to have several adult/boy overnight camping trips during the year, as well as other activities that prepare them for becoming Boy Scouts.

■ Webelos Scouts have some distinctive choices in their uniform. (You'll find "Webelos Uniform and Insignia" starting on page 456.)

Webelos Scouts are still Cub Scouts. They take part in Cub Scout pack meetings, events, and outings. But the Webelos den also makes its own plans and enjoys many activities too advanced for younger boys.

Protecting Your Children Against Drugs and Child Abuse

Every day, more than 3,000 teenagers start smoking. An American is killed in an alcohol-related accident every 22 minutes. Drinking and driving is the number one killer of teenagers. A variety of illegal, life-ruining drugs are widely available to teens and even younger children. And many children are victims of verbal, physical, or sexual abuse or neglect.

Scout leaders share your concern about the way young people will react if approached by drug dealers or by friends who have drugs to share. We all want children and teens to know how to *recognize, resist,* and *report* abuse.

DRUGS:
Deadly
A DANGEROUS GAME.
DON'T PLAY IT.

Although the reporting of child abuse incidents to authorities has increased significantly in recent years, this isn't true of drug use. Many children try to keep their drug problems a secret, fearing what might happen if the truth comes out.

Drug abuse and child abuse can be devastating to children and families. Explain to your children that their bodies belong to them alone. Tell them to say "NO" to anyone who offers them drugs, including alcohol and tobacco, and to anyone who touches them in an inappropriate manner.

It's important for you to know what's going on in your children's lives, to let them know they can talk about anything with you, to assure them you'll listen with understanding and love. The Boy Scouts of America urges you to take part in your children's activities. Become acquainted with their friends, their friends' parents, and their Scouting leaders.

In the Den

How the Webelos Den Works

The Webelos den has three leaders. They'll need your help if the den is to be successful.

■ The *Webelos den leader* is an adult who plans and directs the den activities. Appointed by the pack committee, the den leader must be at least 21 years old and a U.S. citizen. There also should be an assistant Webelos den leader.

■ The *Webelos den chief* is a Boy Scout, a Varsity Scout, or a Venturer who has been a Boy Scout. The den chief is trained to help the den leader, especially in leading games and teaching skills.

■ The *Webelos denner* is a Webelos Scout elected by the other boys to help the den leader and den chief.

The den meets each week at the home of the den leader or at a central meeting place, such as the chartered organization's building. The den leader, Webelos Scouts, and parents set the time and place.

Activity Badge Fun

Each month, the projects and many of the activities at den meetings are centered around one of the 20 activity badges Webelos Scouts may earn. If you have skills or knowledge in any of the activity badge areas, the den leader may ask you to help.

Family members often help the den at its meetings. When your boy joins the Webelos den, you may be asked to fill out a questionnaire to indicate your skills and interests that relate to the activity badge areas, the Webelos badge, and the Arrow of Light Award requirements. Your Webelos den leader might ask you to help when the boys are scheduled to work in an area you've noted.

An engineer, for example, could be involved with the Engineer activity badge. The requirements are challenging for a boy but simple for an engineer. He or she could explain what an engineer does and guide the boys in building a catapult, if the den chooses that project.

If you're skilled with tools and know about home repairs and car and bicycle care, you could help with Handyman activity badge projects. Take a look at the activity badge requirements in your boy's *Webelos Scout Book*—Sportsman, Scientist, Communicator, Showman, and the rest—and see where you might fit in. Sharing what you know with your boy and his friends will be a great experience. (In addition to the activity badge areas, family members will have other opportunities to help at meetings and events.)

The Webelos den leader (or another adult the leader designates) signs or initials each requirement your boy completes. After passing the necessary requirements for one activity badge, he'll receive his badge (a small metal emblem to attach to his cap) during a pack meeting ceremony.

Encourage and help your boy earn as many of the 20 activity badges as possible, plus the Webelos badge and the Arrow of Light Award.

Requirements for all badges and awards are in this *Webelos Scout Book*.

The Webelos Den at Pack Meetings

The role of the Webelos den in pack meetings differs from that of the younger Cub Scouts. The Webelos den may present an exhibit of projects or a demonstration of skills they've learned in exploring their activity badge for the month. Or they could come up with a skit or stunt that ties their activity badge to the younger Cub Scouts' theme for the month.

The Webelos Scouts are old enough to handle certain responsibilities at pack meetings. They may be asked to set up chairs, usher people to their seats, and direct them to the den exhibits.

During the pack meeting recognition ceremony, your boy will receive any badges he has earned. Be sure to attend so you can pin on his new badge. He'll be proud of his accomplishment and proud to have you doing the honors.

When he has earned the Arrow of Light Award (or is 11 years old or has completed the fifth grade), he'll be ready to continue along the Scouting trail that leads to a Boy Scout troop. This will be a highlight of his young life, and you'll want to share the ceremony with him. His graduation will take place at a pack meeting—his last.

Fun and Responsibility for You and Your Webelos Scout

Webelos Scouting offers much to you and your boy: challenging new experiences, ways to grow more knowledgeable and skilled, and ways to have fun. At the same time, it presents responsibilities for both of you.

Webelos Scouting asks four things of you as a parent:

- **Most important, provide a home for your boy** where he finds love and security.

- **Help your boy.** Much of his work in activity badge areas and for the Webelos badge and Arrow of Light Award will be done in the den, but he'll do some requirements at home. Be prepared to help.

- **Take an interest in his Webelos activities.** He needs to know that you approve of what he's doing, you're interested in what he's learning, you want to help him, and you're proud of his accomplishments.

- **Pursue leadership in the den and pack.** Some parents and guardians of Webelos Scouts may be asked to serve as den leader, assistant den leader, Cubmaster, assistant Cubmaster, or pack committee member. If you are asked, please serve if you can. Your boy will be proud of you.

The opportunity to work with your boy at this age is a precious one. Keep in mind the Cub Scout motto, "Do Your Best." If you and your boy strive for your best in Webelos Scouting, you'll have a great, productive time together.

Advancement: You Can Help

Your Part at Home

When your boy has some of his activity badge work to do at home, he may ask you for help. Your assistance and encouragement will mean a lot to him.

For the Outdoorsman badge, for example, he can choose from requirements that include backyard camping, cookouts, and family camping trips. It's natural for you to be the one to okay his work on such projects. For the Family Member and Fitness badges, you'll approve almost all of the requirements. Whenever he asks you to oversee his work and sign the badge scoreboard, make sure he does his best.

Webelos Badge and Arrow of Light Award

Your boy will practice his skills and study for the Webelos badge and Arrow of Light Award at den meetings. But if he wants to continue practicing and studying at home, encourage and help him.

For details on all the activity badges and other awards, see this *Webelos Scout Book.*

The Den's Outdoor Program

Webelos Scouts take part in more outdoor activities than younger Cub Scouts. Your boy will get a taste of the outdoor life of the Boy Scout and learn some of the skills he needs for it.

Hiking

The boys will go on occasional nature hikes with the Webelos den leader and some parents and guardians. Whether or not you go along, ensure a good experience for your boy by helping him prepare. He'll need good socks, comfortable walking shoes, proper clothing, and food to take on the trail.

Overnight Camping

The policy of the Boy Scouts of America is to encourage several overnight camping trips and other challenging outdoor activities for Webelos Scouts. You'll always have a major part in these overnighters. Don't worry if you're not an experienced camper. The den leader and other adults will help you, and you and your boy will have fun learning about camping together.

These campouts are for boys AND their adult partners. Without the adults, there can be no trips.

The cooperation of adults is essential. The den leader cannot be expected to take full responsibility for the health and safety of six or eight boys at an overnight campout. Each boy must be the special responsibility of his adult partner. If you or another adult family member can't attend, find a responsible adult to go with your boy.

Remember that no adult should be responsible for more than his or her own boy.

Planning the Overnighter

You'll have a hand in planning the details of the campout at a meeting of all participating adults. If you have special outdoor skills, the den leader may plan an activity in which you can instruct the Webelos Scouts.

Here are some of the topics for the meeting:

Where you're going. The site may be decided before the meeting. It won't be a rugged, pioneering type of camp. Your boy won't experience that kind of camping until he's a Boy Scout.

Webelos overnighters should take place in warm weather, at sites reasonably close to home. The events can be held at suitable public campgrounds, local council camps, or privately owned facilities. Usually tents are used. Tent camping provides an element of adventure that boys find exciting. Any nearby cabins or shelters should serve only as emergency protection and a base for toilet facilities, water, etc.

Each adult and boy team brings the tent and other equipment they'll use. Equipment can be borrowed from a Boy Scout troop or rented.

How you'll get there. At the meeting, you and the other adults will make plans to share transportation to the campsite.

Who will cook. You and your boy will cook for yourselves, so bring food and cooking equipment from home. Plan simple menus together. (This *Webelos Scout Book* has some suggestions.)

Cooking and heating of food can be done on charcoal grills provided at the camp or brought from home. Adults who own propane and liquid fuel stoves or lanterns may use them, if allowed by local camping property authorities, but **under no circumstances should boys be permitted to handle liquid fuels or stoves or lanterns fired by such fuel.** Such equipment should be considered personal gear, and adult owners must assume full personal responsibility for these items and for fuel.

Water supply. Be sure the water supply at the camp is safe. If it has not been tested, bring water from home for drinking and cooking. Water will also be needed for cleanup and for fire protection.

 ## Webelos Uniform and Insignia

The Basic Uniform

The basic Webelos uniform is either the blue uniform your boy may have worn as a Cub Scout or the tan shirt and olive green trousers he'll wear as a Boy Scout. The choice is yours and your boy's, and it may be made at any time. If your boy has been a Cub Scout, he might wear his blue uniform until he outgrows it and then switch to the tan and olive green uniform.

The following are worn with either uniform:

- **Webelos cap:** Two-tone blue cap with a bill. The Webelos Scout insignia (light blue and gold fleur-de-lis embroidered on dark blue background with gold border) is centered above the bill.

- **Neckerchief:** Gold, green, and red plaid, with the Webelos insignia centered 1 inch from the point. The neckerchief slide may be the official Webelos slide or a homemade one.

How to Put on the Neckerchief

The Webelos neckerchief may be worn either over or under the collar, but all Webelos Scouts in the pack wear it the same way. If it is worn over the collar, the collar should be turned under.

Roll the long edge over several times, to about 6 inches from the tip. Place the rolled neckerchief around the neck. Pull the neckerchief slide up snugly. Tie the loose ends or leave them loose, according to the rule of your pack.

The neckerchief should fit smoothly on the back of the shirt. It should measure about 6 inches from the top of the fold down to the tip.

Obtaining a Uniform

The uniform and uniform accessories may be purchased at stores that are distributors for the Boy Scouts of America. Your den leader or Cubmaster will know the location of the nearest one.

Suggest that your boy earn his uniform by working for it. You might arrange to pay him for special chores around the house. Or he might work around the neighborhood—shoveling snow, running errands, taking care of pets while their owners are away, etc.

Some Cub Scout packs maintain a uniform "bank" with "experienced" uniforms for new members.

Placement of Awards

Activity badges are small metal emblems. Your boy earns one each time he completes the requirements for one of the 20 activity badges. They are pinned onto the light blue front panel of the Webelos cap. The shield inside the cap should be folded down when attaching awards and then folded up to cover the backs of the pins.

Another way to wear the activity badges is to pin them to the Webelos badge colors, which are optional. The colors are three ribbons—one gold, one green, one red—fastened together at the top by a pin with the word *Webelos* on it. The colors are pinned to the right shirt sleeve just below the American flag. (The colors will hide the Webelos den patch or number.)

Webelos Scouting's two highest awards, the Webelos badge and the Arrow of Light Award, are cloth patches. They are sewn onto the uniform shirt.

The compass points emblem, an award for earning activity badges beyond those required for the Webelos badge, is worn suspended from the button of the right pocket. Three metal "points" are attached to the emblem when they are earned.

Boys who earned belt loops in the Cub Scout Sports and Academics program as Cub Scouts may continue to wear them. These awards are square metal emblems that slide onto the belt. Webelos Scouts also may earn belt loops.

Webelos Scout Insignia

The diagrams below show you where to place insignia on the sleeves and pockets of the uniform.

Webelos Scouts wear the Bobcat, Wolf, and Bear badges, if they have earned them, on the left pocket of the shirt, as well as the Webelos badge and Arrow of Light Award after they are earned. The Arrow of Light Award is centered above the button on the left pocket flap.

Below the left pocket, the boy may wear all the arrow points he earned as a Cub Scout. Or he may wear two or three on his shirt and place the others on a vest or display them in his room at home.

Temporary insignia or Progress Toward Ranks beads are centered on the right pocket. These are patches given by local Scout councils for participation in a Scouting show, day camp, roundup, or other special event. Only one may be worn at a time.

The Webelos denner and assistant denner wear shoulder cords on the left shoulder. The cord is removed when the term of office ends.

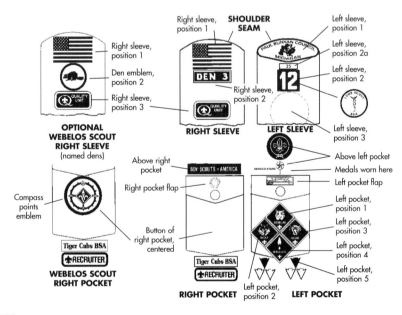

Who Contributes to Scouting?

Many people in your community make Scouting programs possible by contributing their financial support, their skills, and their time. Some of these people are:

- **The boy and his parent or guardian.** It's a good idea for your boy to pay part of his own way with money he has earned and saved. This might include paying for his annual membership fee, weekly den dues, or *Boys' Life* subscription (through the pack budget plan). You may help him buy his Cub Scout books and uniform. Many parents and guardians also help local Scouting by contributing to the United Way and by participating in Friends of Scouting (FOS) (see below).

- **The chartered organization.** The unit's chartered organization contributes by providing pack leadership and a meeting place.

- **The pack.** The pack maintains itself through its budget plan and its own money-earning projects. The adult leaders who volunteer their time, ideas, and effort contribute by making the program happen for boys.

- **The community.** People in the community support the local council and its services financially by participating in United Way and Friends of Scouting and through bequests and other contributions.

Friends of Scouting

Cub Scouting in your area is administered by an organization called the local council. (It's listed in the telephone book under "Boy Scouts of America.")

The local council provides services to Cub Scout packs, Boy Scout troops, Varsity Scout teams, and Venturing crews. It operates camping facilities, conducts training for leaders, plans and runs councilwide events for all members, and works continually to introduce more young people to Scouting. It raises the necessary funds through the United Way and/or other methods.

Each year, usually in the spring, the local council conducts a special funding campaign called Friends of Scouting (FOS). Parents, guardians, Scouters (volunteers and professionals in Scouting), former members, and other friends of Scouting are invited to contribute. A member of your pack committee will be assigned to ask the pack's families to give to FOS. By donating to FOS, you'll help ensure good Scouting for your Webelos Scout.

Together on the Webelos Trail

Your boy sees Webelos Scouting as a chance to have fun, go camping, and make new friends. He also sees it as a step on the way to outdoor adventures in Boy Scouting.

But Webelos Scouting is more than that. For you, it's a new way to grow closer to your boy, share his excitement about his expanding physical and mental skills, and create a warm and open relationship with him.

Join him on the Webelos trail. You'll be glad you did.

> Webelos badge requirement 1 asks your boy to have you read this parent guide. Please sign your name beside that requirement on page 415 in his *Webelos Scout Book*, under "Approved by."

Index

Cub Scout Academics and
  Sports program, 437
    belt loops, 41, 81, 204, 437
    pins, 46, 437
Cub Scout handshake, 10
Cub Scout motto, 10
Cub Scout Promise, 7–8
    in sign language, 193–96
Cub Scout salute, 10
Cub Scout sign, 9

D

den
  how it works, 13, 451
    at pack meetings, 452
den chief, 15, 451
den leader
  defined, 14, 451
  duties of, 451, 452
den meeting
  friends at, 18
  locations suggested, 451
  when and how often, 451
denner, 15, 451
  shoulder cords, 458
diet. *See* nutrition; food; Food Guide
  Pyramid
drama. *See* Showman
drawing, 93, 98
drug abuse, 75–76
dual contests
  arm wrestle, 60
  chest push, 62
  duck fight, 62
  leg wrestle, 62
  pull apart, 61
  stick fight, 61
  stick pull, 60

E

Earth, structure of, 351
earthquakes, 362
ecosystems, 390–91
electricity, 269–72

electrical circuits, 270–71
  replacing a light bulb, 291
  safety with, 272
energy, conservation of at home, 217–18
Engineer, 266–81
  badge requirements, 267
  block and tackle, 275–77
  bridges, 272–74
  catapult, 278
  computers, 279–80
  defined, 267, 268
  electricity, 269–72
  floor plans, 278–79
  property lines, 269
  scoreboard, 281
  surveyors, 269
erosion, 338, 353, 364
exercises
  All the Way, 56
  biceps builder, 54
  butterfly, 57
  curl-ups, 47
  dual contests, 60–62
  50-yard dash, 51
  jump and reach, 51
  leg stretch, 58
  neck builder, 57
  paper crunch, 54
  pull-ups, 48
  push-ups, 49
  600-yard run (walk), 52
  squat thrust, 59
  standing long jump, 50
  stretcher, 56
  toe exercise, 59
  trunk bend, 58
  trunk stretch, 55
  walking, 55
eyes, how they work, 321, 323

F

Family Member, 208–26
  badge requirements, 209–10
  budgeting, 215–16
  cleanliness and
    neatness, 212
  defined, 209

Photo Credits

Courtesy of American Airlines—pages 146, 301

Courtesy of AMTRAK—page 146

Steve Anderson—page 151

Courtesy of Linda Blase, Dallas Theater Center—page 133

Jack Brown—pages 1, 2, 13, 14, 19, 21, 23, 24, 41, 44, 47, 55, 59, 65, 78, 85, 86, 108, 118, 133, 144, 155, 156, 171, 181, 182, 188, 189, 208, 217, 228, 230, 251, 252, 266, 277, 279, 282, 288, 290, 291, 298, 327, 328, 348, 366, 370, 382, 394, 440–43

Courtesy of Casa Mañana, Fort Worth, Texas—page 137

Jack Kelly Clark, courtesy of University of California Statewide IPM Project—page 379

Tina Collins—page 274

Courtesy of Dallas Area Rapid Transit—page 146

Courtesy of Dallas Opera, Dallas, Texas—page 138

Philip Greenspun—pages 331, 404

Philip Greenspun/Roy Jansen—page 178

Roy Jansen—front cover; pages 40, 88, 90, 91, 92, 95, 97, 120, 149, 150, 190, 197, 199, 208, 211, 214, 218, 219, 220, 221, 222, 223, 243, 268, 296, 337, 344, 350, 365, 367, 373, 401, 405, 444

Roy Jansen/KFWB-News 98—page 189

Chris Michaels—pages 48, 51, 57, 58, 106, 167, 186, 321

Courtesy of NASA—page 314

Joe Schwartz—page 306

Courtesy of U.S. Department of the Interior, U.S. Geological Survey, David A. Johnston Cascades Volcano Observatory, Vancouver, Washington—page 359

Courtesy of Pat Vanecek, University of Texas Health Science Center, Dallas Department of Ophthalmology—page 321